BENCHMARK SERIES

Microsoft®
Excel®
2016
Level 1

Rutkosky • Roggenkamp • Rutkosky

PARADIGM
EDUCATION SOLUTIONS

St. Paul

Senior Vice President	Linda Hein
Editor in Chief	Christine Hurney
Director of Production	Timothy W. Larson
Production Editor	Jen Weaverling
Cover and Text Designer	Valerie King
Copy Editors	Communicáto, Ltd.; Page to Portal, LLC
Senior Design and Production Specialist	Jack Ross; PerfecType
Assistant Developmental Editors	Mamie Clark, Katie Werdick
Testers	Janet Blum, Fanshawe College; Traci Post
Instructional Support Writers	Janet Blum, Fanshawe College; Brienna McWade
Indexer	Terry Casey
Vice President Information Technology	Chuck Bratton
Digital Projects Manager	Tom Modl
Vice President Sales and Marketing	Scott Burns
Director of Marketing	Lara Weber McLellan

Trademarks: Microsoft is a trademark or registered trademark of Microsoft Corporation in the United States and/or other countries. Some of the product names and company names included in this book have been used for identification purposes only and may be trademarks or registered trade names of their respective manufacturers and sellers. The authors, editors, and publisher disclaim any affiliation, association, or connection with, or sponsorship or endorsement by, such owners.

We have made every effort to trace the ownership of all copyrighted material and to secure permission from copyright holders. In the event of any question arising as to the use of any material, we will be pleased to make the necessary corrections in future printings.

Cover Photo Credits: © Photomall/Dreamstime.com. **Getting Started Photo Credits:** Page 3: Leungchopan/Shutterstock.com.

Paradigm Publishing is independent from Microsoft Corporation, and not affiliated with Microsoft in any manner. While this publication may be used in assisting individuals to prepare for a Microsoft Office Specialist certification exam, Microsoft, its designated program administrator, and Paradigm Publishing do not warrant that use of this publication will ensure passing a Microsoft Office Specialist certification exam.

ISBN 978-0-76386-938-0 (print)
ISBN 978-0-76386-940-3 (digital)

© 2017 by Paradigm Publishing, Inc.
875 Montreal Way
St. Paul, MN 55102
Email: educate@emcp.com
Website: ParadigmCollege.com

Printed in the United States of America

23 22 21 20 19 18 17 16   1 2 3 4 5 6 7 8 9 10 11 12

Brief Contents

Contents

Preface

Benchmark Series: Microsoft® Excel 2016 is designed for students who want to learn how to use this powerful spreadsheet program to manipulate numerical data in resolving issues related to finances or others numbers-based information. No prior knowledge of spreadsheets is required. After successfully completing a course using this textbook and digital courseware, students will be able to:

- Create and edit spreadsheets worksheets of varying complexity
- Format cells, columns, and rows as well as entire workbooks in a uniform, attractive style
- Analyze numerical data and project outcomes to make informed decisions
- Plan, research, create, revise, and publish worksheets and workbooks to meet specific communication needs
- Given a workplace scenario requiring a numbers-based solution, assess the information requirements and then prepare the materials that achieve the goal efficiently and effectively

Upon completing the text, students can expect to be proficient in using Excel to organize, analyze, and present information.

Well-designed textbook pedagogy is important, but students learn technology skills through practice and problem solving. Technology provides opportunities for interactive learning as well as excellent ways to quickly and accurately assess student performance. To this end, this textbook is supported with SNAP 2016, Paradigm's web-based training and assessment learning management system. Details about SNAP as well as additional student courseware and instructor resources can be found on page xiv.

Achieving Proficiency in Excel 2016

Since its inception several Office versions ago, the *Benchmark Series* has served as a standard of excellence in software instruction. Elements of the *Benchmark Series* function individually and collectively to create an inviting, comprehensive learning environment that produces successful computer users. The following visual tour highlights the structure and features that comprise the highly popular *Benchmark* model.

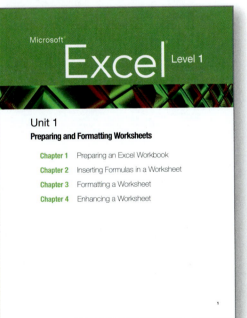

Microsoft

Excel Level 1

Unit 1
Preparing and Formatting Worksheets

Chapter 1 Preparing an Excel Workbook
Chapter 2 Inserting Formulas in a Worksheet
Chapter 3 Formatting a Worksheet
Chapter 4 Enhancing a Worksheet

Unit Openers display the unit's four chapter titles. *Excel Level 1* contains two units; each unit concludes with a comprehensive unit performance assessment.

Student Textbook and eBook

Chapter Openers present the performance objectives and an overview of the skills taught.

Precheck quizzes allow students to check their current skills before starting chapter work.

Data Files are provided for each chapter from the ebook. A prominent note reminds students to copy the appropriate chapter data folder and make it active.

Students with SNAP access are reminded to launch the Precheck quiz and chapter tutorials from their SNAP Assignments page.

Projects Build Skill Mastery within Realistic Context

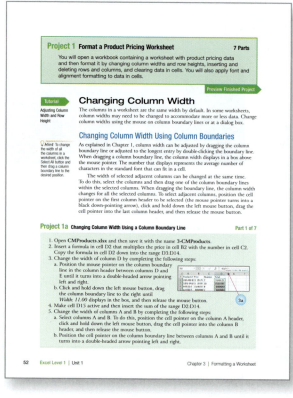

Multipart Projects provide a framework for instruction and practice on software features. A project overview identifies tasks to accomplish and key features to use in completing the work.

Preview Finished Project shows how the file will look after students complete the project.

Tutorials provide interactive, guided training and measured practice.

Hint margin notes offer useful tips on how to use features efficiently and effectively.

Typically, a file remains open throughout all parts of the project. Students save their work incrementally. At the end of the project, students save, print, and then close the file.

Quick Steps provide feature summaries for reference and review.

Between project parts, the text presents instruction on the features and skills necessary to accomplish the next section of the project.

Step-by-Step Instructions guide students to the desired outcome for each project part. Screen captures illustrate what the screen should look like at key points.

Magenta Text identifies material to type.

Check Your Work allows students to confirm they have completed the project activity correctly.

Chapter Review Tools Reinforce Learning

Chapter Summary reviews the purpose and execution of key features.

Commands Review summarizes visually the major features and alternative methods of access.

At the end of each chapter, students are encouraged to go to the Workbook ebook to access study tools and assessment activities.

Workbook eBook Activities Provide a Hierarchy of Learning Assessments

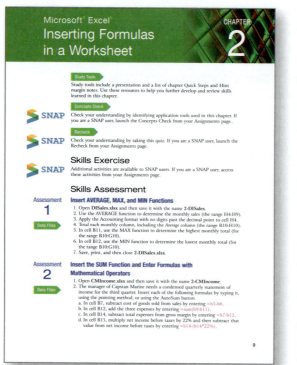

Study Tools are presentations with audio support and a list of chapter Quick Steps and Hint margin notes designed to help students further develop and review skills learned in the chapter.

Concepts Check is an objective completion exercise that allows students to assess their comprehension and recall of application features, terminology, and functions.

Recheck concept quizzes for each chapter enable students to check how their skills have improved after completing chapter work.

Skills Exercises are available to SNAP 2016 users. SNAP will automatically score student work, which is performed live in the application, and provide detailed feedback.

Skills Assessment exercises ask students to develop both standard and customized types of spreadsheets without how-to directions.

Visual Benchmark assessments test problem-solving skills and mastery of application features.

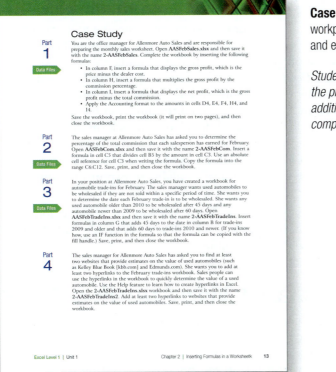

Case Study requires analyzing a workplace scenario and then planning and executing a multipart project.

Students search the web and/or use the program's Help feature to locate additional information required to complete the Case Study.

Unit Performance Assessments Deliver Cross-Disciplinary, Comprehensive Evaluation

Assessing Proficiency exercises check mastery of features.

Writing Activities involve applying application skills in a communication context.

Internet Research projects reinforce research and information processing skills.

Job Study at the end of Unit 2 presents a capstone assessment requiring critical thinking and problem solving.

SNAP Training and Assessment

SNAP is a web-based training and assessment program and learning management system (LMS) for learning Microsoft Office 2016. SNAP is comprised of rich content, a sophisticated grade book, and robust scheduling and analytics tools. SNAP courseware supports the *Benchmark Series* content and delivers live-in-the-application assessments for students to demonstrate their skills mastery. Interactive tutorials increase skills-focused moments with guided training and measured practice. SNAP provides automatic scoring and detailed feedback on the many activities, exercises, and quizzes to help identify areas where additional support is needed, evaluating student performance both at an individual and course level. The *Benchmark Series* SNAP course content is also available to export into any LMS system that supports LTI tools.

Paradigm Education Solutions provides technical support for SNAP through 24-7 chat at ParadigmCollege.com. In addition, an online User Guide and other SNAP training tools for using SNAP are available.

Student eBook and *Workbook* eBook

The student ebook and *Workbook* ebook available through SNAP or online at Paradigm.bookshelf.emcp.com provide access to the *Benchmark Series* content from any device (desktop, tablet, and smartphone) anywhere, through a live Internet connection. The versatile ebook platform features dynamic navigation tools including a linked table of contents and the ability to jump to specific pages, search for terms, bookmark, highlight, and take notes. The ebooks offer live links to the interactive content and resources that support the print textbook, including the student data files, Precheck and Recheck quizzes, and interactive tutorials. The *Workbook* ebook also provides access to presentations with audio support and to end-of-section Concept Check, Skills Assessment, Visual Benchmark, Case Study, and end-of-unit Performance Assessment activities.

Instructor eResources eBook

All instructor resources are available digitally through a web-based ebook at Paradigm.bookshelf.emcp.com. The instructor materials include these items:

- Planning resources, such as lesson plans, teaching hints, and sample course syllabi
- Presentation resources, such as PowerPoint slide shows with lecture notes
- Assessment resources, including live and annotated PDF model answers for chapter work and workbook activities, rubrics for evaluating student work, and chapter-based exam banks

Several computer applications are combined to make the Microsoft Office 2016 application suite. The applications are known as *software*, and they contain instructions that tell the computer what to do. Some of the applications in the suite include Word, a word processing applicaton; Excel, a spreadsheet applicaton; Access, a database applicaton; and PowerPoint, a presentation applicaton.

Identifying Computer Hardware

The Microsoft Office suite can run on several types of computer equipment, referred to as *hardware*. You will need access to a laptop or a desktop computer system that includes a PC/tower, monitor, keyboard, printer, drives, and mouse. If you are not sure what equipment you will be operating, check with your instructor. The computer systems shown in Figure G.1 consists of six components. Each component is discussed separately in the material that follows.

Figure G.1 Computer System

PC/tower

USB drive

monitor

printer

keyboard

mouse

1

Figure G.2 PC/Tower

PC/Tower

The PC, also known as the *tower*, is the brain of the computer and is where all processing occurs. A PC/tower consists of components such as the Central Processing Unit (CPU), hard drives, and video cards plugged into a motherboard. The motherboard is mounted inside the case, which includes input and output ports for attaching external peripherals (as shown in Figure G.2). When a user provides input through the use of peripherals, the PC/tower computes that input and outputs the results. Similar hardware is included in a laptop, but the design is more compact to allow for mobility.

Monitor

Hint Monitor size is measured diagonally. For example, the distance from the bottom left corner to the top right corner of the monitor.

A computer monitor looks like a television screen. It displays the visual information that the computer is outputting. The quality of display for monitors varies depending on the type of monitor and the level of resolution. Monitors can also vary in size—generally from 13 inches to 26 inches or larger.

Keyboard

The keyboard is used to input information into the computer. The number and location of the keys on a keyboard can vary. In addition to letters, numbers, and symbols, most computer keyboards contain function keys, arrow keys, and a numeric keypad. Figure G.3 shows an enhanced keyboard.

The 12 keys at the top of the keyboard, labeled with the letter F followed by a number, are called *function keys*. Use these keys to perform functions within each of the Office applications. To the right of the regular keys is a group of special or dedicated keys. These keys are labeled with specific functions that will be performed when you press the key. Below the special keys are arrow keys. Use these keys to move the insertion point in the document screen.

Some keyboards include mode indicator lights. When you select certain modes, a light appears on the keyboard. For example, if you press the Caps Lock key, which disables the lowercase alphabet, a light appears next to Caps Lock. Similarly, pressing the Num Lock key will disable the special functions on the numeric keypad, which is located at the right side of the keyboard.

Figure G.3 Keyboard

function keys

media center

function keys

mode indicator lights

special or dedicated keys

special or dedicated keys

alphanumeric keys

arrow keys or insertion point control keys

numeric, insertion point control, and special keys

Drives and Ports

A PC includes drives and ports that allow you to input and output data. For example, a hard drive is a disk drive inside of the PC that stores data that may have been inputted or outputted. Other drives may include CD, DVD and BluRay disc drives, although newer computers may not include these drives, because USB flash drives are becoming the preferred technology. Ports are the "plugs" on the PC, and are used to connect devices to the computer, such as the keyboard and mouse, the monitor, speakers, a USB flash drive and so on. Most PCs will have a few USB ports, at least one display port, an audio cable port, and possibly an ethernet port (used to physically connect to the Internet or a network).

Printer

An electronic version of a file is known as a *soft copy*. If you want to create a hard copy of a file, you need to print it. To print documents you will need to access a printer (as shown in Figure G.4), which will probably be either a laser printer or an ink-jet printer. A laser printer uses a laser beam combined with heat and pressure to print documents, while an ink-jet printer prints a document by spraying a fine mist of ink on the page.

Figure G.4 Printer

Mouse

Most functions and commands in the Microsoft Office suite are designed to be performed using a mouse or a similar pointing device. A mouse is an input device that sits on a flat surface next to the computer. You can operate a mouse with your left or right hand. Moving the mouse on the flat surface causes a corresponding pointer to move on the screen, and clicking the left or right mouse buttons allows you to select various objects and commands. Figure G.5 shows an example of a mouse.

Using the Mouse The applications in the Microsoft Office suite can be operated with the keyboard and a mouse. The mouse generally has two buttons on top, which you press to execute specific functions and commands. A mouse may also contain a wheel, which can be used to scroll in a window or as a third button. To use the mouse, rest it on a flat surface or a mouse pad. Put your hand over it with your palm resting on top of the mouse and your index finger resting on the left mouse button. As you move your hand, and thus the mouse, a corresponding pointer moves on the screen.

When using the mouse, you should understand four terms — point, click, double-click, and drag. When operating the mouse, you may need to point to a specific command, button, or icon. To *point* means to position the mouse pointer on the desired item. With the mouse pointer positioned on the item, you may need to click a button on the mouse to select the item. To *click* means to quickly tap a button on the mouse once. To complete two steps at one time, such as choosing and then executing a function, double-click the mouse button. To *double-click* means to tap the left mouse button twice in quick succession. The term *drag* means to click and hold down the left mouse button, move the mouse pointer to a specific location, and then release the button.

> 💡 *Hint* This textbook will use the verb *click* to refer to the mouse and the verb press to refer to a key on the keyboard.

Using the Mouse Pointer The mouse pointer will look different depending on where you have positioned it and what function you are performing. The following are some of the ways the mouse pointer can appear when you are working in the Office suite:

- The mouse pointer appears as an I-beam (called the *I-beam pointer*) when you are inserting text in a file. The I-beam pointer can be used to move the insertion point or to select text.
- The mouse pointer appears as an arrow pointing up and to the left (called the *arrow pointer*) when it is moved to the Title bar, Quick Access Toolbar, ribbon, or an option in a dialog box, among other locations.
- The mouse pointer becomes a double-headed arrow (either pointing left and right, pointing up and down, or pointing diagonally) when you perform certain functions such as changing the size of an object.

Figure G.5 Mouse

- In certain situations, such as when you move an object or image, the mouse pointer displays with a four-headed arrow attached. The four-headed arrow means that you can move the object left, right, up, or down.
- When a request is being processed or when an application is being loaded, the mouse pointer may appear as a moving circle. The moving circle means "please wait." When the process is completed, the circle is replaced with a normal mouse pointer.
- When the mouse pointer displays as a hand with a pointing index finger, it indicates that more information is available about an item. The mouse pointer also displays as a hand with a pointing index finger when you hover the mouse over a hyperlink.

Touchpad

If you are working on a laptop computer, you may use a touchpad instead of a mouse. A *touchpad* allows you to move the mouse pointer by moving your finger across a surface at the base of the keyboard. You click and right-click by using your thumb to press the buttons located at the bottom of the touchpad. Some touchpads have special features such as scrolling or clicking something by tapping the surface of the touchpad instead of pressing a button with a thumb.

TouchScreen

Smartphones, tablets, and touch monitors all use TouchScreen technology (as shown in Figure G.6), which allows users to directly interact with the objects on the screen by touching them with fingers, thumbs, or a stylus. Multiple fingers or both thumbs can be used on most modern touchscreens, giving users the ability to zoom, rotate, and manipulate items on the screen. While a lot of activities in this textbook can be completed using a device with a touchscreen, a mouse or touchpad might be required to complete a few activities.

Figure G.6 Touchscreen

Choosing Commands

Once an application is open, you can use several methods in the application to choose commands. A command is an instruction that tells the application to do something. You can choose a command using the mouse or the keyboard. When an application such as Word or PowerPoint is open, the ribbon contains buttons and options for completing tasks, as well as tabs you can click to display additional buttons and options. To choose a button on the Quick Access Toolbar or on the ribbon, position the tip of the mouse arrow pointer on the button and then click the left mouse button.

The Office suite provides accelerator keys you can press to use a command in an application. Press the Alt key on the keyboard to display KeyTips that identify the accelerator key you can press to execute a command. For example, if you press the Alt key in a Word document with the Home tab active, KeyTips display as shown in Figure G.7. Continue pressing accelerator keys until you execute the desired command. For example, to begin checking the spelling in a document, press the Alt key, press the R key on the keyboard to display the Review tab, and then press the letter S on the keyboard.

Choosing Commands from Drop-Down Lists

To choose a command from a drop-down list with the mouse, position the mouse pointer on the option and then click the left mouse button. To make a selection from a drop-down list with the keyboard, type the underlined letter in the option.

Some options at a drop-down list may appear in gray (dimmed), indicating that the option is currently unavailable. If an option at a drop-down list displays preceded by a check mark, it means the option is currently active. If an option at a drop-down list displays followed by an ellipsis (…), clicking that option will display a dialog box.

Choosing Options from a Dialog Box

A dialog box contains options for applying formatting or otherwise modifying a file or data within a file. Some dialog boxes display with tabs along the top that provide additional options. For example, the Font dialog box shown in Figure G.8 contains two tabs—the Font tab and the Advanced tab. The tab that displays in the front is the active tab. To make a tab active using the mouse, position the arrow pointer on the tab and then click the left mouse button. If you are using the keyboard, press Ctrl + Tab or press Alt + the underlined letter on the tab.

To choose an option from a dialog box with the mouse, position the arrow pointer on the option and then click the left mouse button. If you are using the keyboard, press the Tab key to move the insertion point forward from option to option. Press Shift + Tab to move the insertion point backward from option to option. You can also press and hold down the Alt key and then press the

Figure G.7 Word Home Tab KeyTips

Figure G.8 Word Font Dialog Box

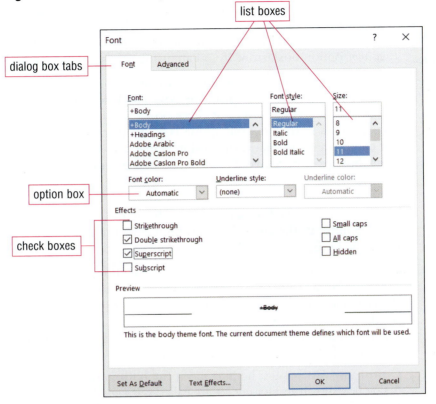

underlined letter of the option. When an option is selected, it displays with a blue background or surrounded by a dashed box called a *marquee*. A dialog box contains one or more of the following elements: list boxes, option boxes, check boxes, text boxes, option buttons, measurement boxes, and command buttons.

List Boxes and Option Boxes The fonts available in the Font dialog box, shown in Figure G.8, are contained in a list box. To make a selection from a list box with the mouse, move the arrow pointer to the option and then click the left mouse button.

Some list boxes may contain a scroll bar. This scroll bar will display at the right side of the list box (a vertical scroll bar) or at the bottom of the list box (a horizontal scroll bar). Use a vertical scroll bar or a horizontal scroll bar to move through the list if the list is longer (or wider) than the box. To move down a list using a vertical scroll bar, position the arrow pointer on the down arrow, and then click and hold down the left mouse button. To scroll up through the list, position the arrow pointer on the up arrow, and then click and hold down the left mouse button. You can also move the arrow pointer above the scroll box and click the left mouse button to scroll up the list or move the arrow pointer below the scroll box and click the left mouse button to move down the list. To navigate in a list with a horizontal scroll bar, click the left arrow to scroll to the left of the list or click the right arrow to scroll to the right of the list.

To use the keyboard to make a selection from a list box, move the insertion point into the box by holding down the Alt key and pressing the underlined letter of the desired option. Press the Up and/or Down Arrow keys on the keyboard to move through the list, and press the Enter key when the desired option is selected.

In some dialog boxes where there is not enough room for a list box, lists of options are contained in a drop-down list box called an *option box*. Option boxes display with a down arrow. For example, in Figure G.8, the font color options are contained in an option box. To display the different color options, click the *Font color* option box arrow. If you are using the keyboard, press Alt + C.

Check Boxes

Some dialog boxes contain options preceded by a box. A check mark may or may not appear in the box. The Word Font dialog box shown in Figure G.8 displays a variety of check boxes within the *Effects* section. If a check mark appears in the box, the option is active (turned on). If the check box does not contain a check mark, the option is inactive (turned off). Any number of check boxes can be active. For example, in the Word Font dialog box, you can insert a check mark in several of the boxes in the *Effects* section to activate the options.

To make a check box active or inactive with the mouse, position the tip of the arrow pointer in the check box and then click the left mouse button. If you are using the keyboard, press Alt + the underlined letter of the option.

Text Boxes

Some options in a dialog box require you to enter text. For example, the boxes below the *Find what* and *Replace with* options at the Excel Find and Replace dialog box shown in Figure G.9 are text boxes. In a text box, type text or edit existing text. Edit text in a text box in the same manner as normal text. Use the Left and Right Arrow keys on the keyboard to move the insertion point without deleting text and use the Delete key or Backspace key to delete text.

Command Buttons

The buttons at the bottom of the Excel Find and Replace dialog box shown in Figure G.9 are called *command buttons*. Use a command button to execute or cancel a command. Some command buttons display with an ellipsis (...), which means another dialog box will open if you click that button. To choose a command button with the mouse, position the arrow pointer on the button and then click the left mouse button. To choose a command button with the keyboard, press the Tab key until the command button is surrounded by a marquee and then press the Enter key.

Option Buttons

The Word Insert Table dialog box shown in Figure G.10 contains options in the *AutoFit behavior* section preceded by option buttons. Only one option button can be selected at any time. When an option button is selected, a blue or black circle displays in the button. To select an option button with the mouse, position the tip of the arrow pointer inside the option button or on the option and then click the left mouse button. To make a selection with the keyboard, press and hold down the Alt key, press the underlined letter of the option, and then release the Alt key.

Figure G.9 Excel Find and Replace Dialog Box

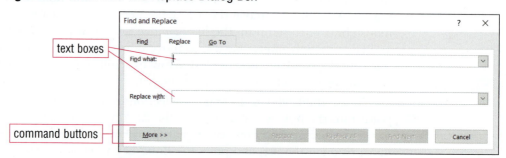

Figure G.10 Word Insert Table Dialog Box

measurement boxes

option buttons

💡 **Hint** In addition to using the up and down arrows, you can change the current measurement by selecting it and then typing the new measurement using the keyboard.

Measurement Boxes Some options in a dialog box contain measurements or amounts you can increase or decrease. These options are generally located in a measurement box. For example, the Word Insert Table dialog box shown in Figure G.10 contains the *Number of columns* and *Number of rows* measurement boxes. To increase a number in a measurement box, position the tip of the arrow pointer on the up arrow at the right of the measurement box and then click the left mouse button. To decrease the number, click the down arrow. If you are using the keyboard, press and hold down the Alt key and then press the underlined letter for the option, press the Up Arrow key to increase the number or the Down Arrow key to decrease the number, and then release the Alt key.

Choosing Commands with Keyboard Shortcuts

Applications in the Office suite offer a variety of keyboard shortcuts you can use to execute specific commands. Keyboard shortcuts generally require two or more keys. For example, the keyboard shortcut to display the Open dialog box in an application is Ctrl + F12. To use this keyboard shortcut, press and hold down the Ctrl key, press the F12 function on the keyboard, and then release the Ctrl key. For a list of keyboard shortcuts, refer to the Help files.

Choosing Commands with Shortcut Menus

The software applications in the Office suite include shortcut menus that contain commands related to different items. To display a shortcut menu, position the mouse pointer over the item for which you want to view more options, and then click the right mouse button or press Shift + F10. The shortcut menu will appear wherever the insertion point is positioned. For example, if the insertion point is positioned in a paragraph of text in a Word document, clicking the right mouse button or pressing Shift + F10 will cause the shortcut menu shown in Figure G.11 to display in the document screen (along with the Mini toolbar).

To select an option from a shortcut menu with the mouse, click the option. If you are using the keyboard, press the Up or Down Arrow key until the option is selected and then press the Enter key. To close a shortcut menu without choosing an option, click outside the shortcut menu or press the Esc key.

Figure G.11 Word Shortcut Menu

Working with Multiple Programs

As you learn the various applications in the Microsoft Office suite, you will notice many similarities between them. For example, the steps to save, close, and print are virtually the same whether you are working in Word, Excel, or PowerPoint. This consistency between applications greatly enhances your ability to transfer knowledge learned in one application to another within the suite. Another benefit to using Microsoft Office is the ability to have more than one application open at the same time and to integrate content from one program with another. For example, you can open Word and create a document, open Excel and create a spreadsheet, and then copy the Excel spreadsheet into Word.

When you open an application, a button containing an icon representing the application displays on the taskbar. If you open another application, a button containing an icon representing that application displays to the right of the first application button on the taskbar. Figure G.12 shows the taskbar with Word, Excel, Access, and PowerPoint open. To move from one program to another, click the taskbar button representing the desired application.

Customizing Settings

Before beginning computer projects in this textbook, you may need to customize your monitor's settings, change the DPI display setting, and turn on the display of file extensions. Projects in the chapters in this textbook assume that the monitor display is set at 1600 × 900 pixels, the DPI set at 125%, and that the display of file extensions is turned on. If you are unable to make changes to the monitor's resolution or the DPI settings, the projects can still be completed successfully. Some references in the text might not perfectly match what you see on your

Figure G.12 Taskbar with Word, Excel, Access, and PowerPoint Open screen, so some mental adjustments may need to be made for certain steps. For example, an item in a drop-down gallery might appear in a different column or row than what is indicated in the step instructions.

Before you begin learning the applications in the Microsoft Office 2016 suite, take a moment to check the display settings on the computer you are using. Your monitor's display settings are important because the ribbon in the Microsoft Office suite adjusts to the screen resolution setting of your computer monitor. A computer monitor set at a high resolution will have the ability to show more buttons in the ribbon than will a monitor set to a low resolution. The illustrations in this textbook were created with a screen resolution display set at 1600 × 900 pixels. In Figure G.13, the Word ribbon is shown three ways: at a lower screen resolution (1366 × 768 pixels), at the screen resolution featured throughout this textbook, and at a higher screen resolution (1920 × 1080 pixels). Note the variances in the ribbon in all three examples. If possible, set your display to 1600 × 900 pixels to match the illustrations you will see in this textbook.

Figure G.13 The Home Tab Displayed on a Monitor Set at Different Screen Resolutions

1366 × 768 screen resolution

1600 × 900 screen resolution

1920 × 1080 screen resolution

Project 1 Setting Monitor Display to 1600 × 900

Note: The resolution settings may be locked on lab computers. Also, some laptop screens and small monitors may not be able to display in a 1600 × 900 resolution.

1. At the Windows 10 desktop, right-click in a blank area of the screen.
2. At the shortcut menu, click the *Display settings* option.

3. At the Settings window with the SYSTEM screen active, scroll down and then click *Advanced display settings*.

4. Scroll down the Settings window until the *Resolution* option box is visible and take note of the current resolution setting. If the current resolution is already set to 1600 × 900, skip ahead to Step 8.
5. Click in the Resolution option box and then click the 1600 × 900 option at the drop-down list.

6. Click the Apply button.
7. Click the Keep Changes button.
8. Click the Close button.

Project 2 Changing the DPI Setting

Note: The DPI settings may be locked on lab computers. Also, some laptop screens and small monitors may not allow the DPI settings to be changed.

1. At the Windows 10 desktop, right-click in a blank area of the screen.
2. At the shortcut menu, click the *Display settings* option.
3. At the Settings window, take note of the current DPI percentage next to the text *Change the size of text, apps, and other items*. If the percentage is already set to 125%, skip to Step 5.
4. Click the slider bar below the text *Change the size of text, apps, and other items* and hold down the left mouse button, drag to the right until the DPI percentage is 125%, and then release the mouse button.

Identify   Detect

125%

Change the size of text, apps, and other items: 100% (

Orientation

Landscape

4

5. Close the computer window.

Project 3 Displaying File Extensions

1. At the Windows 10 desktop, click the File Explorer button on the taskbar.

2. At the File Explorer window, click the View tab.
3. Click the *File name extensions* check box in the Show/hide group to insert a check mark.

This PC

| File | Computer | View |

Preview pane   Medium icons   Small icons
Details pane   List   Details
Navigation   Tiles   Content
pane

Sort
by

☐ Item check boxes
☑ File name extensions
☑ Hidden items

Hide selected items

Panes   Layout   Current view   Show/hide

3

Downloads   Desktop   Documents
Documents
Pictures   Downloads   Music

4. Close the computer window.

Completing Computer Projects

Some projects in this textbook require that you open an existing file. Project files are saved on OneDrive in a zip file. Before beginning projects and assessments in this book and the accompanying ebook, copy the necessary folder from the zip file to your storage medium (such as a USB flash drive) using File Explorer. Begin downloading the files for this book by going to the ebook and clicking the Ancillary Links button that displays when the ebook displays this page or any chapter opener page with the Data Files tab on it.

Project 4 Downloading Files to a USB Flash Drive

Note: OneDrive is updated periodically, so the steps to download files may vary from the steps below.

1. Insert your USB flash drive into an available USB port.
2. Navigate to this textbook's ebook. If you are a SNAP user, navigate to the ebook by clicking the textbook ebook link on your Assignments page. If you are not a SNAP user, launch your browser and go to http://paradigm.bookshelf.emcp.com, log in, and then click the textbook ebook thumbnail. *Note: The steps in this activity assume you are using the Microsoft Edge browser. If you are using a different browser, the following steps may vary.*
3. Navigate to the ebook page that corresponds to this textbook page.
4. Click the Ancillary Links button in the menu. The menu that appears may be at the top of the window or along the side of the window, depending on the size of the window.

5. At the Ancillary Links dialog box, click the Data Files: All Files hyperlink.

6. Click the Download hyperlink at the top of the window.
7. Click the Open button in the message box when the DataFiles.zip finishes downloading.
8. Right-click the DataFiles folder in the Content pane.
9. Click the *Copy* option in the shortcut menu.

10. Click the USB flash drive that displays in the Navigation pane at the left side of the File Explorer window.
11. Click the Home tab in the File Explorer window.
12. Click the Paste button in the Clipboard group.

13. Close the File Explorer window by clicking the Close button in the upper right corner of the window.

Project 5 Deleting a File

Note: Check with your instructor before deleting a file.

1. At the Windows 10 desktop, open File Explorer by clicking the File Explorer button on the taskbar.
2. Click the *Downloads* folder in the navigation pane.
3. Right-click *DataFiles.zip*.
4. Click the *Delete* option at the shortcut menu.

Unit 1

Preparing and Formatting Worksheets

Microsoft® Excel®

Preparing an Excel Workbook

CHAPTER 1

Performance Objectives

Upon successful completion of Chapter 1, you will be able to:

1 Identify the various elements of an Excel workbook
2 Create a workbook
3 Enter data in a worksheet
4 Save a workbook
5 Edit data in a worksheet
6 Print a worksheet
7 Close a workbook and close Excel
8 Use the AutoComplete, AutoCorrect, and AutoFill features
9 Open a workbook
10 Pin and unpin a workbook and folder to and from the *Recent* option list
11 Insert a formula using the AutoSum button
12 Select cells and data within cells
13 Apply basic formatting to cells in a workbook
14 Use the Tell Me feature
15 Use the Help feature

Precheck

Check your current skills to help focus your study.

Many companies use spreadsheets to organize numerical and financial data and to analyze and evaluate information. An Excel spreadsheet can be used for such activities as creating financial statements, preparing budgets, managing inventory, and analyzing cash flow. In addition, numbers and values can be easily manipulated to create "What if?" situations. For example, using a spreadsheet, a person in a company can ask questions such as "What if the value in this category is decreased? How will that change affect the department budget?" Questions like these can be easily answered using the information in an Excel spreadsheet. Change the value in a category and Excel will recalculate formulas for the other values. In this way, a spreadsheet can be used not only for creating financial statements or budgets but also as a planning tool.

Data Files

Before beginning the chapter work, copy the EL1C1 folder to your storage medium and then make EL1C1 the active folder.

SNAP

If you are a SNAP user, launch the Precheck and Tutorials from your Assignments page.

Project 1 Prepare a Worksheet with Employee Information **3 Parts**

You will create a worksheet containing employee information, edit the contents, and then save and close the workbook.

Preview Finished Project

Tutorial

Opening a Blank Workbook

Creating a Worksheet

Open Excel by clicking the *Excel 2016* tile at the Windows Start menu.(Depending on your operating system, these steps may vary.) At the Excel 2016 opening screen, click the *Blank workbook* template. This displays a workbook with a blank worksheet, as shown in Figure 1.1. The elements of a blank Excel worksheet are described in Table 1.1.

A file created in Excel is referred to as a *workbook*. An Excel workbook consists of an individual worksheet (or *sheet*) by default but it can contain multiple worksheets, like the sheets of paper in a notebook. Notice the tab named *Sheet1*, at the bottom of the Excel window. The area containing the gridlines in the Excel window is called the *worksheet area*. Figure 1.2 identifies the elements of the worksheet area. Create a worksheet in the worksheet area that will be saved as part of a workbook. Columns in a worksheet are labeled with letters of the alphabet and rows are labeled with numbers. The intersection of columns and rows create a box, which is referred to as a *cell*. A cell is where data and formulas are entered.

Figure 1.1 Blank Excel Worksheet

Table 1.1 Elements of an Excel Worksheet

Feature	Description
active cell	location in the worksheet that displays typed data or is affected by a command
cell pointer	when this icon appears, select cells by clicking or dragging the mouse
Collapse the Ribbon button	when clicked, removes the ribbon from the screen (Redisplay the ribbon by double-clicking a tab, except the File tab.)
dialog box launcher	click to open a dialog box with more options for that group
File tab	displays the backstage area that contains options for working with and managing files
Formula bar	displays the contents stored in the active cell
horizontal and vertical scroll bars	used to view various parts of the worksheet beyond the current screen
Name box	displays the active cell address or name assigned to the active cell
New sheet button	click to insert a new worksheet in the workbook
Quick Access Toolbar	contains buttons for commonly used commands that can be executed with a single mouse click
ribbon	contains the tabs with commands and buttons
sheet tab	identifies the current worksheet in the workbook
Status bar	displays the current mode, action messages, view buttons, and Zoom slider bar
tab	contains commands and buttons organized into groups
Tell Me text box	provides information and guidance on how to perform a function
Title bar	displays the workbook name followed by the application name
worksheet area	contains the cells used to create a worksheet

Figure 1.2 Elements of the Worksheet Area

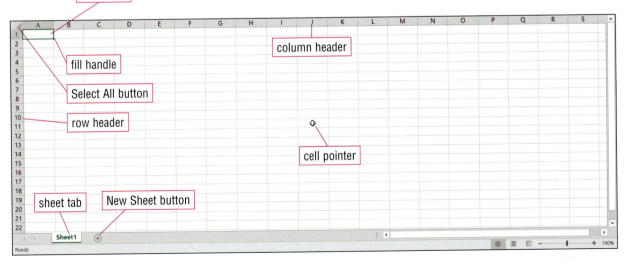

The horizontal and vertical lines that define the cells in the worksheet area are called *gridlines*. When a cell is active (displays with a green border), the cell address, also called the *cell reference*, displays in the Name box. The cell reference includes the column letter and row number. For example, if the first cell of the worksheet is active, the cell reference *A1* displays in the Name box. A green border surrounds the active cell. Any number of adjacent cells can be made active and form a range. A range is typically identified by the first cell reference and last cell reference separated by a colon. For example, the range A1:C1 contains the cells A1, B1, and C1.

Entering Data in a Worksheet

Tutorial

Entering Data

 Find & Select

Hint To make a cell active, position the cell pointer in the cell and then click the left mouse button.

Hint Ctrl + G is the keyboard shortcut to display the Go To dialog box.

Enter data such as text, a number, or a value in a cell. To enter data in a cell, make the cell active and then type the data. To make the next cell active, press the Tab key. Table 1.2 displays additional commands for making a specific cell active.

Another method for making a cell active is to use the Go To feature. To use this feature, click the Find & Select button in the Editing group on the Home tab and then click *Go To*. At the Go To dialog box, type the cell reference in the *Reference* text box and then click OK.

Before typing data into the active cell, check the Status bar. The word *Ready* should display at the left side. As data is typed in a cell, the word *Ready* changes to *Enter*. Data typed in a cell displays in the cell and in the Formula bar. If the data entered in a cell is longer than the cell can accommodate, the data overlaps the next cell to the right. (It does not become a part of the next cell—it simply overlaps it. How to change column widths to accommodate data is explained later in this chapter.)

Table 1.2 Commands for Making a Specific Cell Active

To make this cell active	Press
cell below current cell	Enter
cell above current cell	Shift + Enter
next cell	Tab
previous cell	Shift + Tab
cell at beginning of row	Home
next cell in direction of arrow	Up, Down, Left, or Right Arrow key
last cell in worksheet	Ctrl + End
first cell in worksheet	Ctrl + Home
cell in next window	Page Down
cell in previous window	Page Up
cell in window to right	Alt + Page Down
cell in window to left	Alt + Page Up

If data entered in a cell consists of text and the text does not fit into the cell, it overlaps the next cell. If, however, a number is entered in a cell and the number is too long to fit in the cell, Excel changes the display of the number to number symbols *(###)*. This change is made because Excel does not want to mislead users by a number when only a portion of it displays in the cell.

Along with the keyboard, the mouse can be used to make a specific cell active. To make a specific cell active with the mouse, position the mouse pointer, which displays as a white plus symbol (+) (called the *cell pointer*), in the cell and then click the left mouse button. The cell pointer displays as a white plus sign when positioned in a cell in the worksheet and displays as an arrow pointer when positioned on other elements of the Excel window, such as options and buttons on tabs and scroll bars.

Scroll through a worksheet using the horizontal and/or vertical scroll bars. Scrolling shifts the display of cells in the worksheet area but does not change the active cell. Scroll through a worksheet until the desired cell is visible and then click in the cell.

Saving a Workbook

Tutorial

Saving with the Same Name

Tutorial

Saving with a New Name

Save

Save an Excel workbook, which consists of one or more worksheets, by clicking the Save button on the Quick Access Toolbar or by clicking the File tab and then clicking the *Save As* option at the backstage area. At the Save As backstage area, click the *Browse* option and the Save As dialog box displays. At the Save As dialog box, click the desired location in the Navigation pane, type a name for the workbook in the *File name* text box, and then press the Enter key or click the Save button. Bypass the Save As backstage area and go directly to the Save As dialog box by using the keyboard shortcut F12.

To save an Excel workbook in the EL1C1 folder on your storage medium, display the Save As dialog box, click the drive representing your storage medium in the Navigation pane, and then double-click *EL1C1* in the Content pane.

A workbook file name can contain up to 255 characters, including the drive letter and any folder names, and it can include spaces. A workbook cannot have the same name first in uppercase and then in lowercase letters. Also, some symbols cannot be used in a file name, such as the following:

Quick Steps

Save a Workbook
1. Click Save button on Quick Access Toolbar.
2. At Save As backstage area, click *Browse* option.
3. At Save As dialog box, navigate to folder.
4. Type workbook name.
5. Press Enter.

Hint Ctrl + S is the keyboard shortcut to save a workbook.

forward slash (/)

backslash (\\)

greater-than symbol (>)

less-than symbol (<)

pipe symbol (|)

question mark (?)

quotation mark (")

colon (:)

asterisk (*)

1. Open Excel by clicking the *Excel 2016* tile at the Windows Start menu. (Depending on your operating system, these steps may vary.)
2. At the Excel 2016 opening screen, click the *Blank workbook* template. (This opens a workbook with a blank worksheet.)
3. At the blank Excel worksheet, create the worksheet shown in Figure 1.3 by completing the following steps:
   a. Press the Enter key to make cell A2 the active cell.
   b. Type Employee in cell A2.
   c. Press the Tab key. (This makes cell B2 active.)
   d. Type Location and then press the Tab key. (This makes cell C2 active.)
   e. Type Benefits and then press the Enter key to move the insertion point to cell A3.
   f. Type Avery in cell A3.
   g. Continue typing the data shown in Figure 1.3. (For commands that make specific cells active, refer to Table 1.2.)
4. After typing the data shown in the cells in Figure 1.3, save the workbook by completing the following steps:
   a. Click the Save button on the Quick Access Toolbar.
   b. At the Save As backstage area, click the *Browse* option.
   c. At the Save As dialog box, navigate to the EL1C1 folder in the Navigation pane and then double-click the *EL1C1* folder in the Content pane.
   d. Select the text in the *File name* text box and then type 1-EmpBene.
   e. Press the Enter key or click the Save button.

Check Your Work

Figure 1.3 Project 1a

	A	B	C	D
1				
2	Employee	Location	Benefits	
3	Avery			
4	Connors			
5	Estrada			
6	Juergens			
7	Mikulich			
8	Talbot			
9				

Editing Data in a Cell

Edit data being typed in a cell by pressing the Backspace key to delete the character to the left of the insertion point or pressing the Delete key to delete the character to the right of the insertion point. To change the data in a cell, click in the cell to make it active and then type the new data. When a cell containing data is active, anything typed will take the place of the existing data.

If only a portion of the data in a cell needs to be edited, double-click in the cell. This makes the cell active, moves the insertion point inside the cell, and displays the word *Edit* at the left side of the Status bar. Move the insertion point using the arrow keys or the mouse and then make the needed corrections. Press the Home key to move the insertion point to the first character in the cell or Formula bar or press the End key to move the insertion point to the last character.

When the editing of data in a cell is complete, be sure to change out of the Edit mode. To do this, make another cell active by pressing the Enter key, the Tab key, or Shift + Tab. Another way to change out of the Edit mode and return to the Ready mode is clicking in another cell or clicking the Enter button on the Formula bar.

If the active cell does not contain data, the Formula bar displays only the cell reference (by column letter and row number). As data is typed, two buttons become active on the Formula bar to the right of the Name box, as shown in Figure 1.4. Click the Cancel button to delete the current cell entry. (A cell entry can also be deleted by pressing the Delete key.) Click the Enter button when finished typing or editing the cell entry. Click the Enter button on the Formula bar and the word *Enter* (or *Edit*) at the left side of the Status bar changes to *Ready*.

Figure 1.4 Buttons on the Formula Bar

Project 1b Editing Data in a Cell
Part 2 of 3

1. With **1-EmpBene.xlsx** open, double-click in cell A7 (contains *Mikulich*).
2. Move the insertion point immediately left of the *k* and then type c. (This changes the spelling to *Mickulich*.)
3. Click in cell A4 (contains *Connors*), type Bryant, and then press the Tab key. (Clicking only once allows you to type over the existing data.)
4. Edit cell C2 by completing the following steps:
   a. Click the Find & Select button in the Editing group on the Home tab and then click *Go To* at the drop-down list.

b. At the Go To dialog box, type c2 in the
   Reference text box and then click OK.
c. Type Classification (over *Benefits*).
5. Click in any other cell.
6. Click the Save button on the Quick Access
   Toolbar to save the workbook again.

Check Your Work

Tutorial

Printing a
Worksheet

💡 *Hint* Ctrl + P is
the keyboard shortcut
to display the Print
backstage area.

Printing a Worksheet

With a workbook open, click the File tab and the Info backstage area displays, as shown in Figure 1.5. Use buttons and options at the backstage area to perform functions such as opening, closing, saving, and printing a workbook. Click the Back button (in the upper left corner of the backstage area) to exit the backstage area without completing an action or press the Esc key on the keyboard.

Print a worksheet from the Print backstage area, as shown in Figure 1.6. To display this backstage area, click the File tab and then click the *Print* option. The Print backstage area can also be displayed with the keyboard shortcut Ctrl + P.

Figure 1.5 Info Backstage Area

Click the Back button to redisplay the worksheet.

Information about the worksheet displays in this area of the Info backstage area.

options

Book1 - Excel

Student Name

Info

Info
New
Open
Save
Save As
Save as Adobe PDF
Print
Share
Export
Publish
Close

Account
Options
Feedback

Protect Workbook
Control what types of changes people can make to this workbook.

Inspect Workbook
Before publishing this file, be aware that it contains:
☐ Author's name and absolute path

Manage Workbook
Check in, check out, and recover unsaved changes.
☐ There are no unsaved changes.

Browser View Options
Pick what users can see when this workbook is viewed on the Web.

Properties *
Size   Not saved yet
Title   Add a title
Ta...   Add a tag
Categories   Add a category

Related Dates
Last Modified
Created   Today, 6:23 PM
Last Printed

Related People
Author
              Student Name
              Add an author
Last Modified By   Not saved yet
Show All Properties

Figure 1.6 Print Backstage Area

Click the Print button to send the worksheet to the specified printer.

worksheet preview

Print option

navigation buttons

Quick Steps

Print a Worksheet
1. Click File tab.
2. Click *Print* option.
3. Click Print button.

Click the Print button in the Print backstage area to send the worksheet to the printer and use the *Copies* measurement box to specify the number of copies to be printed. Below the Print button are two categories: *Printer* and *Settings*. Use the gallery in the *Printer* category to specify the printer. The *Settings* category contains a number of galleries, each with options for specifying how the workbook will be printed. Use the galleries to specify whether the pages are collated when printed; what page orientation, page size, and margins the workbook should have; and whether the worksheet will be scaled to print all rows and columns of data on one page.

Another method for printing a workbook is to add the Quick Print button on the Quick Access Toolbar and then click the button. This sends the workbook directly to the printer without displaying the Print backstage area. To insert this button on the Quick Access Toolbar, click the Customize Quick Access Toolbar button at the right side of the toolbar and then click *Quick Print* at the drop-down list. To remove the Quick Print button from the Quick Access Toolbar, right-click the button and then click *Remove from Quick Access Toolbar* at the drop-down list.

Tutorial

Closing a Workbook and Closing Excel

Closing a Workbook

To close an Excel workbook without closing Excel, click the File tab and then click the *Close* option. Using the keyboard shortcut Ctrl + F4 will also close a workbook.

Quick Steps

Close a Workbook
1. Click File tab.
2. Click *Close* option.

Close

Closing Excel

To close Excel, click the Close button in the upper right corner of the screen. The Close button contains an *X* and, if the mouse pointer is positioned on the button, a ScreenTip displays with the name *Close*. Pressing the keyboard shortcut Alt + F4 will also close Excel.

Using Automatic Entering Features

Excel contains several features that help enter data into cells quickly and efficiently. These features include AutoComplete, which automatically inserts data in a cell that begins the same as a previous entry; AutoCorrect, which automatically corrects many common typographical errors; and AutoFill, which automatically inserts words, numbers, or formulas in a series.

Using AutoComplete

The AutoComplete feature automatically inserts data in a cell that begins the same as a previous entry. If the data inserted by AutoComplete is the correct data, press the Tab key or the Enter key. If it is not the correct data, simply continue typing the correct data. This feature can be very useful in a worksheet that contains repetitive data entries. For example, consider a worksheet that repeats the word *Payroll*. The second and subsequent times this word is to be inserted in a cell, simply typing the letter *P* will cause AutoComplete to insert the entire word.

Using AutoCorrect

The AutoCorrect feature automatically corrects many common typing errors. To see what symbols and words are included in AutoCorrect, click the File tab and then click *Options*. At the Excel Options dialog box, click *Proofing* in the left panel and then click the AutoCorrect Options button in the right panel. This displays the AutoCorrect dialog box with the AutoCorrect tab selected, as shown in Figure 1.7, with a list box containing the replacement data.

Figure 1.7 AutoCorrect Dialog Box with AutoCorrect Tab Selected

Type the text displayed in the first column of this list box in a worksheet and then press the spacebar and the text is replaced by the text in the second column of this list box.

At the AutoCorrect dialog box, type the text shown in the first column in the list box and then press the spacebar and the text in the second column is inserted in the cell. Along with symbols, the AutoCorrect dialog box contains commonly misspelled words and common typographical errors.

Project 1c **Inserting Data in Cells with AutoCorrect and AutoComplete** Part 3 of 3

1. With **1-EmpBene.xlsx** open, make cell A1 active.
2. Type the text in cell A1, as shown in Figure 1.8. Insert the ® symbol by typing (r) and then pressing the Enter key. (AutoCorrect will change (r) to ®.)
3. Type the remaining text in the cells. When you type the *W* in *West* in cell B5, the AutoComplete feature will insert *West*. Accept this by pressing the Tab key. (Pressing the Tab key accepts *West* and also makes the cell to the right active.) Use the AutoComplete feature to enter *West* in cells B6 and B8 and *North* in cell B7. Use AutoComplete to enter the second and subsequent occurrences of *Salaried* and *Hourly*.
4. Click the Save button on the Quick Access Toolbar.
5. Print **1-EmpBene.xlsx** by clicking the File tab, clicking the *Print* option, and then clicking the Print button at the Print backstage area. (The gridlines will not print.)

6. Close the workbook by clicking the File tab and then clicking the *Close* option at the backstage area.

Check Your Work

Figure 1.8 Project 1c

	A	B	C	D
1	Team Net®			
2	Employee	Location	Classification	
3	Avery	West	Hourly	
4	Bryant	North	Salaried	
5	Estrada	West	Salaried	
6	Juergens	West	Salaried	
7	Mickulich	North	Hourly	
8	Talbot	West	Hourly	
9				

Project 2 **Open and Format a Workbook and Insert Formulas**   **3 Parts**

You will open an existing workbook and insert formulas to find the sums and averages of numbers.

Preview Finished Project

Tutorial

Entering Data Using the Fill Handle

Using AutoFill

When a cell is active, a thick green border surrounds it and a small green square displays in the bottom right corner of the border. This green square is called the AutoFill *fill handle* (see Figure 1.2 on page 5). Use the fill handle to fill a range of cells with the same data or with consecutive data. For example, suppose the year 2018 is to be inserted in a row or column of cells. To do this quickly, type *2018* in the first cell, position the mouse pointer on the fill handle, click and hold down the left mouse button, drag across or down into the cells in which the year is to be inserted, and then release the mouse button.

The fill handle can also be used to insert a series in a row or column of cells. For example, suppose a worksheet is being created with data for all the months in the year. Type *January* in the first cell, position the mouse pointer on the fill handle, click and hold down the left mouse button, drag down or across into 11 more cells, and then release the mouse button. Excel automatically inserts the other 11 months in the year in the proper order. When using the fill handle, the cells must be adjacent. Table 1.3 identifies the sequences inserted in cells by Excel when specific types of data are entered.

Certain sequences—such as *2, 4* and *Jan 12, Jan 13*—require that both cells be selected before using the fill handle. If only the cell containing *2* is active, the fill handle will insert *2*s in the selected cells. The list in Table 1.3 is only a sampling of what the fill handle can do. A variety of other sequences can be inserted in a worksheet using the fill handle.

An Auto Fill Options button displays when cells are filled with data using the fill handle. Click this button and a list of options displays for filling the cells. By default, data and formatting are filled in each cell. Use the Auto Fill Options button to choose to fill only the formatting in the cells or fill only the data without the formatting. Other fill options include choosing to copy data into the selected cells or to fill the data as a series.

Hint When filling cells with the fill handle, press and hold down the Ctrl key if you want to copy the same data instead of displaying the next instance in the series.

 Auto Fill Options

Table 1.3 AutoFill Fill Handle Series

Enter this data*	And the fill handle will insert this sequence in adjacent cells*
January	February, March, April, and so on
Jan	Feb, Mar, Apr, and so on
Jan 15, Jan 16	17-Jan, 18-Jan, 19-Jan, and so on
Monday	Tuesday, Wednesday, Thursday, and so on
Product 1	Product 2, Product 3, Product 4, and so on
Qtr 1	Qtr 2, Qtr 3, Qtr 4
2, 4	6, 8, 10, and so on

* Commas represent data in separate cells.

Tutorial

Opening a
Workbook from a
Removable Disk

Opening a Workbook

Open an Excel workbook at the Open dialog box. To display this dialog box, click the File tab and then click the *Open* option. This displays the Open backstage area. Other methods of displaying the Open backstage area include using the keyboard shortcut Ctrl + O and inserting an Open button on the Quick Access Toolbar. At the Open backstage area, click the *Browse* option. At the Open dialog box, navigate to the desired folder and then double-click the workbook name in the Content pane. Bypass the Open backstage area and go directly to the Open dialog box by using the keyboard shortcut Ctrl + F12.

Tutorial

Opening from the
Recent Option List

Opening a Workbook from the *Recent* Option List

With the *Recent* option selected in the middle panel at the Open backstage area, a list displays with the most recently opened workbooks. Up to 25 workbook names display in the list by default. Open a workbook from this list by clicking the workbook name.

Pinning and Unpinning Workbooks and Folders

Quick Steps

Open a Workbook
1. Click File tab.
2. Click *Open* option.
3. Click *Browse* option.
4. Navigate to folder.
5. Double-click workbook name.

Pin a Workbook to Recent Option List
1. Click File tab.
2. Click *Open* option.
3. Position mouse pointer over workbook name.
4. Click left-pointing push pin.

Unpin a Workbook from *Recent* Option List
1. Click File tab.
2. Click *Open* option.
3. Position mouse pointer over workbook name.
4. Click down-pointing push pin.

If a workbook is opened on a regular basis, consider pinning it to the *Recent* option list. To pin a workbook, position the mouse pointer over the workbook name and then click the left-pointing push pin at the right of the workbook name. The left-pointing push pin changes to a down-pointing push pin and the pinned workbook is inserted into a new category named *Pinned*. The *Pinned* category displays at the top of the *Recent* option list. The next time the Open backstage area displays, the pinned workbook displays in the *Pinned* category at the top of the *Recent* option list.

A workbook can also be pinned to the Recent list at the Excel 2016 opening screen. When a workbook is pinned, it displays at the top of the Recent list and the *Recent* option list at the Open backstage area. To "unpin" a workbook from the Recent or *Recent* option list, click the pin to change it from a down-pointing push pin to a left-pointing push pin. More than one workbook can be pinned to a list. Another method for pinning and unpinning documents is to use the shortcut menu. Right-click a workbook name and then click the option *Pin to list* or *Unpin from list*.

In addition to workbooks, folders can be pinned to a list at the Save As backstage area. The third panel in the Save As backstage area displays a list of the most recently opened folders and groups them into categories such as *Today*, *Yesterday*, and *Last Week*. Pin a folder or folders to the list and a *Pinned* category is created; the folder names display in the category.

Project 2a Inserting Data in Cells with the Fill Handle   Part 1 of 3

1. Open **FillCells.xlsx** by completing the following steps:
   a. Click the File tab and then click the *Open* option.
   b. With the *This PC* option selected, click the *Browse* option.
   c. Navigate to the to the EL1C1 folder on your storage medium and then double-click **FillCells.xlsx**.
2. Save the workbook with the name **1-FillCells** by completing the following steps:
   a. Press F12 to display the Save As dialog box.
   b. Press the Home key on the keyboard to position the insertion point at the beginning of the name in the *File name* text box and then type 1-.
   c. Click the Save button.

3. Add data to cells as shown in Figure 1.9. Begin by making cell B1 active and then typing *January*.

4. Position the mouse pointer on the fill handle for cell B1, click and hold down the left mouse button, drag across into cell G1, and then release the mouse button.

5. Type a sequence and then use the fill handle to fill the remaining cells by completing the following steps:

   a. Make cell A2 active and then type *Year 1*.
   b. Make cell A3 active and then type *Year 3*.
   c. Select cells A2 and A3 by clicking in cell A2 and holding down the left mouse button, dragging into cell A3, and then releasing the mouse button.
   d. Drag the fill handle for cell A3 down into cell A5. (This inserts *Year 5* in cell A4 and *Year 7* in cell A5.)

6. Use the fill handle to fill adjacent cells with a number but not the formatting by completing the following steps:
   a. Make cell B2 active. (This cell contains *100* with bold formatting.)
   b. Drag the fill handle for cell B2 to the right into cell E2. (This inserts *100* in cells C2, D2, and E2.)
   c. Click the Auto Fill Options button at the bottom right of the selected cells.
   d. Click the *Fill Without Formatting* option at the drop-down list.

7. Use the fill handle to apply formatting only by completing the following steps:
   a. Make cell B2 active.
   b. Drag the fill handle down into cell B5.
   c. Click the Auto Fill Options button and then click *Fill Formatting Only* at the drop-down list.

8. Make cell A10 active and then type *Qtr 1*.
9. Drag the fill handle for cell A10 into cell A13.
10. Save **1-FillCells.xlsx**.

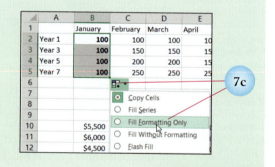

Check Your Work

Figure 1.9 Project 2a

	A	B	C	D	E	F	G
1		January	February	March	April	May	June
2	Year 1	**100**	100	100	100	125	125
3	Year 3	**150**	150	150	150	175	175
4	Year 5	**200**	200	200	150	150	150
5	Year 7	**250**	250	250	250	250	250
6							
7							
8							
9							
10	Qtr1	$5,500	$6,250	$7,000	$8,500	$5,500	$4,500
11	Qtr2	$6,000	$7,250	$6,500	$9,000	$4,000	$5,000
12	Qtr3	$4,500	$8,000	$6,000	$7,500	$6,000	$5,000
13	Qtr4	$6,500	$8,500	$7,000	$8,000	$5,500	$6,000
14							

Entering Formulas

Quick Steps

Enter a Formula Using the AutoSum button
1. Click in cell.
2. Click AutoSum button.
3. Check range identified and make changes if necessary.
4. Press Enter.

Excel is a powerful decision-making tool for manipulating data to answer questions in "What if?" situations. Insert a formula in a worksheet and then manipulate the data to make projections, answer specific questions, and plan for the future. For example, the manager of a department might use an Excel worksheet to prepare a department budget and then determine how hiring a new employee or increasing the volume of production will affect the budget.

Insert a formula in a worksheet to perform calculations on values. A formula contains a mathematical operator, value, cell reference, cell range, and function. Formulas can be written that add, subtract, multiply, and/or divide values. Formulas can also be written that calculate averages, percentages, minimum and maximum values, and much more. The AutoSum button in the Editing group on the Home tab inserts a formula to calculate the total of a range of cells.

Using the AutoSum Button to Add Numbers

Tutorial

Entering Formulas Using the AutoSum Button

 AutoSum

Hint You can use the keyboard shortcut Alt + = to insert the SUM function in a cell.

Use the AutoSum button in the Editing group on the Home tab to insert a formula. The AutoSum button adds numbers automatically with the SUM function. Make active the cell in which the formula will be inserted (this cell should be empty) and then click the AutoSum button. Excel looks for a range of cells containing numbers above the active cell. If no cell above contains numbers, then Excel looks to the left of the active cell. Excel suggests the range of cells to be added. If the suggested range is not correct, drag through the range of cells with the mouse and then press the Enter key. Double-click the AutoSum button to automatically insert the SUM function with the range Excel chooses.

Project 2b Adding Values with the AutoSum Button   Part 2 of 3

1. With **1-FillCells.xlsx** open, make cell A6 active and then type Total.
2. Make cell B6 active and then calculate the sum of the cells by clicking the AutoSum button in the Editing group on the Home tab.
3. Excel inserts the formula *=SUM(B2:B5)* in cell B6. This is the correct range of cells, so press the Enter key.

4. Make cell C6 active and then click the AutoSum button in the Editing group.
5. Excel inserts the formula *=SUM(C2:C5)* in cell C6. This is the correct range of cells, so press the Enter key.

6. Make cell D6 active.
7. Double-click the AutoSum button. This inserts the formula =*SUM(D2:D5)* in cell D6 and inserts the sum *700*.
8. Insert the sum in cells E6, F6, and G6.
9. Save **1-FillCells.xlsx**.

Check Your Work

Quick Steps
Insert an Average
Formula Using the
AutoSum Button
1. Click in cell.
2. Click AutoSum button arrow.
3. Click *Average*.
4. Specify range.
5. Press Enter.

Using the AutoSum Button to Average Numbers

A common function in a formula is the AVERAGE function. With this function, a range of cells are added together and then the total is divided by the number of cell entries. The AVERAGE function is available on the AutoSum button. Click the AutoSum button arrow and a drop-down list displays with a number of common functions.

Tutorial

Copying Formulas

Using the Fill Handle to Copy a Formula

Quick Steps
Copy a Formula Using
the Fill Handle
1. Insert formula in cell.
2. Make active cell containing formula.
3. Using fill handle, drag into cells to contain formula.

The same basic formula can be inserted in other cells in a worksheet. When copying a formula to other locations in a worksheet, use a relative cell reference. Copy a formula containing relative cell references and the cell references change. For example, insert the formula =*SUM(A2:C2)* in cell D2 and then copy it relatively to cell D3 and the formula in cell D3 displays as =*SUM(A3:C3)*. Use the fill handle to copy a formula relatively in a worksheet. To do this, position the mouse pointer on the fill handle until the mouse pointer turns into a thin black cross, click and hold down the left mouse button, drag and select the cells, and then release the mouse button.

Project 2c Inserting the AVERAGE Function and Copying a Formula Relatively   Part 3 of 3

1. With **1-FillCells.xlsx** open, make cell A14 active and then type Average.
2. Insert the average of the range B10:B13 by completing the following steps:
   a. Make cell B14 active.
   b. Click the AutoSum button arrow in the Editing group and then click *Average* at the drop-down list.
   c. Excel inserts the formula =*AVERAGE(B10:B13)* in cell B14. This is the correct range of cells, so press the Enter key.
3. Copy the formula relatively to the range C14:G14 by completing the following steps:
   a. Make cell B14 active.
   b. Position the mouse pointer on the fill handle, click and hold down the left mouse button, drag across into cell G14, and then release the mouse button.

9							
10	Qtr1	$5,500	$6,250	$7,000	$8,500	$5,500	$4,500
11	Qtr2	$6,000	$7,250	$6,500	$9,000	$4,000	$5,000
12	Qtr3	$4,500	$8,000	$6,000	$7,500	$6,000	$5,000
13	Qtr4	$6,500	$8,500	$7,000	$8,000	$5,500	$6,000
14	Average	$5,625	$7,500	$6,625	$8,250	$5,250	$5,125
15							

4. Save, print, and then close **1-FillCells.xlsx**.

Check Your Work

Project 3 **Format a Monthly Expenses Worksheet** **2 Parts**

You will open a workbook containing a monthly expenses worksheet and then change the column width, merge and center cells, and apply number formatting to numbers in cells.

Preview Finished Project

Tutorial

Selecting Cells

Selecting Cells

Use a variety of methods for formatting cells in a worksheet. For example, change the alignment of data in cells or rows or add character formatting. To identify the cells that are to be affected by the formatting, select the specific cells.

Selecting Cells Using the Mouse

Select specific cells, columns, or rows in a worksheet using the mouse. Table 1.4 displays the methods for selecting cells using the mouse.

Hint The first cell in a range displays with a white background and is the active cell.

Selected cells, except the active cell, display with a gray background (this may vary) rather than a white background. The active cell is the first cell in the selection block and displays in the normal manner (white background with black data). Selected cells remain selected until another cell is clicked with the mouse or an arrow key is pressed on the keyboard.

Selecting Cells Using the Keyboard

Keys on the keyboard can be used to select specific cells within a worksheet. Table 1.5 displays the commands for selecting specific cells. If a worksheet contains data, Ctrl + A selects all cells containing data. If a worksheet contains groups of data separated by empty cells, Ctrl + A or Ctrl + Shift + spacebar selects a group of cells rather than all the cells.

Selecting Data within Cells

The selection commands presented in Table 1.4 and Table 1.5 select the entire cell. Specific characters within a cell can also be selected. To do this with the

Table 1.4 Selecting with the Mouse

To select this	Do this
column	Position the cell pointer on the column header (a letter) and then click the left mouse button.
row	Position the cell pointer on the row header (a number) and then click the left mouse button.
adjacent cells	Drag with the mouse into specific cells to select them.
nonadjacent cells	Press and hold down the Ctrl key while clicking the column header, row header, or specific cells.
all cells in worksheet	Click the Select All button. (Refer to Figure 1.2 on page 5.)

Table 1.5 Selecting Cells Using the Keyboard

To select	Press
cells in direction of arrow key	Shift + arrow key
from active cell to beginning of row	Shift + Home
from active cell to beginning of worksheet	Shift + Ctrl + Home
from active cell to last cell in worksheet containing data	Shift + Ctrl + End
entire column	Ctrl + spacebar
entire row	Shift + spacebar
cells containing data	Ctrl + A
groups of data separated by empty cells	Ctrl + Shift + spacebar

Hint Select nonadjacent columns or rows by holding down the Ctrl key while selecting cells.

mouse, position the cell pointer in a cell and then double-click the left mouse button. Drag with the I-beam pointer through the data to be selected. Data selected within a cell displays with a gray background. To select data in a cell using the keyboard, press and hold down the Shift key and then press the arrow key that moves the insertion point in the desired direction. All the data the insertion point passes through will be selected. Press the F8 function key to turn on the Extend Selection mode, move the insertion point in the desired direction to select the data, and then press F8 to turn off the Extend Selection mode. When the Extend Selection mode is on, the words *Extend Selection* display at the left side of the Status bar.

Applying Basic Formatting

Quick Steps

Change Column Width
Drag column boundary line.
OR
Double-click column boundary line.

Merge and Center Cells
1. Select cells.
2. Click Merge & Center button on Home tab.

Excel provides a wide range of formatting options that can be applied to cells in a worksheet. Some basic formatting options that are helpful when creating a worksheet include changing the column width, merging and centering cells, and formatting numbers.

Changing Column Width

If data such as text or numbers overlaps in a cell, increase the width of the column to accommodate the data. To do this, position the mouse pointer on the gray boundary line between columns in the column header (Figure 1.2 identifies the column header) until the pointer turns into a double-headed arrow pointing left and right and then drag the boundary to the new location. If the column contains data, double-click the column boundary line at the right side to automatically adjust the width of the column to accommodate the longest entry.

Merging and
Centering Cells

Merge &
Center

Merging and Centering Cells

As explained earlier in this chapter, if the typed text is longer than the cell can accommodate, the text overlaps the next cell to the right (unless the text typed is numbers). Merge cells to accommodate the text and also center the text within the merged cells. To merge cells and center the text, select the cells and then click the Merge & Center button in the Alignment group on the Home tab.

Project 3a Changing Column Width and Merging and Centering Cells   **Part 1 of 2**

1. Open **MoExps.xlsx** and then save it with the name **1-MoExps**.
2. Change column widths by completing the following steps:
   a. Position the mouse pointer in the column header on the boundary line between columns A and B until the pointer turns into a double-headed arrow pointing left and right.

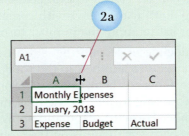

   b. Double-click the left mouse button.
   c. Position the mouse pointer in the column header on the boundary line between columns E and F and then double-click the left mouse button.
   d. Position the mouse pointer in the column header on the boundary line between columns F and G and then double-click the left mouse button.
3. Merge and center cells by completing the following steps:
   a. Select the range A1:C1.
   b. Click the Merge & Center button in the Alignment group on the Home tab.

   c. Select the range A2:C2.
   d. Click the Merge & Center button.
   e. Select cells E1 and F1 and then click the Merge & Center button.
4. Save **1-MoExps.xlsx**.

Check Your Work

Formatting Numbers

Numbers in a cell by default align at the right and decimals and commas do not display unless they are typed in the cell. Change the format of numbers with buttons in the Number group on the Home tab. Symbols that can be added when a number is formatted include a percent symbol (%), a comma (,), and a dollar symbol ($). For example, if the number *$45.50* is typed in a cell, Excel automatically applies the Currency format to the number. If *45%* is entered in a cell, Excel automatically applies the Percentage format to the number. The Number group on the Home tab contains five buttons that are used to format numbers in cells. The five buttons are shown and described in Table 1.6.

Specify the formatting for numbers in cells in a worksheet before typing the numbers or format existing numbers in a worksheet. The Increase Decimal and Decrease Decimal buttons in the Number group on the Home tab change how many digits display after the decimal point. The Number group on the Home tab also contains the *Number Format* option box. Click the *Number Format* option box arrow and a drop-down list displays with common number formats. Click a format at the drop-down list to apply the number format to the cell or selected cells.

A general guideline in accounting is to insert a dollar symbol before the first amount in a column and before the total amount but not before the number amounts between them. Format a worksheet following this guideline by applying the Accounting format to the first amount and total amount using the Accounting Number Format button and applying the Accounting format to the number amounts between them using the Comma Style button. To differentiate between the two Accounting formats, steps in this textbook will use the term *Accounting format* when the Accounting Number Format button in the Number group on the Home tab is to be clicked. The term *Comma format* will be used when the Comma Style button is to be clicked.

Table 1.6 Number Formatting Buttons

Click this button		To do this
$ ▾	Accounting Number Format	Add a dollar symbol, any necessary commas, and a decimal point followed by two digits even if none are typed; right-align the number in the cell.
%	Percent Style	Multiply the cell value by 100 and display the result with a percent symbol; right-align the number in the cell.
,	Comma Style	Add any necessary commas and a decimal point followed by two digits even if none are typed; right-align the number in the cell.
.0 .00	Increase Decimal	Increase the number of digits displayed after the decimal point in the selected cell.
.00 .0	Decrease Decimal	Decrease the number of digits displayed after the decimal point in the selected cell.

1. With **1-MoExps.xlsx** open, make cell B13 active and then double-click the AutoSum button. (This inserts the total of the numbers in the range B4:B12.)
2. Make cell C13 active and then double-click the AutoSum button.
3. Apply the Accounting format to cells by completing the following steps:
   a. Select cells B4 and C4.
   b. Click the Accounting Number Format button in the Number group on the Home tab.
   c. Decrease the number of digits displayed after the decimal point to none by clicking the Decrease Decimal button in the Number group two times.

   d. Select cells B13 and C13.
   e. Click the Accounting Number Format button.
   f. Click the Decrease Decimal button two times.
4. Apply the Comma format to numbers by completing the following steps:
   a. Select the range B5:C12.
   b. Click the Comma Style button in the Number group.
   c. Click the Decrease Decimal button two times.

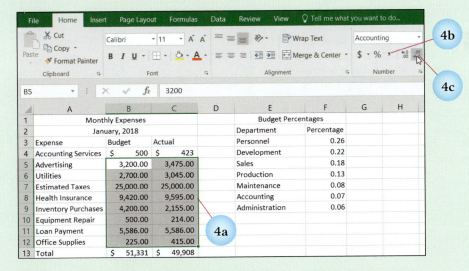

5. Apply the Percentage format to numbers by completing the following steps:
   a. Select the range F3:F9.
   b. Click the Percent Style button in the Number group on the Home tab.
6. Click in cell A1.
7. Save **1-MoExps.xlsx**.

Check Your Work

You will use the Tell Me feature to learn how to change the font size of text and display the Excel Help window with information about wrapping text. You will use the Help feature to learn more about entering data in cells, changing the font color, and printing a workbook.

Preview Finished Project

Tutorial

Using the Tell Me Feature

Quick Steps

Use the Tell Me Feature
1. Click in *Tell Me* text box.
2. Type topic or feature.
3. Click option at drop-down list.

Using the Tell Me Feature

Excel 2016 includes a Tell Me feature that provides information and guidance on how to complete certain actions. Use the Tell Me feature by clicking in the *Tell Me* text box on the ribbon to the right of the View tab and then typing a term, function, or action. As text is typed in the *Tell Me* text box, a drop-down list displays with options that are refined as more text is typed, which is referred to as "word-wheeling." The drop-down list contains options for completing the function, displaying information on the function from sources on the web, or displaying information on the action in the Excel Help window.

The Tell Me drop-down list also includes a Smart Lookup option. Clicking the Smart Lookup option opens the Smart Lookup task pane, as shown in Figure 1.10, at the right side of the screen with information on the typed text from a variety of Internet sources. Smart Lookup can also be accessed using the Smart Lookup button on the Review tab or by selecting a cell, right-clicking in the selected cell, and then clicking the *Smart Lookup* option at the shortcut menu.

Figure 1.10 Smart Lookup Task Pane

With the *Explore* option selected, the Smart Lookup task pane displays information about the topic or feature from various Internet sources.

With the *Define* option selected, the Smart Lookup task pane displays definitions of the topic or feature from various Internet sources.

Close button

Smart Lookup

Explore | Define

Explore Wikipedia

Line wrap and word wrap - Wikipedia,
Line breaking, also known as word wrapping, is the process of breaking a section of text into lines such that it will fit...

Wrap - Wikipedia, the free encycloped
Word wrap, how text is continued onto the next line; Vehicle wrap, a coloured polymer used to cover a car's paintwork, for ...

More

Web search

Line wrap and word wrap - Wikipedia,
https://en.wikipedia.org/wiki/Word_wrap
Line breaking, also known as word

1. With **1-MoExps.xlsx** open, select the range A1:E1.
2. Click in the *Tell Me* text box and then type font size.
3. At the drop-down list, click the *Font Size* option.
4. At the side menu, click the *14* option. (This increases the font size of the text in the range A1:E1, and the height of row 1 automatically adjusts to accommodate the larger text.)
5. Use the Tell Me feature to display the Excel Help window with information on wrapping text by completing the following steps:
   a. Click in the *Tell Me* text box and then type wrap text.
   b. Click the *Get Help on "wrap text"* option.

   c. At the Excel Help window, click a hyperlink to an article that interests you.
   d. After reading the information on wrapping text, close the Excel Help window by clicking the Close button in the upper right corner of the window.
6. Display information on scrolling in a workbook in the Smart Lookup task pane by completing the following steps:
   a. Click in the *Tell Me* text box and then type scrolling.
   b. Click the *Smart Lookup on "scrolling"* option. (The first time you use the Smart Lookup feature, the Smart Lookup task pane displays a message indicating that data will be sent to Bing and suggesting that you read the privacy statement for more details. At this message, click the Got it button.)
   c. If two options—*Explore* and *Define*—display at the top of the Smart Lookup task pane, click the *Define* option. This will display a definition of the word *scrolling* in the Smart Lookup task pane.
   d. Close the Smart Lookup task pane by clicking the Close button in the upper right corner of the task pane.
7. Save, print, and then close **1-MoExps.xlsx**.

Check Your Work

Using Help

Microsoft Excel includes a Help feature that contains information about Excel features and commands. This on-screen reference manual is similar to Windows Help and the Help features in Word, PowerPoint, and Access. Press the keyboard shortcut F1 to display the Excel Help window, as shown in Figure 1.11.

Alternatively, type a term, function, or action in the *Tell Me* text box and then click the *Get Help on* option to open the Excel Help file with articles related to the typed text. In the Excel Help window, type a topic, feature, or question in the search text box and then press the Enter key or click the Search help button. Articles related to the search text display in the Excel Help window. Click an article and the article information displays in the Excel Help window. If the article contains a Show All hyperlink, click the hyperlink and the article expands to show additional information related to the topic. When the Show All hyperlink is clicked, it becomes the Hide All hyperlink.

The Excel Help window contains five buttons to the left of the search text box, as identified in Figure 1.11. Use the Back and Forward buttons to navigate in the window. Click the Home button to return to the Excel Help window opening screen. Print information on a topic or feature by clicking the Print button and then clicking the Print button at the Print dialog box. Make the text in the Excel Help window larger by clicking the Use Large Text button.

Quick Steps
Use the Help Feature
1. Press F1.
2. Click in search text box.
3. Type term, function, or action.
4. Press Enter.
OR
1. Click in *Tell Me* text box.
2. Type term, function, or action.
3. Click *Get Help on* option.

Figure 1.11 Excel Help Window

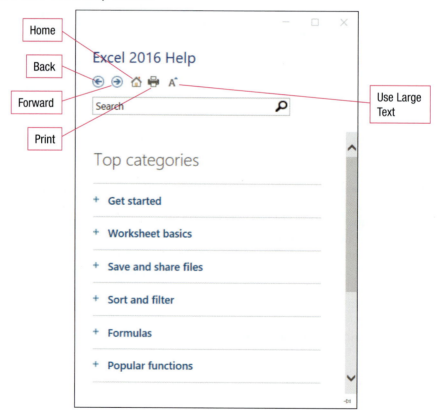

Getting Help from a ScreenTip

Hover the mouse pointer over a button and a ScreenTip displays with information about the button. Some button ScreenTips display with a Help icon and the <u>Tell me more</u> hyperlink. Click the <u>Tell me more</u> hyperlink text or press the F1 function key and the Excel Help window opens with information about the button feature.

Project 4b Using the Help Feature   **Part 2 of 3**

1. At the blank screen, press Ctrl + N to display a blank workbook. (Ctrl + N is the keyboard shortcut to open a blank workbook.)
2. Click in the *Tell Me* text box and then type enter data.
3. Click the *Get Help on "enter data"* option.
4. When the Excel Help window displays with a list of articles, click the article <u>Enter data manually in worksheet cells</u> hyperlink.
5. When the article displays, read the information about entering data in cells.
6. Click the Print button in the Excel Help window to display the Print dialog box. If you want to print the information about the topic, click the Print button; otherwise, click the Cancel button to close the dialog box.
7. Click the Use Large Text button in the Excel Help window to increase the size of the text.
8. Click the Use Large Text button again to return the text to the normal size.
9. Click the Back button to return to the previous window.
10. Click the Forward button to return to the article on entering data manually in worksheet cells.
11. Click the Home button to return to the original Excel Help window screen.
12. Click the Close button to close the Excel Help window.
13. Hover the mouse pointer over the Font Color button in the Alignment group on the Home tab until the ScreenTip displays and then click the <u>Tell me more</u> hyperlink at the bottom of the ScreenTip.
14. At the Excel Help window, read the information and then close the window.

Getting Help in a Dialog Box or at the Backstage Area

Some dialog boxes and the backstage area contain a Help button that, when clicked, displays the Excel Help window with specific information about the dialog box or backstage area. After reading and/or printing the information, close the dialog box by clicking the Close button in the upper right corner of the dialog box or close the backstage area by clicking the Back button or pressing the Esc key.

Project 4c Getting Help in a Dialog Box and Backstage Area **Part 3 of 3**

1. At the blank workbook, click the File tab and then click the *Print* option.
2. At the Print backstage area, click the Microsoft Excel Help button in the upper right corner of the backstage area.
3. At the Excel Help window, click the hyperlink to an article on printing that interests you. Read the article and then close the Excel Help window.
4. Click the Back button to return to the blank workbook.
5. At the blank workbook, click the Number group dialog box launcher.
6. At the Format Cells dialog box with the Number tab selected, click the Help button in the upper right corner of the dialog box.

7. Click the hyperlink to the article on available number formats.
8. Read the article, close the Excel Help window, and then close the Format Cells dialog box.
9. Close the blank workbook.

Chapter Summary

- A file created in Excel is called a *workbook* and consists of individual worksheets.
- The intersection of a column and a row in a worksheet is referred to as a *cell*. Gridlines are the horizontal and vertical lines that define cells.
- When the insertion point is positioned in a cell, the cell name (also called the *cell reference*) displays in the Name box at the left side of the Formula bar. The cell name includes the column letter and row number.
- If the data entered in a cell consists of text (letters) and does not fit into the cell, it overlaps the cell to the right. If the data consists of numbers and does not fit into the cell, the numbers change to number symbols (###).
- Save a workbook by clicking the Save button on the Quick Access Toolbar or by clicking the File tab and then clicking the *Save As* option. At the Save As backstage area, click the *Browse* option. At the Save As dialog box, navigate to the desired folder, type the workbook name in the *File name* text box, and then press the Enter key.
- To replace data in a cell, click in the cell and then type the new data. To edit data within a cell, double-click in the cell and then make the necessary changes.
- Print a workbook by clicking the File tab, clicking the *Print* option, and then clicking the Print button.

- Close a workbook by clicking the File tab and then clicking the *Close* option or by using the keyboard shortcut Ctrl + F4.
- Close Excel by clicking the Close button in the upper right corner of the screen or using the keyboard shortcut Alt + F4.
- The AutoComplete feature automatically inserts a previous entry if the character or characters being typed in a cell match a previous entry. The AutoCorrect feature corrects many common typographical errors. The AutoFill fill handle adds the same or consecutive data into a range of cells.
- Open a workbook by clicking the File tab and then clicking the *Open* option. At the Open backstage area, click the *Browse* option. At the Open dialog box, double-click the workbook.
- Use the AutoSum button in the Editing group on the Home tab to find the total or average of data in columns or rows.
- Select all the cells in a column by clicking the column header. Select all the cells in a row by clicking the row header. Select all the cells in a worksheet by clicking the Select All button immediately to the left of the column headers.
- Change the column width by dragging or double-clicking the column boundary line.
- Merge and center adjacent cells by selecting them and then clicking the Merge & Center button in the Alignment group on the Home tab.
- Format numbers in cells with buttons in the Number group on the Home tab.
- The Tell Me feature provides information and guidance on how to complete actions. The *Tell Me* text box is located on the ribbon to the right of the View tab.
- Use the Tell Me feature, click a hyperlink in a button ScreenTip, or press F1 to display the Excel Help window. At this window, type a topic in the search text box and then press the Enter key.
- Some dialog boxes and the backstage area contain a Help button that, when clicked, displays information specific to the dialog box or backstage area.

Commands Review

FEATURE	RIBBON TAB, GROUP/OPTION	BUTTON	KEYBOARD SHORTCUT
Accounting format	Home, Number	$ ▾	
AutoSum	Home, Editing	Σ	Alt + =
close Excel		✕	Alt + F4
close workbook	File, *Close*		Ctrl + F4
Comma format	Home, Number	,	
decrease decimal place	Home, Number	.00 →.0	
Excel Help window			F1
Go To dialog box	Home, Editing	🔍	Ctrl + G
increase decimal place	Home, Number	←.0 .00	
merge and center cells	Home, Alignment	↔	
Open backstage area	File, *Open*		Ctrl + O
Percentage format	Home, Number	%	Ctrl + Shift + %
Print backstage area	File, *Print*		Ctrl + P
Save As backstage area	File, *Save As*	💾	Ctrl + S

Workbook

Chapter study tools and assessment activities are available in the *Workbook* ebook. These resources are designed to help you further develop and demonstrate mastery of the skills learned in this chapter.

Microsoft Excel

Inserting Formulas in a Worksheet

Performance Objectives

Upon successful completion of Chapter 2, you will be able to:

1 Write formulas with mathematical operators

2 Type a formula in the Formula bar

3 Copy a formula

4 Identify common formula and function errors

5 Use the Insert Function dialog box to insert a formula in a cell

6 Write formulas with the AVERAGE, MAX, MIN, COUNT, COUNTA, NOW, and TODAY functions

7 Display formulas

8 Use absolute and mixed cell references in formulas

Precheck

Check your current skills to help focus your study.

Excel is a powerful decision-making tool that contains data that can be manipulated in "What if?" situations. Insert a formula in a worksheet and then manipulate the data to make projections, answer specific questions, and plan for the future. For example, the owner of a company might prepare a worksheet on production costs and then determine the impact on company revenues if production is increased or decreased. Insert a formula in a worksheet to perform calculations on values. A formula contains a mathematical operator, value, cell reference, cell range, and function. Formulas can be written that add, subtract, multiply, and/or divide values. Formulas can also be written that calculate averages, percentages, minimum and maximum values, and much more. As you learned in Chapter 1, Excel includes an AutoSum button in the Editing group on the Home tab that inserts a formula to calculate the total of a range of cells, along with some other commonly used formulas. Along with the AutoSum button, Excel includes a Formulas tab that offers a variety of functions, which are built-in formulas, to create formulas.

Data Files

Before beginning chapter work, copy the EL1C2 folder to your storage medium and then make EL1C2 the active folder.

SNAP

If you are a SNAP user, launch the Precheck and Tutorials from your Assignments page.

Project 1 **Insert Formulas in a Worksheet**   **4 Parts**

You will open a worksheet containing data and then insert formulas to calculate differences, salaries, and percentages of budgets.

Preview Finished Project

Tutorial

Entering Formulas Using the Keyboard

Hint After typing a formula in a cell, press the Enter key, the Tab key, Shift + Tab, or click the Formula bar.

Writing Formulas with Mathematical Operators

As explained in Chapter 1, the AutoSum button in the Editing group on the Home tab creates a formula. A formula can also be written using mathematical operators. Commonly used mathematical operators and their purposes are displayed in Table 2.1. When writing a formula, begin it with the equals sign (=). For example, to create a formula that divides the contents of cell B2 by the contents of cell C2 and inserts the result in cell D2, make D2 the active cell and then type *=b2/c2*. The column reference letters used in formulas can be entered as either lowercase or uppercase letters. If the column reference letters are entered in a formula in lowercase, Excel will automatically convert the column reference letters to uppercase.

Table 2.1 Mathematical Operators

Operator	Purpose	Operator	Purpose
+	addition	/	division
-	subtraction	%	percentage
*	multiplication	^	exponentiation

Tutorial

Copying Formulas

  Fill

Quick Steps

Copy a Formula Relatively
1. Insert formula in cell.
2. Select cell containing formula and all cells to which the formula is to be copied.
3. Click Fill button.
4. Click direction option.

Copying a Formula with Relative Cell References

In many worksheets, the same basic formula is used repetitively. In a situation where a formula is copied to other locations in a worksheet, use a relative cell reference. Copy a formula containing relative cell references and the cell references change. For example, if the formula *=SUM(A2:C2)* is entered in cell D2 and then copied relatively into cell D3, the formula in cell D3 displays as *=SUM(A3:C3)*. (Additional information on cell references is provided later in this chapter in the section "Using an Absolute Cell Reference in a Formula.")

To copy a formula relatively in a worksheet, use the Fill button or the fill handle. (You used the fill handle to copy a formula in Chapter 1.) To use the Fill button, select the cell containing the formula and all the cells to which the formula is to be copied and then click the Fill button in the Editing group on the Home tab. At the Fill button drop-down list, click the direction. For example, click the *Down* option if the formula is being copied down the worksheet.

1. Open **HCReports.xlsx** and then save it with the name **2-HCReports**.
2. Insert a formula by completing the following steps:
   a. Make cell D3 active.
   b. Type the formula =c3-b3.
   c. Press the Enter key.
3. Copy the formula into the range D4:D10 by completing the following steps:
   a. Select the range D3:D10.
   b. Click the Fill button in the Editing group on the Home tab and then click *Down* at the drop-down list.

4. Save **2-HCReports.xlsx**.
5. With the worksheet open, make the following changes to cell contents:
   B4: Change *48,290* to *46425*
   C6: Change *61,220* to *60000*
   B8: Change *55,309* to *57415*
   B9: Change *12,398* to *14115*
6. Make cell D3 active, apply the Accounting format by clicking the Accounting Number Format button in the Number group on the Home tab, and then click the Decrease Decimal button two times to decrease the digits past the decimal point to none.
7. Save **2-HCReports.xlsx**.

Check Your Work

As explained in Chapter 1, the fill handle can be used to copy a formula up, down, left, or right within a worksheet. To use the fill handle, insert the data in the cell (text, value, formula, etc.). With the cell active, position the mouse pointer on the fill handle until the mouse pointer turns into a thin black cross. Click and hold down the left mouse button, drag and select the cells, and then release the mouse button. When dragging a cell containing a formula, a relative version of the formula is copied to the selected cells.

Checking Cell References in a Formula

Hint Use the fill handle to copy a relative version of a formula.

To verify if a formula is using the correct cell references, double-click in a cell containing a formula and the cells referenced in the formula display with a colored border and shading in the worksheet. This feature makes it easy to identify which cells are being referenced in a formula and is helpful when trying to identify errors that may occur in a formula.

1. With **2-HCReports.xlsx** open, insert a
   formula by completing the following steps:
   a. Make cell D15 active.
   b. Click in the Formula bar text box and then
      type =c15*b15.
   c. Click the Enter button on the Formula bar.
2. Copy the formula into the range D16:D20 by
   completing the following steps:
   a. Make sure cell D15 is still the active cell.
   b. Position the mouse pointer on the fill handle
      at the lower right corner of cell D15 until
      the pointer turns into a thin black cross.
   c. Click and hold down the left mouse button,
      drag into cell D20, and then release the
      mouse button.
3. Save **2-HCReports.xlsx**.
4. Double-click in cell D20 to display the formula
   with cell references color coded to ensure the
   formula was copied relatively and then press
   the Enter key to exit Edit mode.
5. Make the following changes to cell contents in
   the worksheet:
      B16: Change *20* to *28*
      C17: Change *18.75* to *19.10*
      B19: Change *15* to *24*
6. Select the range D16:D20 and then apply the
   Comma format by clicking the Comma Style
   button in the Number group on the Home tab.
7. Save **2-HCReports.xlsx**.

1c   1b

IF			✕	✓	f_x	=c15*b15	
	A	B	C	D

	A	B	C	D
1	**Highland Construction**			
2	**Customer**	**Actual**	**Planned**	**Difference**
3	Sellar Corporation	$ 30,349	$ 34,109	$ 3,760
4	Main Street Photos	46,425	48,100	1,675
5	Sunset Automotive	34,192	32,885	(1,307)
6	Linstrom Enterprises	63,293	60,000	(3,293)
7	Morcos Media	29,400	30,500	1,100
8	Green Valley Optics	57,415	58,394	979
9	Detailed Designs	14,115	13,100	(1,015)
10	Arrowstar Company	87,534	86,905	(629)
11				
12				
13				
14	**Name**	**Hours**	**Rate**	**Salary**
15	Carolyn Bentley	35	$ 23.15	=c15*b15
16	Lindon Cassini	20	19.00	

	Name	Hours	Rate	Salary
13				
14	**Name**	**Hours**	**Rate**	**Salary**
15	Carolyn Bentley	35	$ 23.15	$ 810.25
16	Lindon Cassini	20	19.00	$ 380.00
17	Michelle DeFord	40	18.75	$ 750.00
18	Javier Farias	24	16.45	$ 394.80
19	Deborah Gould	15	11.50	$ 172.50
20	William Jarman	15	11.50	$ 172.50
21				

2c

Check Your Work

Tutorial

Entering Formulas
Using the Mouse

Quick Steps

Write a Formula
by Pointing
1. Click in cell that will
   contain formula.
2. Type equals sign.
3. Click in cell to
   be referenced in
   formula.
4. Type mathematical
   operator.
5. Click in next cell
   reference.
6. Press Enter.

Writing a Formula by Pointing

The formulas written in Projects 1a and Project 1b used cell references such as
=*c3-b3*. Another method for writing a formula is to "point" to the specific cells that
are to be part of the formula. Creating a formula by pointing is more accurate than
typing the cell reference because a mistake can be made when the cell reference is
typed.

   To write a formula by pointing, click in the cell that will contain the
formula, type the equals sign to begin the formula, and then click in the cell to
be referenced in the formula. This inserts a moving border around the cell and
changes the mode from Enter to Point. (The word *Point* displays at the left side
of the Status bar.) Type the mathematical operator and then click in the next
cell reference. Continue in this manner until all the cell references are specified
and then press the Enter key. This ends the formula and inserts the result of the
calculation in the active cell. When a formula is written by pointing, the range of
cells to be included in the formula can be selected.

1. With **2-HCReports.xlsx** open, enter a formula by pointing that calculates the percentage of actual budget by completing the following steps:
   a. Make cell D25 active.
   b. Type the equals sign (=).
   c. Click in cell B25. (This inserts a moving border around the cell and changes the mode from Enter to Point.)
   d. Type the forward slash symbol (/).
   e. Click in cell C25.
   f. Make sure the formula in D25 is *=B25/C25* and then press the Enter key.

23				
24	**Expense**	**Actual**	**Budget**	**% of Actual**
25	Salaries	$ 126,000	$ 124,000	=B25/C25
26	Commissions	58,000	54,500	
27	Media space	8,250	10,100	
28	Travel expenses	6,350	6,000	
29	Dealer display	4,140	4,500	
30	Payroll taxes	2,430	2,200	
31	Telephone	1,450	1,500	
32				

1a-1f

2. Make cell D25 active, click the fill handle and hold down the left mouse button, drag into cell D31, and then release the mouse button.
3. Save **2-HCReports.xlsx**.

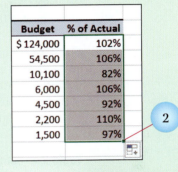

Budget	% of Actual
$ 124,000	102%
54,500	106%
10,100	82%
6,000	106%
4,500	92%
2,200	110%
1,500	97%

2

Check Your Work

Determining the Order of Operations

Tutorial

Determining the Order of Operations

If a formula contains two or more operators, Excel uses the same order of operations used in algebra. From left to right in a formula, this order is negations (negative number—a number preceded by -) first, then percentages (%), then exponentiations (^), followed by multiplications (*), divisions (/), additions (+), and subtractions (-). To change the order of operations, put parentheses around the part of the formula that is to be calculated first. For example, if cells A1, B1, and C1 all contain the value 5, the result of the formula *=a1+b1*c1* will be 30 (because 5*5=25 and 5+25=30). However, if parentheses are placed around the first two cell references so the formula displays as *=(a1+b1)*c1*, the result will be 50 (because 5+5=10 and 10*5=50).

Excel requires each left parenthesis to be paired with a right parenthesis. If a formula is missing a left or right parenthesis, a message box will display explaining that an error exists in the formula and providing a possible correction, which can be accepted or declined. This feature is useful when creating a formula that contains multiple layers of parentheses (called *nested parentheses*) because it will identify any missing left or right parentheses in the formula. Parentheses can also be used in various functions to further determine the order of operations.

Using the Trace Error Button

Trace Error

When typing or editing data in a worksheet, a button may display near the active cell. The general term for this button is *smart tag*. The display of the smart tag button varies depending on the action performed. In Project 1d, you will insert a formula that causes a smart tag button named the Trace Error button to appear. When the Trace Error button appears, a small dark-green triangle also displays in the upper left corner of the cell. Click the Trace Error button and a drop-down list displays with options for updating the formula to include specific cells, getting help with the error, ignoring the error, editing the error in the Formula bar, and completing an error check. In Project 1d, two of the formulas you insert return the correct results. You will click the Trace Error button, read about what Excel perceives to be the error, and then tell Excel to ignore the error.

Identifying Common Formula Errors

Excel is a sophisticated program that requires data input and formula creation to follow strict guidelines in order to function properly. When guidelines that specify how data or formulas are entered are not followed, Excel will display one of many error codes. When an error is identified with a code, determining and then fixing the problem is easier than if no information is provided. Table 2.2 lists some common error codes.

Most errors in Excel result from the user incorrectly inputting data into a worksheet. However, most error messages will not display until the data is used in a formula or function. Common mistakes made while inputting data include placing text in a cell that requires a number, entering data in the wrong location, and entering numbers in an incorrect format. Other errors result from entering a formula or function improperly. A formula will often display an error message if it is trying to divide a number by 0 or contains a circular reference (that is, when a formula within a cell uses the results of that formula in the same cell).

Table 2.2 Common Error Codes

Error Code	Meaning
#DIV/O	A formula is attempting to divide a number by 0.
#N/A	An argument parameter has been left out of a function.
#NAME?	A function name is not entered correctly.
#NUM!	An argument parameter does not meet a function's requirements.
#REF!	A referenced cell no longer exists within a worksheet.
#VALUE	The data entered is the wrong type (for example, text instead of numbers).

Project 1d Writing a Formula by Pointing That Calculates Percentage of Down Time

1. With **2-HCReports.xlsx** open, enter a formula by pointing that calculates the percentage of equipment down time by completing the following steps:
   a. Make cell B45 active.
   b. Type the equals sign followed by the left parenthesis (=().
   c. Click in cell B37. (This inserts a moving border around the cell and changes the mode from Enter to Point.)
   d. Type the minus symbol (-).
   e. Click in cell B43.
   f. Type the right parenthesis followed by the forward slash ()/).
   g. Click in cell B37.
   h. Make sure the formula in cell B45 is *=(B37-B43)/B37* and then press the Enter key.

2. Make cell B45 active, click the fill handle and hold down the left mouse button, drag into cell G45, and then release the mouse button.

3. Enter a formula by dragging into a range of cells by completing the following steps:
   a. Click in cell B46 and then click the AutoSum button in the Editing group on the Home tab.
   b. Select the range B37:D37.
   c. Click the Enter button on the Formula bar. (This inserts *7,260* in cell B46.)

4. Click in cell B47 and then complete steps similar to those in Step 3 to create a formula that totals hours available from April through June (the range E37:G37). (This inserts *7,080* in cell B47.)

5. Click in cell B46 and notice the Trace Error button. Complete the following steps to read about the error and then tell Excel to ignore it:
   a. Click the Trace Error button.
   b. At the drop-down list, click the *Help on this error* option.
   c. Read the information in the Excel Help window and then close the window.
   d. Click the Trace Error button again and then click *Ignore Error* at the drop-down list.

6. Remove the dark-green triangle from cell B47 by completing the following steps:
   a. Click in cell B47.
   b. Click the Trace Error button and then click *Ignore Error* at the drop-down list.

7. Save, print, and then close **2-HCReports.xlsx**.

Check Your Work

Inserting Formulas with Functions

In Project 2b in Chapter 1, the AutoSum button was used to insert the formula *=SUM(b2:b5)* in a cell. The beginning section of the formula, *=SUM*, is called a *function*, and it is a built-in formula. Using a function takes fewer keystrokes when creating a formula. For example, using the *=SUM* function made it unnecessary to type each cell to be included in the formula with the plus symbol (+) between cell entries.

Excel provides other functions for writing formulas. A function operates on what is referred to as an *argument*. An argument may consist of a constant, a cell reference, or another function. In the formula *=SUM(b2:b5)*, the cell range *(b2:b5)* is an example of a cell reference argument. An argument may also contain a *constant*. A constant is a value entered directly into the formula. For example, in the formula *=SUM(b3:b9,100)*, the cell range *b3:b9* is a cell reference argument and *100* is a constant. In this formula, 100 is always added to the sum of the cells.

The phrase *returning the result* is used to describe when a value calculated by the formula is inserted in a cell. The term *returning* refers to the process of calculating the formula and the term *result* refers to the value inserted in the cell.

fx Insert Function

Type a function in a cell in a worksheet or use the Insert Function button on the Formula bar or the Formulas tab to write the formula. Figure 2.1 displays the Formulas tab, which provides the Insert Function button and other buttons for inserting functions in a worksheet. The Function Library group on the Formulas tab contains a number of buttons for inserting functions from a variety of categories, such as *Financial*, *Logical*, *Text*, and *Date & Time*.

Click the Insert Function button on the Formula bar or the Formulas tab and the Insert Function dialog box displays, as shown in Figure 2.2. At the Insert Function dialog box, the most recently used functions display in the *Select a function* list box. Choose a function category by clicking the *Or select a category* option box arrow and then clicking the category at the drop-down list. Use the *Search for a function* search box to locate a specific function.

Figure 2.1 Formulas Tab

Figure 2.2 Insert Function Dialog Box

The most recently used functions display in this list box.

Click this option box arrow to display a list of categories.

Hint You can also display the Insert Function dialog box by clicking the AutoSum button arrow and then clicking *More Functions*.

With the function category selected, choose a function in the *Select a function* list box and then click OK. This displays a Function Arguments dialog box, like the one shown in Figure 2.3. At this dialog box, enter in the *Number1* text box the range of cells to be included in the formula, any constants to be included as part of the formula, or another function.

Type a cell reference or a range of cells in an argument text box or point to a cell or select a range of cells with the mouse pointer. Pointing to cells or selecting a range of cells using the mouse pointer is the preferred method of entering data into an argument text box because there is less chance of making errors. After entering a range of cells, a constant, or another function, click OK.

More than one argument can be included in a function. If the function contains more than one argument, press the Tab key to move the insertion point to the *Number2* text box and then enter the second argument. If the function dialog box covers a specific cell or cells, move the dialog box by positioning the mouse pointer on the dialog box title bar, clicking and holding down the left mouse button, dragging the dialog box to a different location, and then releasing the mouse button.

Figure 2.3 Example of a Function Arguments Dialog Box

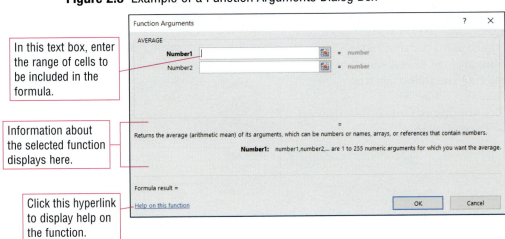

In this text box, enter the range of cells to be included in the formula.

Information about the selected function displays here.

Click this hyperlink to display help on the function.

Excel performs over 300 functions that are divided into these 13 categories: *Financial, Date & Time, Math & Trig, Statistical, Lookup & Reference, Database, Text, Logical, Information, Engineering, Cube, Compatibility,* and *Web.* Clicking the AutoSum button in the Function Library group on the Formulas tab or the Editing group on the Home tab automatically adds numbers with the SUM function. The SUM function is included in the *Math & Trig* category. In some projects in this chapter, formulas will be written with functions in other categories, including *Statistical* and *Date & Time.*

Excel includes the Formula AutoComplete feature that displays a drop-down list of functions. To use this feature, click in the cell or in the Formula bar text box, type the equals sign, and then type the first letter of the function. This displays a drop-down list with functions that begin with the letter. Double-click the function, enter the cell references, and then press the Enter key.

Tutorial

Using Statistical Functions

Writing Formulas with Statistical Functions

Write formulas with statistical functions such as AVERAGE, MAX, MIN, and COUNT. The AVERAGE function returns the average (arithmetic mean) of the arguments. The MAX function returns the largest value in a set of values and the MIN function returns the smallest value in a set of values. Use the COUNT or COUNTA functions to count the number of cells that contain numbers or letters within the specified range.

Finding Averages A common function in a formula is the AVERAGE function. With this function, a range of cells are added together and then divided by the number of cells. In Project 2a, you will use the AVERAGE function, to add all the test scores for a student and then divide that number by the total number of scores. You will use the Insert Function button to simplify the creation of the formula containing an AVERAGE function.

One of the advantages to using formulas in a worksheet is that the data can be easily manipulated to answer certain questions. In Project 2a, you will learn the impact of retaking certain tests on the final average score.

Project 2a Averaging Test Scores in a Worksheet

Part 1 of 4

1. Open **DWTests.xlsx** and then save it with the name **2-DWTests**.
2. Use the Insert Function button to find the average of test scores by completing the following steps:
   a. Make cell E4 active.
   b. Click the Insert Function button on the Formula bar.

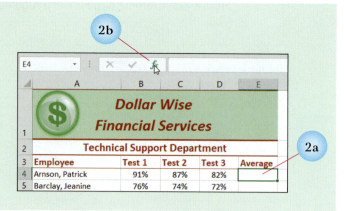

c. At the Insert Function dialog box, click the *Or select a category* option box arrow and then click *Statistical* at the drop-down list.

d. Click *AVERAGE* in the *Select a function* list box.

e. Click OK.

f. At the Function Arguments dialog box, make sure *B4:D4* displays in the *Number1* text box. (If not, type b4:d4 in the *Number1* text box.)

g. Click OK.

3. Copy the formula by completing the following steps:

a. Make sure cell E4 is still active.

b. Position the mouse pointer on the fill handle until the pointer turns into a thin black cross.

c. Click and hold down the left mouse button, drag into cell E16, and then release the mouse button.

4. Save and then print **2-DWTests.xlsx**.

5. After viewing the averages of test scores, you notice that a couple of students have low averages. You decide to see what happens to these average scores if students retake the tests on which they scored the lowest. You decide that a student can score a maximum of 70% on a retake of the test. Make the following changes to test scores to see how the changes affect the test averages:

  B9: Change *50* to *70*
  C9: Change *52* to *70*
  D9: Change *60* to *70*
  B10: Change *62* to *70*
  B14: Change *0* to *70*
  D14: Change *0* to *70*
  D16: Change *0* to *70*

6. Save and then print **2-DWTests.xlsx**. (Compare the test averages of Teri Fisher-Edwards, Stephanie Flanery, Claude Markovits, and Douglas Pherson to see how retaking the tests affects their final test averages.)

Check Your Work

When a function such as the AVERAGE function calculates cell entries, it ignores certain cell entries. The AVERAGE function will ignore text in cells and blank cells (not zeros). For example, in the worksheet containing test scores, a couple of cells contained 0%. This entry was included in the averaging of the test scores. To prevent including that particular test in the average, enter text in the cell such as *N/A* (for *not applicable*) or leave the cell blank.

Finding Maximum and Minimum Values The MAX function in a formula returns the maximum value in a cell range and the MIN function returns the minimum value in a cell range. For example, the MAX and MIN functions in a worksheet containing employee hours can be used to determine which employee worked the most hours and which worked the least. In a worksheet containing sales commissions, the MAX and MIN functions can be used to identify the salesperson who earned the highest commission and the one who earned the lowest.

Insert a MAX or a MIN function into a formula in the same manner as an AVERAGE function. In Project 2b, you will use the Formula AutoComplete feature to insert the MAX function in cells to determine the highest test score average and the Insert Function button to insert the MIN function to determine the lowest test score average.

Project 2b Finding Maximum and Minimum Values in a Worksheet

Part 2 of 4

1. With **2-DWTests.xlsx** open, type the following in the specified cells:
   A19: Highest Test Average
   A20: Lowest Test Average
   A21: Average of Completed Tests
2. Insert a formula to identify the highest test score average by completing the following steps:
   a. Make cell B19 active.
   b. Type =m. (This displays the Formula AutoComplete list.)
   c. Double-click MAX in the Formula AutoComplete list.
   d. Type e4:e16) and then press the Enter key.
3. Insert a formula to identify the lowest test score average by completing the following steps:
   a. Make sure cell B20 is active.
   b. Click the Insert Function button on the Formula bar.
   c. At the Insert Function dialog box, make sure *Statistical* is selected in the *Or select a category* option box and then click *MIN* in the *Select a function* list box. (You will need to scroll down the list to display *MIN*.)
   d. Click OK.
   e. At the Function Arguments dialog box, type e4:e16 in the *Number1* text box.
   f. Click OK.
4. Insert a formula to determine the average of the completed test scores by completing the following steps:
   a. Make cell B21 active.
   b. Click the Formulas tab.
   c. Click the Insert Function button in the Function Library group.
   d. At the Insert Function dialog box, make sure *Statistical* is selected in the *Or select a category* option box and then click *AVERAGE* in the *Select a function* list box.
   e. Click OK.
   f. At the Function Arguments dialog box, make sure the insertion point is positioned in the *Number1* text box with existing text selected, use the mouse pointer to select the range E4:E16 in the worksheet (you may need to move the dialog box to display the cells), and then click OK.

5. Save and then print **2-DWTests.xlsx**.
6. Change the *70%* values (which were previously *0%*) in cells B14, D14, and D16 to *N/A*. (This will cause the average test scores for Claude Markovits and Douglas Pherson to increase and will change the average of completed tests.)
7. Save and then print **2-DWTests.xlsx**.

Check Your Work

Counting Numbers in a Range Use the COUNT function to count the numeric values in a range and use the COUNTA function to count the cells in a range containing any characters. In Project 2c, you will use the COUNT function to specify the number of students who have completed Test 3. In the worksheet, the cells containing the text *N/A* are not counted by the COUNT function. Additionally, you will use the COUNTA function to determine how many students should have completed Test 3 by counting the cells that contain test scores and the text N/A.

Project 2c Counting the Number of Students Taking Tests

Part 3 of 4

1. With **2-DWTests.xlsx** open, make cell A22 active.
2. Type Test 3 Completed.
3. Make cell B22 active.
4. Insert a formula counting the number of students who have completed Test 3 by completing the following steps:
   a. With cell B22 active, click in the Formula bar text box.
   b. Type =c.
   c. At the Formula AutoComplete list, scroll down the list until *COUNT* displays and then double-click *COUNT*.
   d. Type d4:d16) and then press the Enter key.

5. Count the number of students who have completed Test 3 by completing the following steps:
   a. Make cell A23 active.
   b. Type Test 3 Administered.
   c. Make cell B23 active.
   d. Click the Insert Function button on the Formula bar.
   e. At the Insert Function dialog box, make sure *Statistical* is selected in the *Or select a category* option box.
   f. Scroll down the list of functions in the *Select a function* list box until *COUNTA* is visible and then double-click *COUNTA*.
   g. At the Function Arguments dialog box, type d4:d16 in the *Value1* text box and then click OK.
6. Save and then print **2-DWTests.xlsx**.

Check Your Work

Tutorial

Using Date and
Time Functions

 Date & Time

Writing Formulas with the NOW and TODAY Functions

The NOW and TODAY functions are part of the *Date & Time* category of functions. The NOW function returns the current date and time in a date-and-time format. The TODAY function returns the current date in a date format. Both the NOW and TODAY functions automatically update when a workbook is opened. To access the NOW and TODAY functions, click the Date & Time button in the Function Library group on the Formulas tab. The formulas can also be accessed at the Insert Function dialog box.

 Calculate Now

The NOW and TODAY functions can also be updated without closing and then reopening the workbook. To update a workbook that contains a NOW or TODAY function, click the Calculate Now button in the Calculation group on the Formulas tab or press the F9 function key.

Tutorial

Displaying
Formulas

 Show
Formulas

💡 **Hint** Press Ctrl + `
to display the formulas
in a worksheet rather
than the results.

Displaying Formulas

In some situations, displaying the formulas in a worksheet, rather than the results, may be useful—for example, to display formulas for auditing purposes or to check formulas for accuracy. Display all the formulas in a worksheet, rather than the results, by clicking the Formulas tab and then clicking the Show Formulas button in the Formula Auditing group. The display of formulas can also be turned on with the keyboard shortcut Ctrl + `. (This symbol is the grave accent, generally located to the left of the 1 key on the keyboard.) To turn off the display of formulas, press Ctrl + ` or click the Show Formulas button on the Formulas tab.

Project 2d Using the NOW Function and Displaying Formulas

Part 4 of 4

1. With **2-DWTests.xlsx** open, make cell A26 active and then type Prepared by:.
2. Make cell A27 active and then type your first and last names.
3. Insert the current date and time by completing the following steps:
    a. Make cell A28 active.
    b. Click the Date & Time button in the Function Library group on the Formulas tab and then click *NOW* at the drop-down list.
    c. At the Function Arguments dialog box telling you that the function takes no argument, click OK.
4. Update the time in cell A28 by completing the following steps:
    a. Wait for 1 minute.
    b. Click the Calculate Now button in the Calculation group on the Formulas tab.
5. Click the Show Formulas button in the Formula Auditing group to turn on the display of formulas.
6. Print the worksheet with the formulas. (The worksheet will print on two pages.)
7. Press Ctrl + ` to turn off the display of formulas.
8. Save, print, and then close **2-DWTests.xlsx**.

Check Your Work

You will insert a formula containing an absolute cell reference that determines the effect on earnings with specific increases, insert a formula with multiple absolute cell references that determines the weighted average of scores, and use mixed cell references to determine simple interest.

Preview Finished Project

Tutorial

Absolute
Addressing

Using Absolute and Mixed Cell References in Formulas

A reference identifies a cell or range of cells in a worksheet and can be relative, absolute, or mixed. A relative cell reference refers to a cell relative to a position in a formula. An absolute cell reference refers to a cell in a specific location. When a formula is copied, a relative cell reference adjusts while an absolute cell reference remains constant. A mixed cell reference does both: either the column remains absolute and the row is relative or the column is relative and the row remains absolute. Distinguish among relative, absolute, and mixed cell references using the dollar symbol ($). Type a dollar symbol before the column and/or row cell reference in a formula to specify that the column or row is an absolute cell reference.

Using an Absolute Cell Reference in a Formula

In this chapter, you have learned to copy a relative formula. For example, if the formula =SUM(A2:C2) in cell D2 is copied relatively into cell D3, it changes to =SUM(A3:C3). In some situations, a formula may contain an absolute cell reference, which always refers to a cell in a specific location. In Project 3a, you will add a column for projected job earnings and then consider "What if?" situations using a formula with an absolute cell reference. To identify an absolute cell reference, insert a dollar symbol before the row and the column. For example, the absolute cell reference C12 is typed as c12 in a formula.

Project 3a Inserting and Copying a Formula with an Absolute Cell Reference   Part 1 of 4

1. Open **CCReports.xlsx** and then save it with the name **2-CCReports**.
2. Determine the effect of a 10% pay increase on actual job earnings by completing the following steps:
   a. Make cell C3 active, type the formula =b3*b12, and then press the Enter key.
   b. Make cell C3 active and then use the fill handle to copy the formula into the range C4:C10.
   c. Make cell C3 active, click the Accounting Number Format button on the Home tab, and then click the Decrease Decimal button two times.

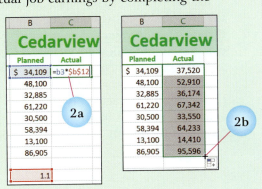

3. Save and then print **2-CCReports.xlsx**.
4. With the worksheet still open, determine the effect of a 10% pay decrease on actual job earnings by completing the following steps:
   a. Make cell B12 active.
   b. Type 0.9 and then press the Enter key.
5. Save and then print the **2-CCReports.xlsx**.
6. Determine the effect of a 20% pay increase on actual job earnings. (To do this, type 1.2 in cell B12 and then press the Enter key.)
7. Save and then print **2-CCReports.xlsx**.

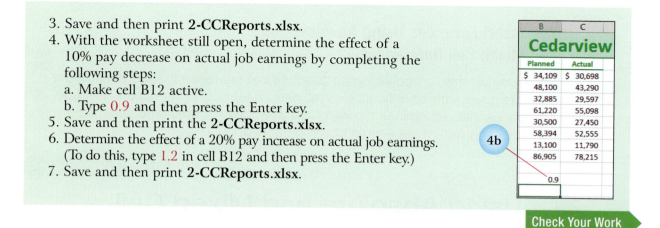

B	C
Cedarview	
Planned	**Actual**
$ 34,109	$ 30,698
48,100	43,290
32,885	29,597
61,220	55,098
30,500	27,450
58,394	52,555
13,100	11,790
86,905	78,215
0.9	

4b

Check Your Work

In Project 3a, you created a formula with one absolute cell reference. A formula also can be created with multiple absolute cell references. For example, in Project 3b, you will create a formula that contains both relative and absolute cell references to determine the average of training scores based on specific weight percentages. In a weighted average, some scores have more value (weight) than others. For example, in Project 3b, you will create a formula that determines the weighted average of training scores that gives more weight to the *Carpentry* percentages than the *Plumbing* or *Electrical* percentages.

Project 3b Inserting and Copying a Formula with Multiple Absolute Cell References

Part 2 of 4

1. With **2-CCReports.xlsx** open, insert the following formulas:
   a. Insert a formula in cell B23 that averages the percentages in the range B17:B22.
   b. Copy the formula in cell B23 into cells C23 and D23.
2. Insert a formula that determines the weighted average of training scores by completing the following steps:
   a. Make cell E17 active.
   b. Type the following formula:
      =b24*b17+c24*c17+d24*d17
   c. Press the Enter key.
   d. Copy the formula in cell E17 into the range E18:E22.
   e. With the range E17:E22 selected, click the Decrease Decimal button three times.
3. Save and then print **2-CCReports.xlsx**.
4. With the worksheet still open, determine the effect on weighted training scores if the weighted values change by completing the following steps:
   a. Make cell B24 active, type 30, and then press the Enter key.
   b. Make cell D24 active, type 40, and then press the Enter key.
5. Save and then print **2-CCReports.xlsx**.

Employee Training				
Name	**Plumbing**	**Electrical**	**Carpentry**	**Weighted Average**
Allesandro	76%	80%	84%	80%
Ellington	66%	72%	64%	67%
Goodman	90%	88%	94%	91%
Huntington	76%	82%	88%	83%
Kaplan-Downing	90%	84%	92%	89%
Larimore	58%	62%	60%	60%
Training Averages	76%	78%	80%	
Training Weights	30%	30%	40%	

4a   4b

Check Your Work

Using a Mixed Cell Reference in a Formula

The formula you created in Step 2a in Project 3a contained a relative cell reference (b3) and an absolute cell reference (b12). A formula can also contain a mixed cell reference. As stated earlier, in a mixed cell reference, either the column remains absolute and the row is relative or the column is relative and the row remains absolute. In Project 3c, you will insert a number of formulas—two of which will contain mixed cell references. You will insert the formula =e29*e$26 to calculate withholding tax and =e29*h$36 to calculate social security tax. The dollar symbol before each row number indicates that the row is an absolute cell reference.

Project 3c Determining Payroll Using Formulas with Absolute and Mixed Cell References

Part 3 of 4

1. With **2-CCReports.xlsx** open, make cell E29 active and then type the following formula that calculates the gross pay, including overtime (press the Enter key after typing each formula):
   =(b29*c29+(b29*b36*d29))
2. Copy the formula in cell E29 into the range E30:E34.
3. Make cell F29 active and then type the following formula that calculates the amount of withholding tax:
   =e29*e$36
4. Copy the formula in cell F29 into the range F30:F34.
5. Make cell G29 active and then type the following formula that calculates the amount of social security tax:
   =e29*h$36
6. Copy the formula in cell G29 into the range G30:G34.
7. Make cell H29 active and then type the following formula that calculates net pay:
   =e29-(f29+g29)
8. Copy the formula in cell H29 into the range H30:H34.
9. Select the range E29:H29 and then click the Accounting Number Format button.
10. Save **2-CCReports.xlsx**.

Check Your Work

As you learned in Project 3c, a formula can contain a mixed cell reference. In Project 3d, you will create the formula =$a41*b$40. In the first cell reference in the formula, $a41, the column is absolute and the row is relative. In the second cell reference, b$40, the column is relative and the row is absolute. The formula containing the mixed cell reference allows you to fill in the column and row data using only one formula.

Identify an absolute or mixed cell reference by typing a dollar symbol before the column and/or row reference or press the F4 function key to cycle through the various cell references. For example, type =a41 in a cell, press the F4 function key, and the cell reference changes to =a41. Press F4 again and the cell reference changes to =a$41. Press F4 a third time and the cell reference changes to =$a41 and press F4 a fourth time and the cell reference changes back to =a41.

1. With **2-CCReports.xlsx** open, make cell B41 the active cell and then insert a formula containing mixed cell references by completing the following steps:
   a. Type =a41 and then press the F4 function key three times. (This changes the cell reference to *$A41*.)
   b. Type *b40 and then press the F4 function key two times. (This changes the cell reference to *B$40*.)
   c. Make sure the formula displays as =$A41*B$40 and then press the Enter key.

39				SIMPL
40			$ 1,000	$ 2,00(
41		5%	=$A41*B$40	
42		6%		

1c

2. Copy the formula to the right by completing the following steps:
   a. Make cell B41 active and then use the fill handle to copy the formula into cell F41.
   b. With the range B41:F41 selected, use the fill handle to copy the formula into cell F51.

SIMPLE INTEREST LOAN TABLE					
	$ 1,000	$ 2,000	$ 3,000	$ 4,000	$ 5,000
5%	$ 50	$ 100	$ 150	$ 200	$ 250
6%					

2a

SIMPLE INTEREST LOAN TABLE					
	$ 1,000	$ 2,000	$ 3,000	$ 4,000	$ 5,000
5%	$ 50	$ 100	$ 150	$ 200	$ 250
6%	$ 60	$ 120	$ 180	$ 240	$ 300
7%	$ 70	$ 140	$ 210	$ 280	$ 350
8%	$ 80	$ 160	$ 240	$ 320	$ 400
9%	$ 90	$ 180	$ 270	$ 360	$ 450
10%	$ 100	$ 200	$ 300	$ 400	$ 500
11%	$ 110	$ 220	$ 330	$ 440	$ 550
12%	$ 120	$ 240	$ 360	$ 480	$ 600
13%	$ 130	$ 260	$ 390	$ 520	$ 650
14%	$ 140	$ 280	$ 420	$ 560	$ 700
15%	$ 150	$ 300	$ 450	$ 600	$ 750

2b

3. Save, print, and then close **2-CCReports.xlsx**.

Check Your Work

Chapter Summary

- Type a formula in a cell and the formula displays in the cell and in the Formula bar. If cell entries are changed, a formula automatically recalculates the values and inserts the result in the cell.

- Write a formula using commonly used operators, such as addition (+), subtraction (-), multiplication (*), division (/), percentage (%), and exponentiation ($^$). When writing a formula, begin with the equals sign (=).

- Copy a formula to other cells in a row or column with the Fill button in the Editing group on the Home tab or with the fill handle in the bottom right corner of the active cell.

- Double-click in a cell containing a formula and the cell references displays with a colored border and cell shading.

- Another method for writing a formula is to point to specific cells that are part of the formula as the formula is being built.
- Excel uses the same order of operations as algebra and that order can be modified by adding parentheses around certain parts of a formula.
- If Excel detects an error in a formula, a Trace Error button appears and a dark-green triangle displays in the upper left corner of the cell containing the formula.
- Excel displays different error codes for different formula errors. An error code helps identify an error in a formula by providing information on the specific issue.
- Excel performs over 300 functions that are divided into 13 categories.
- A function operates on an argument, which may consist of a cell reference, a constant, or another function. When a value calculated by a formula is inserted in a cell, this is referred to as *returning the result*.
- The AVERAGE function returns the average (arithmetic mean) of the arguments. The MAX function returns the largest value in a set of values and the MIN function returns the smallest value in a set of values. The COUNT function counts the number of cells containing numbers within the list of arguments. The COUNTA function counts the number of cells containing any data, numerical or alphabetical.
- The NOW function returns the current date and time and the TODAY function returns the current date.
- Turn on the display of formulas in a worksheet with the Show Formulas button on the Formulas tab or with the keyboard shortcut Ctrl + ` (grave accent).
- A reference identifies a cell or a range of cells in a worksheet and can be relative, absolute, or mixed. Identify an absolute cell reference by inserting a dollar symbol ($) before the column and row. Cycle through the various cell reference options by typing the cell reference and then pressing the F4 function key.

Commands Review

FEATURE	RIBBON TAB, GROUP	BUTTON	KEYBOARD SHORTCUT
cycle through cell references			F4
display formulas	Formulas, Formula Auditing		Ctrl + `
Insert Function dialog box	Formulas, Function Library		Shift + F3
SUM function	Home, Editing OR Formulas, Function Library		Alt + =
update formulas	Formulas, Calculation		F9

Workbook

Chapter study tools and assessment activities are available in the *Workbook* ebook. These resources are designed to help you further develop and demonstrate mastery of the skills learned in this chapter.

Microsoft® Excel®

Formatting a Worksheet

CHAPTER 3

Performance Objectives

Upon successful completion of Chapter 3, you will be able to:

1 Change column widths and row heights

2 Insert rows and columns

3 Delete cells, rows, and columns

4 Clear data in cells

5 Apply formatting to data in cells

6 Apply formatting to selected data using the Mini toolbar

7 Apply a theme and customize the theme font and colors

8 Format numbers

9 Apply formatting at the Format Cells dialog box

10 Repeat the last action

11 Automate formatting with Format Painter

12 Hide and unhide rows and columns

Precheck

Check your current skills to help focus your study.

The appearance of a worksheet on screen and how it looks when printed is called the *format*. In Chapter 1, you learned how to apply basic formatting to cells in a worksheet. Additional types of formatting include changing column width and row height; applying character formatting such as bold, italic, and underlining; specifying number formatting; inserting and deleting rows and columns; and applying borders, shading, and patterns to cells. You can also apply formatting to a worksheet with a theme. A theme is a set of formatting choices that include colors and fonts.

SNAP

If you are a SNAP user, launch the Precheck and Tutorials from your Assignments page.

Data Files

Before beginning chapter work, copy the EL1C3 folder to your storage medium and then make EL1C3 the active folder.

Project 1 **Format a Product Pricing Worksheet**   **7 Parts**

You will open a workbook containing a worksheet with product pricing data and then format it by changing column widths and row heights, inserting and deleting rows and columns, and clearing data in cells. You will also apply font and alignment formatting to data in cells.

Preview Finished Project

Tutorial

Adjusting Column
Width and Row
Height

Changing Column Width

The columns in a worksheet are the same width by default. In some worksheets, column widths may need to be changed to accommodate more or less data. Change column widths using the mouse on column boundary lines or at a dialog box.

Changing Column Width Using Column Boundaries

💡 **Hint** To change
the width of all
the columns in a
worksheet, click the
Select All button and
then drag a column
boundary line to the
desired position.

As explained in Chapter 1, column width can be adjusted by dragging the column boundary line or adjusted to the longest entry by double-clicking the boundary line. When dragging a column boundary line, the column width displays in a box above the mouse pointer. The number that displays represents the average number of characters in the standard font that can fit in a cell.

The width of selected adjacent columns can be changed at the same time. To do this, select the columns and then drag one of the column boundary lines within the selected columns. When dragging the boundary line, the column width changes for all the selected columns. To select adjacent columns, position the cell pointer on the first column header to be selected (the mouse pointer turns into a black down-pointing arrow), click and hold down the left mouse button, drag the cell pointer into the last column header, and then release the mouse button.

Project 1a **Changing Column Width Using a Column Boundary Line**   **Part 1 of 7**

1. Open **CMProducts.xlsx** and then save it with the name **3-CMProducts**.
2. Insert a formula in cell D2 that multiplies the price in cell B2 with the number in cell C2. Copy the formula in cell D2 down into the range D3:D14.
3. Change the width of column D by completing the following steps:
   a. Position the mouse pointer on the column boundary line in the column header between columns D and E until it turns into a double-headed arrow pointing left and right.
   b. Click and hold down the left mouse button, drag the column boundary line to the right until *Width: 11.00* displays in the box, and then release the mouse button.

   3a

4. Make cell D15 active and then insert the sum of the range D2:D14.
5. Change the width of columns A and B by completing the following steps:
   a. Select columns A and B. To do this, position the cell pointer on the column A header, click and hold down the left mouse button, drag the cell pointer into the column B header, and then release the mouse button.
   b. Position the cell pointer on the column boundary line between columns A and B until it turns into a double-headed arrow pointing left and right.

c. Click and hold down the left mouse button, drag the column boundary line to the right until *Width: 10.33* displays in the box, and then release the mouse button.

6. Adjust the width of column C to accommodate the longest entry by double-clicking on the column boundary line between columns C and D.

7. Save **3-CMProducts.xlsx**.

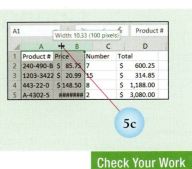

5c

Check Your Work

Changing Column Width at the Column Width Dialog Box

Use the *Column width* measurement box in the Column Width dialog box, shown in Figure 3.1, to specify a column width number. Increase the number to make the column wider and decrease the number to make the column narrower.

Display the Column Width dialog box by clicking the Format button in the Cells group on the Home tab and then clicking *Column Width* at the drop-down list. At the Column Width dialog box, type a measurement number (the number represents the number of characters in the standard font that can fit in the column) and then press the Enter key or click OK.

Format

Quick Steps

Change Column Width
Drag column boundary line.
OR
Double-click column boundary line.
OR
1. Click Format button.
2. Click *Column Width*.
3. Type width.
4. Click OK.

Figure 3.1 Column Width Dialog Box

Column Width	?	X
Column width:	8.11	
OK		Cancel

Type the column width in this measurement box.

Project 1b **Changing Column Width at the Column Width Dialog Box**   **Part 2 of 7**

1. With **3-CMProducts.xlsx** open, change the width of column A by completing the following steps:
   a. Make any cell in column A active.
   b. Click the Format button in the Cells group on the Home tab and then click *Column Width* at the drop-down list.
   c. At the Column Width dialog box, type 12.7 in the *Column width* measurement box.
   d. Click OK to close the dialog box.

2. Make any cell in column B active and then change the width of column B to 12.5 characters by completing steps similar to those in Step 1.

3. Make any cell in column C active and then change the width of column C to 8 characters by completing steps similar to those in Step 1.

4. Save **3-CMProducts.xlsx**.

1c

1d

Check Your Work

Changing Row Height

Quick Steps

Change Row Height
Drag row boundary line.
OR
1. Click Format button.
2. Click *Row Height*.
3. Type height.
4. Click OK.

💡 **Hint** To change the height of all the rows in a worksheet, click the Select All button and then drag a row boundary line to the desired position.

💡 **Hint** Excel measures row height in points and column width in characters.

Change row height in much the same manner as column width. Change row height using the mouse on a row boundary line or at the Row Height dialog box. Change row height using a row boundary line by positioning the cell pointer on the boundary line between rows in the row header until it turns into a double-headed arrow pointing up and down, clicking and holding down the left mouse button, dragging up or down until the row is the desired height, and then releasing the mouse button.

Change the height of adjacent rows by selecting the rows and then dragging one of the row boundary lines within the selected rows. As the boundary line is being dragged, the row height changes for all the selected rows.

As a row boundary line is being dragged, the row height displays in a box above the mouse pointer. The number that displays represents a point measurement. Increase the point size to increase the row height; decrease the point size to decrease the row height.

Another method for changing row height is to use the *Row height* measurement box at the Row Height dialog box, shown in Figure 3.2. Display this dialog box by clicking the Format button in the Cells group on the Home tab and then clicking *Row Height* at the drop-down list.

Figure 3.2 Row Height Dialog Box

Type the row height in this measurement box.

Project 1c Changing Row Height

Part 3 of 7

1. With **3-CMProducts.xlsx** open, change the height of row 1 by completing the following steps:
   a. Position the cell pointer in the row header on the row boundary line between rows 1 and 2 until it turns into a double-headed arrow pointing up and down.
   b. Click and hold down the left mouse button, drag the row boundary line down until *Height: 19.80* displays in the box, and then release the mouse button.

2. Change the height of rows 2 through 14 by completing the following steps:
   a. Select rows 2 through 14. To do this, position the cell pointer on the number *2* in the row header, click and hold down the left mouse button, drag the cell pointer to the number *14* in the row header, and then release the mouse button.
   b. Position the cell pointer on the row boundary line between rows 2 and 3 until it turns into a double-headed arrow pointing up and down.

c. Click and hold down the left mouse button, drag the row boundary line down until *Height: 16.80* displays in the box, and then release the mouse button.

3. Change the height of row 15 by completing the following steps:
   a. Make cell A15 active.
   b. Click the Format button in the Cells group on the Home tab and then click *Row Height* at the drop-down list.
   c. At the Row Height dialog box, type 20 in the *Row height* measurement box and then click OK.

Row Height ? ×

Row height: 20

OK   Cancel

3c

2c

	A	B
	240-490-B	$ 85
3	1203-3422	$ 20
4	443-22-0	$ 148
5	A-4302-5	$ 1,540
6	43-GB-39	$ 45
7	341-453	$ 19
8	CT-342	$ 304
9	83-492	$ 9
10	L-756-M	$ 95
11	340-19	$ 15
12	T-3491-S	$ 450
13	900-599	$ 35
14	43-49CE	$ 120
15	Total	

Height: 16.80 (28 pixels)

4. Save **3-CMProducts.xlsx**.

Check Your Work

Tutorial

Inserting Columns and Rows

Inserting and Deleting Cells, Rows, and Columns

New data may need to be included in an existing worksheet. For example, a row or several rows of new data may need to be inserted into a worksheet or data may need to be removed from a worksheet.

Inserting Rows

Hint When you insert cells, rows, or columns in a worksheet, all the references affected by the insertion automatically adjust.

 Insert

A row or rows can be inserted in an existing worksheet. Insert a row with the Insert button in the Cells group on the Home tab or with options at the Insert dialog box. By default, a row is inserted above the row containing the active cell. To insert a row in a worksheet, select the row below where the row is to be inserted and then click the Insert button. To insert more than one row, select the number of rows to be inserted in the worksheet and then click the Insert button.

Another method for inserting a row is to make a cell active in the row below where the row is to be inserted, click the Insert button arrow, and then click *Insert Sheet Rows*. A row also can be inserted by clicking the Insert button arrow and then clicking *Insert Cells*. This displays the Insert dialog box, as shown in Figure 3.3. At the Insert dialog box, click *Entire row* and then click OK. This inserts a row above the active cell.

Quick Steps

Insert a Row
Click Insert button.
OR
1. Click Insert button arrow.
2. Click *Insert Sheet Rows*.
OR
1. Click Insert button arrow.
2. Click *Insert Cells*.
3. Click *Entire row*.
4. Click OK.

Figure 3.3 Insert Dialog Box

This is the default insert option.

Click this option to insert a row in the worksheet.

Insert ? ×

Insert
○ Shift cells right
● Shift cells down
○ Entire row
○ Entire column

OK   Cancel

1. With **3-CMProducts.xlsx** open, insert two rows at the beginning of the worksheet by completing the following steps:
   a. Make cell A1 active.
   b. Click the Insert button arrow in the Cells group on the Home tab.
   c. At the drop-down list that displays, click *Insert Sheet Rows*.
   d. With cell A1 active, click the Insert button arrow and then click *Insert Sheet Rows* at the drop-down list.
2. Type the text Capstan Marine Products in cell A1.
3. Make cell A2 active and then type Purchasing Department.
4. Change the height of row 1 to 42 points.
5. Change the height of row 2 to 21 points.
6. Insert two rows by completing the following steps:
   a. Select rows 7 and 8 in the worksheet.
   b. Click the Insert button in the Cells group on the Home tab.
7. Type the following data in the specified cells. For the cells that contain money amounts, you do not need to type the dollar symbols:

   A7: 855-495
   B7: 42.75
   C7: 5
   A8: ST039
   B8: 12.99
   C8: 25
8. Make cell D6 active and then use the fill handle to copy the formula down into cells D7 and D8.
9. Save **3-CMProducts.xlsx**.

Check Your Work

Inserting Columns

Quick Steps

Insert a Column
Click Insert button.
OR
1. Click Insert button arrow.
2. Click *Insert Sheet Columns*.
OR
1. Click Insert button arrow.
2. Click *Insert Cells*.
3. Click *Entire column*.
4. Click OK.

Insert columns in a worksheet in much the same way as rows. Insert a column with options from the Insert button drop-down list or with options at the Insert dialog box. By default, a column is inserted immediately to the left of the column containing the active cell. To insert a column in a worksheet, make a cell active in the column immediately to the right of where the new column is to be inserted, click the Insert button arrow, and then click *Insert Sheet Columns* at the drop-down list. To insert more than one column, select the number of columns to be inserted in the worksheet, click the Insert button arrow, and then click *Insert Sheet Columns*.

Another method for inserting a column is to make a cell active in the column immediately to the right of where the new column is to be inserted, click the Insert button arrow, and then click *Insert Cells* at the drop-down list. At the Insert dialog box that displays, click *Entire column*. This inserts a column immediately left of the active cell.

Excel includes an especially helpful and time-saving feature related to inserting columns. When columns are inserted in a worksheet, all the references affected by the insertion automatically adjust.

1. With **3-CMProducts.xlsx** open, insert a column to the left of column A by completing the following steps:
   a. Click in any cell in column A.
   b. Click the Insert button arrow in the Cells group on the Home tab and then click *Insert Sheet Columns* at the drop-down list.
2. Type the following data in each specified cell:
        A3: Company
        A4: RD Manufacturing
        A8: Smithco, Inc.
        A11: Sunrise Corporation
        A15: Geneva Systems
3. Make cell A1 active and then adjust the width of column A to accommodate the longest entry.
4. Insert another column to the left of column B by completing the following steps:
   a. Make cell B1 active.
   b. Click the Insert button arrow and then click *Insert Cells* at the drop-down list.
   c. At the Insert dialog box, click *Entire column*.
   d. Click OK.
5. Type Date in cell B3 and then press the Enter key.
6. Save **3-CMProducts.xlsx**.

Check Your Work

Tutorial

Deleting Columns and Rows

Delete

Hint Display the Delete dialog box by positioning the cell pointer in the worksheet, clicking the right mouse button, and then clicking *Delete* at the shortcut menu.

Deleting Cells, Rows, or Columns

Specific cells in a worksheet or rows or columns in a worksheet can be deleted. To delete a row, select it and then click the Delete button in the Cells group on the Home tab. To delete a column, select it and then click the Delete button. Delete a specific cell by making it active, clicking the Delete button arrow, and then clicking *Delete Cells* at the drop-down list. This displays the Delete dialog box, shown in Figure 3.4. At the Delete dialog box, specify what is to be deleted and then click OK. Delete adjacent cells by selecting them and then displaying the Delete dialog box.

Figure 3.4 Delete Dialog Box

Choose the option that makes the desired change.

Clearing Data in Cells

To delete the cell contents but not the cell, make the cell active or select cells and then press the Delete key. A quick method for clearing the contents of a cell is to right-click in the cell and then click *Clear Contents* at the shortcut menu. Another method for deleting cell content is to make the cell active or select cells, click the Clear button in the Editing group on the Home tab, and then click *Clear Contents* at the drop-down list.

Use options at the Clear button drop-down list to clear the contents of the cell or selected cells as well as the formatting and comments. Click the *Clear Formats* option to remove the formatting from the cell or selected cells while leaving the data. Click the *Clear All* option to clear the contents of the cell or selected cells as well as the formatting.

Project 1f Deleting and Clearing Rows in a Worksheet

1. With **3-CMProducts.xlsx** open, delete column B in the worksheet by completing the following steps:
   a. Click in any cell in column B.
   b. Click the Delete button arrow in the Cells group on the Home tab and then click *Delete Sheet Columns* at the drop-down list.
2. Delete row 5 by completing the following steps:
   a. Select row 5.
   b. Click the Delete button in the Cells group.
3. Clear row contents by completing the following steps:
   a. Select rows 7 and 8.
   b. Click the Clear button in the Editing group on the Home tab and then click *Clear Contents* at the drop-down list.
4. Type the following data in each specified cell:
   A7: Ray Enterprises
   B7: S894-T
   C7: 4.99
   D7: 30
   B8: B-3448
   C8: 25.50
   D8: 12
5. Make cell E6 active and then copy the formula down into cells E7 and E8.
6. Save **3-CMProducts.xlsx**.

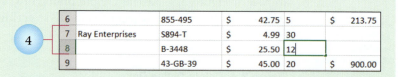

Check Your Work

Applying Formatting

Many of the groups on the Home tab contain options for applying formatting to text in the active cell or selected cells. Use buttons and options in the Font group to apply font formatting to text and use buttons in the Alignment group to apply alignment formatting.

Figure 3.5 Font Group

Use buttons and options in the Font group to apply formatting to cells or the data in cells.

Tutorial

Applying Font Formatting

Applying Font Formatting

Apply a variety of formatting to cells in a worksheet with buttons and options in the Font group on the Home tab. Use buttons and options in the Font group, shown in Figure 3.5, to change the font, font size, and font color; to bold, italicize, and underline data in cells; to change the text color; and to apply a border or add fill to cells.

Use the *Font* option box in the Font group to change the font of the text in a cell and use the *Font Size* option box to specify the size of the text. Apply bold formatting to text in a cell with the Bold button, italic formatting with the Italic button, and underlining with the Underline button.

Click the Increase Font Size button and the text in the active cell or selected cells increases to the next font size in the *Font Size* option box drop-down gallery. Click the Decrease Font Size button and the text in the active cell or selected cells decreases to the next point size.

Use the Borders button in the Font group to insert a border on any or all sides of the active cell or any or all sides of selected cells. The name of the button changes depending on the most recent border applied to a cell or selected cells. Use the Fill Color button to insert color in the active cell or in selected cells. Change the color of the text within a cell with the Font Color button.

Formatting with the Mini Toolbar

Double-click in a cell and then select the data within it and the Mini toolbar displays above the selected data. The Mini toolbar also displays when right-clicking in a cell. The Mini toolbar contains buttons and options for applying font formatting such as font, font size, and font color, as well as bold and italic formatting. Click a button or option on the Mini toolbar to apply formatting to selected text.

Tutorial

Applying Alignment Formatting

Applying Alignment Formatting

The alignment of data in cells depends on the type of data entered. Enter words or text combined with numbers in a cell and the text aligns at the left edge of the cell. Enter numbers in a cell and the numbers align at the right side of the cell. Use options in the Alignment group to align data at the left, center, or right side of the cell; align data at the top, center, or bottom of the cell; increase and/or decrease the indent of data in a cell; and change the orientation of data in a cell.

 Merge & Center

As explained in Chapter 1, selected cells can be merged by clicking the Merge & Center button. If cells are merged, the merged cell can be split into the original cells by selecting the cell and then clicking the Merge & Center button. Click the Merge & Center button arrow and a drop-down list of options displays. Click the *Merge &*

Center option to merge all of the selected cells and to apply center cell alignment. Click the *Merge Across* option to merge each row of selected cells. For example, if three cells and two rows are selected, clicking the *Merge Across* option will merge the three cells in the first row and merge the three cells in the second row, resulting in two cells. Click the *Merge Cells* option to merge all the selected cells but not apply center cell alignment. Use the last option, *Unmerge Cells*, to split cells that were previously merged. If cells that are selected and then merged contain data, only the data in the upper left cell will remain. Data in the other merged cells is deleted.

 Orientation

Click the Orientation button in the Alignment group and a drop-down list displays with options for rotating data in a cell. If the data typed in a cell is longer than the cell, it overlaps the next cell to the right. To wrap the data to the next line within the cell, click the Wrap Text button in the Alignment group.

Wrap Text

Project 1g   Applying Font and Alignment Formatting   Part 7 of 7

1. With **3-CMProducts.xlsx** open, make cell B1 active and then click the Wrap Text button in the Alignment group on the Home tab. (This wraps the company name within the cell.)
2. Select the range B1:C2, click the Merge & Center button arrow in the Alignment group on the Home tab, and then click *Merge Across* at the drop-down list.
3. After looking at the merged cells, you decide to merge additional cells and horizontally and vertically center the text in the cells by completing the following steps:
   a. With the range B1:C2 selected, click the Merge & Center button arrow and then click *Unmerge Cells* at the drop-down list.
   b. Select the range A1:E2.
   c. Click the Merge & Center button arrow and then click the *Merge Across* option at the drop-down list.
   d. Click the Middle Align button in the Alignment group and then click the Center button.

4. Rotate the text in the third row by completing the following steps:
   a. Select the range A3:E3.
   b. Click the Orientation button in the Alignment group and then click *Angle Counterclockwise* at the drop-down list.
   c. After looking at the rotated text, you decide to return the orientation to horizontal by clicking the Undo button on the Quick Access Toolbar.
5. Change the font, font size, and font color for the text in specific cells by completing the following steps:
   a. Make cell A1 active.
   b. Click the *Font* option box arrow in the Font group, scroll down the drop-down gallery, and then click *Bookman Old Style*.
   c. Click the *Font Size* option box arrow in the Font group and then click *22* at the drop-down gallery.

d. Click the Font Color button arrow and then click the *Dark Blue* option (ninth option in the *Standard Colors* section).

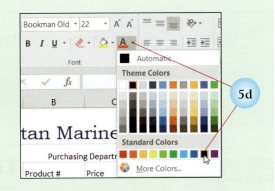

6. Make cell A2 active and then complete steps similar to those in Step 5 to change the font to Bookman Old Style, the font size to 16 points, and the font color to standard dark blue.

7. Select the range A3:E3 and then click the Center button in the Alignment group.

8. With the range A3:E3 still selected, click the Bold button in the Font group and then click the Italic button.

9. Select the range A3:E18 and then change the font to Bookman Old Style.

10. Use the Mini toolbar to apply formatting to selected data by completing the following steps:
    a. Double-click in cell A4.
    b. Select the letters *RD*. (This displays the Mini toolbar above the selected word.)
    c. Click the Increase Font Size button on the Mini toolbar.
    d. Double-click in cell A14.
    e. Select the word *Geneva* and then click the Italic button on the Mini toolbar.

11. Adjust columns A through E to accommodate the longest entry in each column. To do this, select columns A through E and then double-click any selected column boundary line.

12. Select the range D4:D17 and then click the Center button in the Alignment group.

13. Add a double-line bottom border to cell A2 by completing the following steps:
    a. Make cell A2 active.
    b. Click the Borders button arrow in the Font group. (The name of this button varies depending on the last option selected.)
    c. Click the *Bottom Double Border* option at the drop-down list.

14. Add a single-line bottom border to the range A3:E3 by completing the following steps:
    a. Select the range A3:E3.
    b. Click the Borders button arrow and then click the *Bottom Border* option.

15. Apply a fill color to specific cells by completing the following steps:
    a. Select the range A1:E3.
    b. Click the Fill Color button arrow in the Font group.
    c. Click the *Blue, Accent 5, Lighter 80%* color option (ninth column, second row in the *Theme Colors* section).

16. Select the range C5:C17 and then click the Comma Style button.

17. Select the range E5:E17 and then click the Comma Style button.

18. Save, print, and then close **3-CMProducts.xlsx**.

Check Your Work

Project 2 Apply a Theme to a Payroll Worksheet

1 Part

You will open a workbook containing a worksheet with payroll information and then insert text in cells, apply formatting to the cells and cell contents, apply a theme, and then change the theme font and colors.

Tutorial

Applying and Modifying Themes

 Themes

♡ Hint Apply a theme to give your worksheet a professional look.

Applying a Theme

Excel provides a number of themes that can be used to format text and cells in a worksheet. A theme is a set of formatting choices that includes a color theme (a set of colors), a font theme (a set of heading and body text fonts), and an effects theme (a set of lines and fill effects). To apply a theme, click the Page Layout tab and then click the Themes button in the Themes group. At the drop-down gallery that displays, click the desired theme. Position the mouse pointer over a theme and the live preview feature displays the worksheet with the theme formatting applied.

Project 2 Applying a Theme

Part 1 of 1

1. Open **SBAPayroll.xlsx** and then save it with the name **3-SBAPayroll**.
2. Make cell G4 active and then insert a formula that calculates the amount of social security tax. (Multiply the gross pay amount in cell E4 with the social security rate in cell H11; you will need to use the mixed cell reference H$11 when writing the formula.)
3. Copy the formula in cell G4 down into the range G5:G9.
4. Make H4 the active cell and then insert a formula that calculates the net pay (gross pay minus withholding and social security tax).
5. Copy the formula in cell H4 down into the range H5:H9.
6. Increase the height of row 1 to 36.00 points.
7. Make cell A1 active, click the Middle Align button in the Alignment group, click the *Font Size* option box arrow, click *18* at the drop-down gallery, and then click the Bold button.
8. Type Stanton & Barnett Associates in cell A1.
9. Select the range A2:H3 and then click the Bold button in the Font group.
10. Apply a theme and customize the font and colors by completing the following steps:
    a. Make cell A1 active.
    b. Click the Page Layout tab.
    c. Click the Themes button in the Themes group and then click *Wisp* at the drop-down gallery. (You might want to point the mouse to individual themes to see how they affect the formatting of the worksheet.)

d. Click the Colors button in the Themes group and then click *Red Orange* at the drop-down gallery.

e. Click the Fonts button in the Themes group, scroll down the drop-down gallery, and then click *Trebuchet MS*.

11. Select columns A through H and adjust the width of the columns to accommodate the longest entries.

12. Save, print, and then close **3-SBAPayroll.xlsx**.

Check Your Work

Project 3 **Format an Invoices Worksheet**   **2 Parts**

You will open a workbook containing an invoice worksheet and apply number formatting to the numbers in the cells.

Preview Finished Project

Tutorial

Applying Number Formatting

Formatting Numbers

By default, the numbers in a cell align at the right and decimals and commas do not display unless they are typed in the cell. Change the format of numbers with buttons in the Number group on the Home tab or with options at the Format Cells dialog box with the Number tab selected.

Formatting Numbers Using Number Group Buttons

The format symbols available for formatting numbers include a percent symbol (%), comma (,), and dollar symbol ($). For example, type *$45.50* in a cell and Excel automatically applies the Currency format to the number. Type *45%* in a cell and Excel automatically applies the Percentage format to the number. The Number group on the Home tab contains five buttons for formatting numbers in cells. (These buttons were explained in Chapter 1.)

Specify the formatting for numbers in cells in a worksheet before typing the numbers or format existing numbers in a worksheet. Use the Increase Decimal and Decrease Decimal buttons in the Number group on the Home tab to change the number of digits after the decimal point for existing numbers only.

The Number group on the Home tab also contains the *Number Format* option box. Click the *Number Format* option box arrow and a drop-down list displays common number formats. Click a format at the drop-down list to apply the number formatting to the cell or selected cells.

Project 3a   Formatting Numbers with Buttons in the Number Group   Part 1 of 2

1. Open **RPInvoices.xlsx** and then save it with the name **3-RPInvoices**.
2. Make the following changes to column widths:
   a. Change the width of column C to 17.00 characters.
   b. Change the width of column D to 10.00 characters.
   c. Change the width of column E to 7.00 characters.
   d. Change the width of column F to 12.00 characters.
3. Select row 1 and then click the Insert button in the Cells group on the Home tab.
4. Change the height of row 1 to 42.00 points.
5. Select the range A1:F1 and then make the following changes:
   a. Click the Merge & Center button in the Alignment group on the Home tab.
   b. With cell A1 active, change the font size to 24 points and the font color to Green, Accent 6, Darker 50% (last column, sixth row in the *Theme Colors* section).
   c. Click the Fill Color button arrow in the Font group and then click *Gray-50%, Accent 3, Lighter 60%* (seventh column, third row in the *Theme Colors* section).
   d. Click the Borders button arrow in the Font group and then click the *Top and Thick Bottom Border* option.
   e. With cell A1 active, type REAL PHOTOGRAPHY and then press the Enter key.
6. Change the height of row 2 to 24.00 points.
7. Select the range A2:F2 and then make the following changes:
   a. Click the Merge & Center button in the Alignment group.
   b. With cell A2 active, change the font size to 18 points.
   c. Click the Fill Color button in the Font group. (This will fill the cell with the gray color applied in Step 5c.)
   d. Click the Borders button arrow in the Font group and then click the *Bottom Border* option.
8. Make the following changes to row 3:
   a. Change the height of row 3 to 18.00 points.
   b. Select the range A3:F3, click the Bold button in the Font group, and then click the Center button in the Alignment group.
   c. With the cells still selected, click the Borders button.

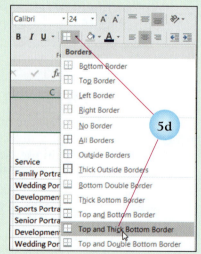

9. Make the following number formatting changes:
   a. Select the range E4:E16 and then click the Percent Style button in the Number group on the Home tab.
   b. With the cells still selected, click the Increase Decimal button in the Number group. (The percentages should include one digit after the decimal point.)

9a   **9b**

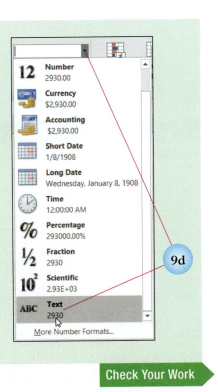

9d

   c. Select the range A4:B16.
   d. Click the *Number Format* option box arrow, scroll down the drop-down list, and then click *Text*.
   e. With the range A4:B16 still selected, click the Center button in the Alignment group.
10. Save **3-RPInvoices.xlsx**.

Check Your Work

Applying Number Formatting at the Format Cells Dialog Box

In addition to using buttons in the Number group, numbers can be formatted with options at the Format Cells dialog box with the Number tab selected, as shown in Figure 3.6. Display this dialog box by clicking the Number group dialog box launcher or by clicking the *Number Format* option box arrow and then clicking *More Number Formats* at the drop-down list. The left side of the dialog

Figure 3.6 Format Cells Dialog Box with Number Tab Selected

Choose a category in this list box and a description of the category displays in the dialog box.

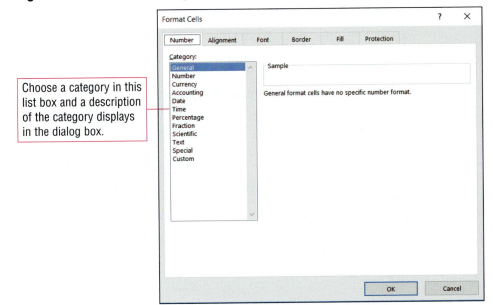

box displays number categories; the default category is *General*. At this setting, no specific formatting is applied to numbers except right alignment in cells. The other number categories are described in Table 3.1.

Table 3.1 Number Formatting Options at the Format Cells Dialog Box

Category	Formatting
Number	Specify the number of digits after the decimal point and whether a "thousand" separator should be used; choose the display of negative numbers; right-align numbers in the cell.
Currency	Apply general monetary values; add a dollar symbol as well as commas and decimal points, if needed; right-align numbers in the cell.
Accounting	Line up the currency symbols and decimal points in a column; add a dollar symbol and two digits after the decimal point; right-align numbers in the cell.
Date	Display the date as a date value; specify the type of formatting desired by clicking an option in the *Type* list box; right-align the date in the cell.
Time	Display the time as a time value; specify the type of formatting desired by clicking an option in the *Type* list box; right-align the time in the cell.
Percentage	Multiply the cell value by 100 and display the result with a percent symbol; add a decimal point followed by two digits by default; change the number of digits with the *Decimal places* option; right-align numbers in the cell.
Fraction	Specify how a fraction displays in the cell by clicking an option in the *Type* list box; right-align a fraction in the cell.
Scientific	Use for very large or very small numbers; use the letter *E* to have Excel move the decimal point a specified number of digits.
Text	Treat a number in the cell as text; the number is displayed in the cell exactly as typed.
Special	Choose a number type, such as *Zip Code*, *Phone Number*, or *Social Security Number*, in the *Type* option list box; useful for tracking list and database values.
Custom	Specify a numbering type by choosing an option in the *Type* list box.

Project 3b Formatting Numbers at the Format Cells Dialog Box

Part 2 of 2

1. With **3-PRInvoices.xlsx** open, make cell F4 active, type the formula =(d4*e4)+d4, and then press the Enter key.
2. Make cell F4 active and then copy the formula down into the range F5:F16.
3. Apply the Accounting format by completing the following steps:
   a. Select the range D4:D16.
   b. Click the Number group dialog box launcher.

3b

c. At the Format Cells dialog box with the Number tab selected, click *Accounting* in the *Category* list box.

d. Make sure a *2* displays in the *Decimal places* option box and a *$* (dollar symbol) displays in the *Symbol* option box.

e. Click OK.

4. Apply the Accounting format to the range F4:F16 by completing actions similar to those in Step 3.

5. Save, print, and then close **3-RPInvoices.xlsx**.

Check Your Work

Project 4 **Format a Company Budget Worksheet** **6 Parts**

You will open a workbook containing a company budget worksheet and then apply formatting to cells with options at the Format Cells dialog box, use Format Painter to apply formatting, and hide and unhide rows and columns.

Preview Finished Project

Tutorial

Applying Formatting at the Format Cells Dialog Box

Applying Formatting at the Format Cells Dialog Box

As explained earlier in this chapter, the Format Cells dialog box with the Number tab selected provides options for formatting numbers. This dialog box also contains other tabs with options for formatting cells.

Aligning and Indenting Data

Align and indent data in cells using buttons in the Alignment group on the Home tab or using options at the Format Cells dialog box with the Alignment tab selected, as shown in Figure 3.7. Display this dialog box by clicking the Alignment group dialog box launcher.

Use options in the *Orientation* section to rotate data. A portion of the *Orientation* section shows points on an arc. Click a point on the arc to rotate the text along that point. Or type a rotation degree in the *Degrees* measurement box. Type a positive number to rotate selected text from the lower left to the upper right of the cell. Type a negative number to rotate selected text from the upper left to the lower right of the cell.

If the data typed in a cell is longer than the cell, it overlaps the next cell to the right. To wrap text to the next line within a cell, insert a check mark in the *Wrap text* check box in the *Text control* section of the dialog box. Insert a check mark in the *Shrink to fit* check box to reduce the size of the text font so all the data fits within the cell. Insert a check mark in the *Merge cells* check box to combine two or more selected cells into a single cell. To enter data on more than one line within a cell, enter the data on the first line and then press Alt + Enter. Pressing Alt + Enter moves the insertion point to the next line within the same cell.

Figure 3.7 Format Cells Dialog Box with Alignment Tab Selected

Specify horizontal and vertical alignment with options in this section.

Use options in this section to control how text fits in a cell.

Rotate text in a cell by clicking a point on the arc or by entering a number in the *Degrees* measurement box.

Project 4a Aligning and Rotating Data in Cells

Part 1 of 6

1. Open **HBCJobs.xlsx** and then save it with the name **3-HBCJobs**.
2. Make the following changes to the worksheet:
   a. Insert a new row at the beginning of the worksheet.
   b. Change the height of row 1 to 66.00 points.
   c. Merge and center the range A1:E1.
   d. Type Harris & Briggs in cell A1 and then press Alt + Enter. (This moves the insertion point down to the next line in the same cell.)
   e. Type Construction and then press the Enter key.
   f. With cell A2 active, type Preferred, press Alt + Enter, type Customer, and then press the Enter key.
   g. Change the width of column A to 22.00 characters.
   h. Change the width of column B to 7.00 characters.
   i. Change the widths of columns C, D, and E to 10.00 characters.
3. Make cell E3 active and then type the formula =d3-c3. Copy this formula down into the range E4:E11.
4. Change the number formatting for specific cells by completing the following steps:
   a. Select the range C3:E3.
   b. Click the Number group dialog box launcher.
   c. At the Format Cells dialog box with the Number tab selected, click *Accounting* in the *Category* list box.
   d. Click the *Decimal places* measurement box down arrow until *0* displays.
   e. Make sure a *$* (dollar symbol) displays in the *Symbol* option box.
   f. Click OK.

5. Select the range C4:E11, click the Comma Style button in the Number group on the Home tab, and then decrease the number of digits that display after the decimal point to 0.

6. Change the orientation of data in cells by completing the following steps:
   a. Select the range B2:E2.
   b. Click the Alignment group dialog box launcher.
   c. At the Format Cells dialog box with the Alignment tab selected, select *0* in the *Degrees* measurement box and then type *45*.
   d. Click OK.

7. Change the vertical alignment of text in cells by completing the following steps:
   a. Select the range A1:E2.
   b. Click the Alignment group dialog box launcher.
   c. At the Format Cells dialog box with the Alignment tab selected, click the *Vertical* option box arrow.
   d. Click *Center* at the drop-down list.
   e. Click OK.

8. Change the horizontal alignment of text in cells by completing the following steps:
   a. Select the range A2:E2.
   b. Click the Alignment group dialog box launcher.
   c. At the Format Cells dialog box with the Alignment tab selected, click the *Horizontal* option box arrow.
   d. Click *Center* at the drop-down list.
   e. Click OK.

9. Change the horizontal alignment and indent of text in cells by completing the following steps:
   a. Select the range B3:B11.
   b. Click the Alignment group dialog box launcher.
   c. At the Format Cells dialog box with the Alignment tab selected, click the *Horizontal* option box arrow and then click *Right (Indent)* at the drop-down list.
   d. Click the *Indent* measurement box up arrow. (This displays *1*.)
   e. Click OK.

10. Save **3-HBCJobs.xlsx**.

Check Your Work

Changing the Font

As explained earlier in this chapter, the Font group on the Home tab contains buttons and options for applying font formatting to data in cells. The font for data in cells can also be changed with options at the Format Cells dialog box with the Font tab selected, as shown in Figure 3.8. Use options at the Format Cells dialog box with the Font tab selected to change the font, font style, font size, and font color; to change the underlining method; and to add effects such as superscript and subscript. Click the Font group dialog box launcher to display this dialog box.

Figure 3.8 Format Cells Dialog Box with Font Tab Selected

Choose a font in this list box. Use the scroll bar at the right side of the box to view the available fonts.

Choose a font style in this list box. The options in the box may vary depending on the selected font.

Choose a font size in this list box or select the current measurement in the option box and then type the measurement.

Apply font effects to text by inserting a check mark in the check box next to the desired effect.

Preview the text with the selected formatting applied.

Project 4b Applying Font Formatting at the Format Cells Dialog Box

Part 2 of 6

1. With **3-HBCJobs.xlsx** open, change the font and font color by completing the following steps:
   a. Select the range A1:E11.
   b. Click the Font group dialog box launcher.
   c. At the Format Cells dialog box with the Font tab selected, scroll down the *Font* option list box and then click *Garamond*.
   d. Click *12* in the *Size* list box.
   e. Click the *Color* option box arrow.
   f. At the color palette that displays, click the *Dark Red* color (first option in the *Standard Colors* section).
   g. Click OK to close the dialog box.
2. Make cell A1 active and then change the font size to 24 points and apply bold formatting.
3. Select the range A2:E2 and then apply bold formatting.
4. Save and then print **3-HBCJobs.xlsx**.

Check Your Work

Adding Borders to Cells

The gridlines that display in a worksheet do not print. As explained earlier in this chapter, use the Borders button in the Font group to add borders to cells that will print. Borders can also be added to cells with options at the Format Cells dialog box with the Border tab selected, as shown in Figure 3.9. Display this dialog box by clicking the Borders button arrow in the Font group and then clicking *More Borders* at the drop-down list.

With options in the *Presets* section, remove borders with the *None* option, add only outside borders with the *Outline* option, and add borders to the insides of selected cells with the *Inside* option. In the *Border* section of the dialog box, specify the side of the cell or selected cells to which the border is to be applied. Choose the line style for the border with options in the *Style* list box. Add color to border lines by clicking the *Color* option box arrow and then clicking a color at the color palette that displays.

Quick Steps

Add Borders to Cells
1. Select cells.
2. Click Borders button arrow.
3. Click border.
OR
1. Select cells.
2. Click Borders button arrow.
3. Click *More Borders*.
4. Use options in dialog box to apply border.
5. Click OK.

Figure 3.9 Format Cells Dialog Box with Border Tab Selected

Click a border style to change the border thickness and whether the border is solid or patterned.

Choose a border color with this option box.

Click the sides, top, and/or bottom of this preview box to insert or remove one or more borders. Or use the buttons to the left and below the preview box.

Project 4c Adding Borders to Cells

Part 3 of 6

1. With **3-HBCJobs.xlsx** open, remove the 45-degree orientation you applied in Project 4a by completing the following steps:
   a. Select the range B2:E2.
   b. Click the Alignment group dialog box launcher.
   c. At the Format Cells dialog box with the Alignment tab selected, select *45* in the *Degrees* measurement box and then type 0.
   d. Click OK.
2. Change the height of row 2 to 33.00 points.

3. Add a thick, standard dark red border line to cells by completing the following steps:
    a. Select the range A1:E11.
    b. Click the Borders button arrow in the Font group and then click the *More Borders* option at the drop-down list.
    c. At the Format Cells dialog box with the Border tab selected, click the *Color* option box arrow and then click the *Dark Red* color (first option in the *Standard Colors* section).
    d. Click the thick single-line option in the *Style* list box in the *Line* section (sixth option in the second column).
    e. Click the *Outline* option in the *Presets* section.
    f. Click OK.

4. Add borders above and below cells by completing the following steps:
    a. Select the range A2:E2.
    b. Click the Borders button arrow in the Font group and then click *More Borders* at the drop-down list.
    c. At the Format Cells dialog box with the Border tab selected, make sure the color is still standard dark red.
    d. Make sure the thick single-line option is still selected in the *Style* list box in the *Line* section.
    e. Click the top border of the sample cell in the *Border* section of the dialog box.
    f. Click the double-line option in the *Style* list box (last option in the second column).
    g. Click the bottom border of the sample cell in the *Border* section of the dialog box.
    h. Click OK.
5. Save **3-HBCJobs.xlsx**.

Check Your Work

Adding Fill and Shading to Cells

To enhance the appearance of cells and data within cells, consider adding fill color. As explained earlier in this chapter, fill color can be added to cells with the Fill Color button in the Font group. Fill color can also be added to cells in a worksheet with options at the Format Cells dialog box with the Fill tab selected, as shown in Figure 3.10. Display the Format Cells dialog box by clicking the Format button in the Cells group and then clicking *Format Cells* at the drop-down list. The dialog box can also be displayed by clicking the Font group, Alignment group, or Number group dialog box launcher. At the Format Cells dialog box, click the Fill tab or right-click in a cell and then click *Format Cells* at the shortcut menu. Choose a fill color for a cell or selected cells by clicking a color choice in the *Background Color* section. To add gradient fill to a cell or selected cells, click the Fill Effects button and then click a style at the Fill Effects dialog box.

Quick Steps

Add Fill and Shading
1. Select cells.
2. Click Fill Color button arrow.
3. Click color.
OR
1. Select cells.
2. Click Format button.
3. Click *Format Cells*.
4. Click Fill tab.
5. Use options in dialog box to apply shading.
6. Click OK.

Repeating the Last Action

To apply the same formatting to other cells in a worksheet, use the Repeat command by pressing the F4 function key or the keyboard shortcut Ctrl + Y. The Repeat command repeats the last action performed.

Quick Steps

Repeat Last Action
1. Apply formatting.
2. Move to location.
3. Press F4 or Ctrl + Y.

Figure 3.10 Format Cells Dialog Box with Fill Tab Selected

Click a color in this color palette to apply a background color to a cell or selected cells.

Click this button to display the Fill Effects dialog box.

Apply a pattern style and/or color with these two options.

1. With **3-HBCJobs.xlsx** open, add a fill color to cell A1 and repeat the formatting by completing the following steps:
   a. Make cell A1 active.
   b. Click the Format button in the Cells group and then click *Format Cells* at the drop-down list.
   c. At the Format Cells dialog box, click the Fill tab.
   d. Click the light gold color in the *Background Color* section (eighth column, second row).

   e. Click OK.
   f. Select the range A2:E2 and then press the F4 function key. (This repeats the application of the light gold fill.)
2. Select row 2, insert a new row, and then change the height of the new row to 12.00 points.
3. Add gradient fill to cells by completing the following steps:
   a. Select the range A2:E2.
   b. Click the Format button in the Cells group and then click *Format Cells* at the drop-down list.
   c. At the Format Cells dialog box, click the Fill tab, if necessary.
   d. Click the Fill Effects button.
   e. At the Fill Effects dialog box, click the *Color 2* option box arrow and then click the *Gold, Accent 4* option (eighth column, first row in the *Theme Colors* section).
   f. Click OK to close the Fill Effects dialog box.
   g. Click OK to close the Format Cells dialog box.
4. Save **3-HBCJobs.xlsx**.

Check Your Work

Formatting with Format Painter

Use the Format Painter button in the Clipboard group on the Home tab to copy formatting to different locations in the worksheet. To use the Format Painter button, make active a cell or selected cells that contain the desired formatting, click the Format Painter button, and then click in the cell or selected cells to which the formatting is to be applied.

Click the Format Painter button and the mouse pointer displays with a paintbrush attached. To apply formatting in a single location, click the Format Painter button. To apply formatting in more than one location, double-click the Format Painter button, selected the desired cells, and then click the Format Painter button to turn off the feature.

Format Painter

---

1. With **3-HBCJobs.xlsx** open, select the range A5:E5.
2. Click the Font group dialog box launcher.
3. At the Format Cells dialog box, click the Fill tab.
4. Click the light green color in the *Background Color* section (last column, second row).
5. Click OK to close the dialog box.
6. Use Format Painter to apply the light green color to rows by completing the following steps:
   a. With the range A5:E5 selected, double-click the Format Painter button in the Clipboard group.
   b. Select the range A7:E7.
   c. Select the range A9:E9.
   d. Select the range A11:E11.
   e. Turn off Format Painter by clicking the Format Painter button.
7. Save and then print **3-HBCJobs.xlsx**.

Check Your Work

Tutorial

Hiding and Unhiding Columns and Rows

Hiding and Unhiding Columns and Rows

If a worksheet contains columns and/or rows of data that is not being used or should not be viewed, consider hiding the columns and/or rows. To hide columns in a worksheet, select the columns, click the Format button in the Cells group on the Home tab, point to *Hide & Unhide*, and then click *Hide Columns*. To hide rows, select the rows, click the Format button in the Cells group, point to *Hide & Unhide*, and then click *Hide Rows*. To make a hidden column visible, select the columns to the left and the right of the hidden column, click the Format button in the Cells group, point to *Hide & Unhide*, and then click *Unhide Columns*. To make a hidden row visible, select the rows above and below the hidden row, click the Format button in the Cells group, point to *Hide & Unhide*, and then click *Unhide Rows*.

If the first row or column is hidden, use the Go To feature to make it visible. To do this, click the Find & Select button in the Editing group on the Home tab and then click *Go To* at the drop-down list. At the Go To dialog box, type *A1* in the *Reference* text box and then click OK. At the worksheet, click the Format button in the Cells group, point to *Hide & Unhide*, and then click *Unhide Columns* or click *Unhide Rows*.

The mouse also can be used to unhide columns or rows. If a column or row is hidden, the light-gray boundary line in the column or row header displays as a slightly thicker gray line. To unhide a column, position the mouse pointer on the

Quick Steps

Hide Columns
1. Select columns.
2. Click Format button.
3. Point to *Hide & Unhide*.
4. Click *Hide Columns*.

Hide Rows
1. Select rows.
2. Click Format button.
3. Point to *Hide & Unhide*.
4. Click *Hide Rows*.

Hint Set the column width to 0 and the column is hidden. Set the row height to 0 and the row is hidden.

---

slightly thicker gray line in the column header until the mouse pointer changes into a left-and-right-pointing arrow with a double line in the middle. (Make sure the mouse pointer displays with two lines between the arrows. If a single line displays, only the size of the visible column will change.) Click and hold down the left mouse button, drag to the right until the column displays at the desired width, and then release the mouse button. Unhide a row in a similar manner. Position the mouse pointer on the slightly thicker gray line in the row header until the mouse pointer changes into an up-and-down-pointing arrow with a double line in the middle. Drag down to display the row and then release the mouse button. If two or more adjacent columns or rows are hidden, unhide each column or row separately.

Project 4f Hiding and Unhiding Columns and Rows

Part 6 of 6

1. With **3-HBCJobs.xlsx** open, hide the row for Linstrom Enterprises and the row for Summit Services by completing the following steps:
   a. Click the row 7 header to select the entire row.
   b. Press and hold down the Ctrl key and then click the row 11 header to select the entire row.
   c. Click the Format button in the Cells group on the Home tab, point to *Hide & Unhide*, and then click *Hide Rows*.
2. Hide the column containing the dollar amounts by completing the following steps:
   a. Click in cell D3 to make it the active cell.
   b. Click the Format button in the Cells group, point to *Hide & Unhide*, and then click *Hide Columns*.
3. Save and then print **3-HBCJobs.xlsx**.
4. Unhide the rows by completing the following steps:
   a. Select rows 6 through 12.
   b. Click the Format button in the Cells group, point to *Hide & Unhide*, and then click *Unhide Rows*.
   c. Click in cell A4.
5. Unhide column D by completing the following steps:
   a. Position the mouse pointer on the thicker gray line between columns C and E in the column header until the pointer turns into a left-and-right-pointing arrow with a double line in the middle.
   b. Click and hold down the left mouse button, drag to the right until *Width: 9.56* displays in a box above the mouse pointer, and then release the mouse button.

6. Save, print, and then close **3-HBCJobs.xlsx**.

Check Your Work

Chapter Summary

- Change column width using the mouse on column boundary lines or using options at the Column Width dialog box. Change row height using the mouse on row boundary lines or using options at the Row Height dialog box.

- Insert a row or column in a worksheet with the Insert button in the Cells group on the Home tab or with options at the Insert dialog box.

- Delete a specific cell by clicking the Delete button arrow and then clicking *Delete Cells* at the drop-down list. At the Delete dialog box, specify if only the cell should be deleted or an entire row or column.

- Delete a selected row or column or multiple rows or columns by clicking the Delete button in the Cells group.

- Delete the cell contents by pressing the Delete key or clicking the Clear button in the Editing group on the Home tab and then clicking *Clear Contents*.

- Apply font formatting with buttons and options in the Font group on the Home tab. Use the Mini toolbar to apply font formatting to selected data in a cell.

- Apply alignment formatting with buttons in the Alignment group on the Home tab. Use the Themes button in the Themes group on the Page Layout tab to apply a theme to cells in a worksheet, which includes formatting such as color, font, and effects. Use the other buttons in the Themes group to customize the theme.

- Format numbers in cells with buttons in the Number group on the Home tab or with options at the Format Cells dialog box with the Number tab selected.

- Apply formatting to cells in a worksheet with options at the Format Cells dialog box, which includes the Number, Alignment, Font, Border, and Fill tabs.

- Press the F4 function key or the keyboard shortcut Ctrl + Y to repeat the last action performed.

- Use the Format Painter button in the Clipboard group on the Home tab to apply formatting to several locations in a worksheet.

- Hide selected columns or rows in a worksheet by clicking the Format button in the Cells group on the Home tab, pointing to *Hide & Unhide*, and then clicking *Hide Columns* or *Hide Rows*.

- To make a hidden column visible, select the columns to the left and right, click the Format button in the Cells group, point to *Hide & Unhide*, and then click *Unhide Columns*.

- To make a hidden row visible, select the rows above and below, click the Format button in the Cells group, point to *Hide & Unhide*, and then click *Unhide Rows*.

Commands Review

FEATURE	RIBBON TAB, GROUP	BUTTON	KEYBOARD SHORTCUT
bold text	Home, Font	B	Ctrl + B
borders	Home, Font		
bottom-align (in row)	Home, Alignment		
center-align (in column)	Home, Alignment		
clear cell or cell contents	Home, Editing		

FEATURE	RIBBON TAB, GROUP	BUTTON	KEYBOARD SHORTCUT
decrease font size	Home, Font		
decrease indent	Home, Alignment		
delete cells, rows, or columns	Home, Cells		
fill color	Home, Font		
font	Home, Font		
font color	Home, Font		
font size	Home, Font		
format	Home, Cells		
Format Painter	Home, Clipboard		
increase font size	Home, Font		
increase indent	Home, Alignment		
insert cells, rows, or columns	Home, Cells		
italicize text	Home, Font		Ctrl + I
left-align (in column)	Home, Alignment		
merge and center cells	Home, Alignment		
middle-align (in row)	Home, Alignment		
number format	Home, Number		
orientation	Home, Alignment		
repeat last action			F4 or Ctrl + Y
right-align (in column)	Home, Alignment		
themes	Page Layout, Themes		
top-align (in row)	Home, Alignment		
underline text	Home, Font		Ctrl + U
wrap text	Home, Alignment		

Workbook

Chapter study tools and assessment activities are available in the *Workbook* ebook. These resources are designed to help you further develop and demonstrate mastery of the skills learned in this chapter.

Microsoft® Excel

Enhancing a Worksheet

Performance Objectives

Upon successful completion of Chapter 4, you will be able to:

1 Change the margins in a worksheet

2 Center a worksheet horizontally and vertically on the page

3 Change page orientation and size

4 Insert and remove a page break in a worksheet

5 Print column and row titles on multiple pages

6 Scale data

7 Insert a background picture

8 Print gridlines and row and column headings

9 Set and clear a print area

10 Insert headers and footers

11 Customize a print job

12 Complete a spelling check

13 Use the Undo and Redo

14 Find and replace data and cell formatting

15 Sort data in cells in ascending and descending order

16 Filter data

Excel contains features you can use to enhance and control the formatting of a worksheet. In this chapter, you will learn how to change worksheet margins, orientation, size, and scale; print column and row titles; print gridlines; and center a worksheet horizontally and vertically on the page. You will also learn how to complete a spelling check on the text in a worksheet, find and replace specific data and formatting in a worksheet, sort and filter data, and plan and create a worksheet.

SNAP

If you are a SNAP user, launch the Precheck and Tutorials from your Assignments page.

Data Files

Before beginning chapter work, copy the EL1C4 folder to your storage medium and then make EL1C4 the active folder.

Project 1 **Format a Yearly Budget Worksheet**   **12 Parts**

You will format a yearly budget worksheet by inserting formulas; changing margins, page orientation, and page size; inserting a page break; printing column headings on multiple pages; scaling data to print on one page; inserting a background picture; inserting headers and footers; and identifying a print area and customizing a print job.

Preview Finished Project

Tutorial

Changing Page
Layout Options

Formatting a Worksheet Page

An Excel worksheet has default page formatting. For example, a worksheet has left and right margins of 0.7 inch and top and bottom margins of 0.75 inch. In addition, a worksheet prints in portrait orientation and its page size is 8.5 inches by 11 inches. These defaults, along with additional settings, can be changed and/or controlled with options on the Page Layout tab.

Changing Margins

The Page Setup group on the Page Layout tab contains buttons for changing the margins and the page orientation and size. In addition, it contains buttons for establishing a print area, inserting a page break, applying a picture background, and printing titles.

Change the worksheet margins by clicking the Margins button in the Page Setup group on the Page Layout tab. This displays a drop-down list of predesigned margin choices. If one of the predesigned choices applies the desired margins, click that option. To customize the margins, click the *Custom Margins* option at the bottom of the Margins button drop-down list. This displays the Page Setup dialog box with the Margins tab selected, as shown in Figure 4.1.

Margins

Quick Steps

**Change Worksheet
Margins**
1. Click Page Layout
   tab.
2. Click Margins button.
3. Click predesigned
   margin.
OR
1. Click Page Layout
   tab.
2. Click Margins button.
3. Click *Custom
   Margins* at drop-
   down list.
4. Change the top, left,
   right, and/or bottom
   measurements.
5. Click OK.

Figure 4.1 Page Setup Dialog Box with Margins Tab Selected

Changes made to the margin measurements are reflected in the sample worksheet page.

Use these options to horizontally and/or vertically center the worksheet on the page.

A worksheet page showing the cells and margins displays in the dialog box. As the top, bottom, left, or right margin measurements are increased or decreased, the sample worksheet page reflects the change. The measurement from the top of the page to the header can be increased or decreased with the *Header* measurement box and the measurement from the footer to the bottom of the page can be changed with the *Footer* measurement box. (Headers and footers are covered later in this chapter.)

Quick Steps

Center a Worksheet Horizontally and/or Vertically

1. Click Page Layout tab.
2. Click Margins button.
3. Click *Custom Margins*.
4. Click *Horizontally* option and/or click *Vertically* check box.
5. Click OK.

Centering a Worksheet Horizontally and/or Vertically

By default, a worksheet prints in the upper left corner of the page. A worksheet can be centered on the page by changing the margins. However, an easier method for centering a worksheet is to use the *Horizontally* and/or *Vertically* check boxes that display in the Page Setup dialog box with the Margins tab selected. Choose one or both of these check boxes and the worksheet page in the preview section displays how the worksheet will print on the page.

Project 1a **Changing Margins and Horizontally and Vertically Centering a Worksheet**   **Part 1 of 12**

1. Open **RPBudget.xlsx** and then save it with the name **4-RPBudget**.
2. Insert the following formulas in the worksheet:
   a. Insert formulas in column N, rows 5 through 10 that sum the totals for all the income items.
   b. Insert formulas in row 11, columns B through N that sum the income amounts and the totals for all the income items.
   c. Insert formulas in column N, rows 14 through 19 that sum the totals for all the expense items.
   d. Insert formulas in row 20, columns B through N that sum the expenses and the totals for all the expense items.
   e. Insert formulas in row 21, columns B through N that subtract the total expenses from the income. (Make cell B21 active and then type the formula =b11-b20. Copy this formula to columns C through N.)
   f. Apply the Accounting format with no digits past the decimal point to cell N5 and cell N14.
3. Click the Page Layout tab.
4. Click the Margins button in the Page Setup group and then click *Custom Margins* at the drop-down list.

5. At the Page Setup dialog box with the Margins tab selected, click the *Top* measurement box up arrow until *3.5* displays.
6. Click the *Bottom* measurement box up arrow until *1.5* displays.
7. Preview the worksheet by clicking the Print Preview button at the bottom of the Page Setup dialog box. The worksheet appears to be a little low on the page so you decide to horizontally and vertically center it by completing the following steps:
   a. Click the <u>Page Setup</u> hyperlink below the galleries in the *Settings* category in the Print backstage area.
   b. Click the Margins tab at the Page Setup dialog box.
   c. Change the *Top* and *Bottom* measurements to *1*.
   d. Click the *Horizontally* check box to insert a check mark.
   e. Click the *Vertically* check box to insert a check mark.
   f. Click OK to close the dialog box.
   g. Look at the preview of the worksheet and then click the Back button to return to the worksheet.
8. Save **4-RPBudget.xlsx**.

Check Your Work

Changing Page Orientation

Orientation

Quick Steps

Change Page Orientation
1. Click Page Layout tab.
2. Click Orientation button.
3. Click orientation at drop-down list.

Click the Orientation button in the Page Setup group and a drop-down list displays with two choices: *Portrait* and *Landscape*. The two choices are represented by sample pages. A sample page that is taller than it is wide shows how the default orientation (*Portrait*) prints data on the page. The other choice, *Landscape*, rotates the data and prints it on a page that is wider than it is tall.

Changing the Page Size

Quick Steps

Change Page Size
1. Click Page Layout tab.
2. Click Size button.
3. Click size at drop-down list.

 Size

By default, an Excel worksheet page size is 8.5 inches by 11 inches. Change this default page size by clicking the Size button in the Page Setup group. At the drop-down list that displays, notice that the default setting is *Letter* and that the measurement *8.5" × 11"* displays below *Letter*. This drop-down list also contains a number of page sizes, such as *Executive* and *Legal*, and a number of envelope sizes.

Project 1b Changing Page Orientation and Size   **Part 2 of 12**

1. With **4-RPBudget.xlsx** open, click the Orientation button in the Page Setup group on the Page Layout tab and then click *Landscape* at the drop-down list.
2. Click the Size button in the Page Setup group and then click *Legal* at the drop-down list.
3. Preview the worksheet by clicking the File tab and then clicking the *Print* option. After viewing the worksheet in the Print backstage area, press the Esc key to return to the worksheet.
4. Save **4-RPBudget.xlsx**.

Check Your Work

Inserting and Removing Page Breaks

Tutorial

Using Page Break Preview

Quick Steps

Insert a Page Break
1. Select column or row.
2. Click Page Layout tab.
3. Click Breaks button.
4. Click *Insert Page Break*.

 Breaks

The default left and right margins of 0.7 inch allow approximately 7 inches of cells across the page (8.5 inches minus 1.4 inches equals 7.1 inches). If a worksheet contains more than 7 inches of cells across the page, a page break is inserted and the remaining columns are moved to the next page. A page break displays as a dashed line along cell borders. Figure 4.2 shows the page break in **4-RPBudget.xlsx** when the paper size is set to *Letter*.

A page break also displays horizontally in a worksheet. By default, a worksheet can contain approximately 9.5 inches of cells down the page. This is because the paper size is set by default at 11 inches. With the default top and bottom margins of 0.75 inch, this allows 9.5 inches of cells to print vertically on one page.

Excel automatically inserts page breaks in a worksheet. To have more control over what cells print on a page, insert a page break. To insert a page break, select a column or row, click the Breaks button in the Page Setup group on the Page

Figure 4.2 Page Break

	January	February	March	April	May	June	July	August	September	October	November	December	Total
Income													
Sublet Rent	$ 1,100	$ 1,100	$ 1,100	$ 1,100	$ 1,100	$ 1,100	$ 1,100	$ 1,100	$ 1,100	$ 1,100	$ 1,100	$ 1,100	$ 13,200
Archway Systems Contract	235	235	235	235	235	235	235	235	235	235	235	235	2,820
Lowell-Briggs Contract	750	750	525	525	-	-	450	450	450	575	575	575	5,625
Wedding Portraits	4,500	2,000	1,500	2,800	4,000	8,250	7,500	6,850	4,500	3,500	3,500	7,000	55,900
Senior Portraits	2,250	1,500	4,500	5,000	3,250	1,000	300	500	650	650	400	400	20,400
Catalog Pictures	-	-	-	-	500	500	500	500	500	-	-	-	2,500
Total Income	$ 8,835	$ 5,585	$ 7,860	$ 9,660	$ 9,085	$ 11,085	$ 10,085	$ 9,635	$ 7,435	$ 6,060	$ 5,810	$ 9,310	$ 100,445
Expenses													
Mortgage	$ 4,230	$ 4,230	$ 4,230	$ 4,230	$ 4,230	$ 4,230	$ 4,230	$ 4,230	$ 4,230	$ 4,230	$ 4,230	$ 4,230	$ 50,760
Utilities	625	550	600	425	400	500	650	700	700	500	550	650	6,850
Insurance	375	375	375	375	375	375	375	375	375	375	375	375	4,500
Equipment Purchases	525	1,250	950	3,500	-	-	-	-	-	-	-	-	6,225
Supplies	750	750	1,500	1,250	1,500	2,500	2,250	1,750	950	850	850	2,000	16,900

page break

Layout tab, and then click *Insert Page Break* at the drop-down list. A page break is inserted immediately left of the selected column or immediately above the selected row.

To insert both horizontal and vertical page breaks at the same time, make a cell active, click the Breaks button in the Page Setup group, and then click *Insert Page Break*. This causes a horizontal page break to be inserted immediately above the active cell and a vertical page break to be inserted at the left side of the active cell. To remove a page break, select the column or row or make the cell active, click the Breaks button in the Page Setup group, and then click *Remove Page Break* at the drop-down list.

A page break that is automatically inserted by Excel may not be visible in a worksheet. One way to display the page break is to display the worksheet in the Print backstage area. Return to the worksheet and the page break will display in the worksheet.

Excel provides a page break view that displays worksheet pages and page breaks. To display this view, click the Page Break Preview button in the view area at the right side of the Status bar or click the View tab and then click the Page Break Preview button in the Workbook Views group. This causes the worksheet to display similarly to the worksheet shown in Figure 4.3. The word *Page* along with the page number displays in gray behind the cells in the worksheet. A dashed blue line indicates a page break inserted automatically by Excel and a solid blue line indicates a page break inserted manually.

Move a page break by positioning the arrow pointer on the blue line, holding down the left mouse button, dragging the line to the desired location, and then releasing the mouse button. To return to Normal view, click the Normal button in the view area on the Status bar or click the View tab and then click the Normal button in the Workbook Views group.

Page Break Preview

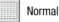 **Hint** You can edit a worksheet in Page Break Preview.

Normal

Figure 4.3 Worksheet in Page Break Preview

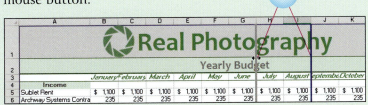

Move a page break by dragging it to the new location.

Project 1c Inserting a Page Break in a Worksheet

Part 3 of 12

1. With **4-RPBudget.xlsx** open, click the Size button in the Page Setup group on the Page Layout tab and then click *Letter* at the drop-down list.
2. Click the Margins button and then click *Custom Margins* at the drop-down list.
3. At the Page Setup dialog box with the Margins tab selected, click in the *Horizontally* check box to remove the check mark, click in the *Vertically* check box to remove the check mark, and then click OK to close the dialog box.
4. Insert a page break between columns I and J by completing the following steps:
   a. Select column J.
   b. Click the Breaks button in the Page Setup group and then click *Insert Page Break* at the drop-down list. Click in any cell in column I.
5. View the worksheet in Page Break Preview by completing the following steps:
   a. Click the Page Break Preview button in the view area at the right side of the Status bar.
   b. View the pages and page breaks in the worksheet.
   c. You decide to include the first six months of the year on one page. To do this, position the arrow pointer on the vertical blue line until the arrow pointer displays as a left-and-right-pointing arrow, click and hold down the left mouse button, drag the line to the left so it is positioned between columns G and H, and then release the mouse button.

Printing Column and Row Titles on Multiple Pages

The columns and rows in a worksheet are usually titled. For example, in 4-RPBudget.xlsx, the column titles include *Income, Expenses, January, February, March*, and so on. The row titles include the income and expenses categories. If a worksheet prints on more than one page, having column and/or row titles print on each page provides context for understanding the text and values in columns and rows. To do this, click the Print Titles button in the Page Setup group on the Page Layout tab. This displays the Page Setup dialog box with the Sheet tab selected, as shown in Figure 4.4.

At the Page Setup dialog box with the Sheet tab selected, specify the range of row cells to print on every page in the *Rows to repeat at top* text box. Type a cell range using a colon. For example, to print the range A1:J1 on every page, type *a1:j1* in the *Rows to repeat at top* text box. Type the range of column cells to print on every page in the *Columns to repeat at left* text box. To make rows and columns easy to identify on the printed page, specify that row and/or column headings print on each page.

Print Titles

Quick Steps

Print Column and Row Titles
1. Click Page Layout tab.
2. Click Print Titles button.
3. Type row range in *Rows to repeat at top* option.
4. Type column range in *Columns to repeat at left* option.
5. Click OK.

Figure 4.4 Page Setup Dialog Box with Sheet Tab Selected

Type the row range in this text box.

Type the column range in this text box.

1. With **4-RPBudget.xlsx** open, click the Page Layout tab and then click the Print Titles button in the Page Setup group.
2. At the Page Setup dialog box with the Sheet tab selected, click in the *Columns to repeat at left* text box.
3. Type a1:a21.
4. Click OK to close the dialog box.
5. Save and then print **4-RPBudget.xlsx**.

Page Setup			?	X
Page	Margins	Header/Footer	**Sheet**	

Print area:

Print titles

Rows to repeat at top:

Columns to repeat at left: a1:a21

③

Check Your Work

Scaling Data

Use buttons in the Scale to Fit group on the Page Layout tab to adjust the printed output by a percentage to fit the number of pages specified. For example, if a worksheet contains too many columns to print on one page, click the *Width* option box arrow in the Scale to Fit group on the Page Layout tab and then click *1 page*. This reduces the size of the data so all the columns display and print on one page. Manually adjust the scale of a worksheet by clicking the up or down arrows in the *Scale* measurement box, or by typing a percentage into the *Scale* measurement box and pressing the Enter key.

Width

1. With **4-RPBudget.xlsx** open, display the Page Setup dialog box with the Sheet tab selected.
2. Select and then delete the text that displays in the *Columns to repeat at left* text box and then click the OK button.
3. Click the *Width* option box arrow in the Scale to Fit group on the Page Layout tab and then click the *1 page* option at the drop-down list.

4. Display the Print backstage area, notice that all the cells that contain data display on one page in the worksheet, and then return to the worksheet.
5. Change the margins by completing the following steps:
   a. Click the Margins button in the Page Setup group and then click *Custom Margins* at the drop-down list.
   b. At the Page Setup dialog box with the Margins tab selected, select the current number in the *Top* measurement box and then type 3.5.
   c. Select the current number in the *Left* measurement box and then type 0.3.
   d. Select the current number in the *Right* measurement box and then type 0.3.
   e. Click OK to close the Page Setup dialog box.
6. Specify that you want row titles to print on each page by completing the following steps:
   a. Click the Print Titles button in the Page Setup group on the Page Layout tab.
   b. Click in the *Rows to repeat at top* text box and then type a3:n3.
   c. Click OK to close the dialog box.

Page Setup			
Page	Margins	Header/Footer	**Sheet**

Print area:

Print titles

Rows to repeat at top: a3:n3

Columns to repeat at left:

6b

7. Save and then print **4-RPBudget.xlsx**. (The worksheet prints on two pages and the row titles are repeated on the second page.)

8. At the worksheet, return to the default margins by clicking the Page Layout tab, clicking the Margins button, and then clicking the *Normal* option at the drop-down list.

9. Prevent titles from printing on the second and subsequent pages by completing the following steps:
   a. Click the Print Titles button in the Page Setup group.
   b. At the Page Setup dialog box with the Sheet tab selected, select and then delete the text in the *Rows to repeat at top* text box.
   c. Click OK to close the dialog box.

10. Change the scaling back to the default by completing the following steps:
    a. Click the *Width* option box arrow in the Scale to Fit group and then click *Automatic* at the drop-down list.
    b. Click the *Scale* measurement box up arrow until *100%* displays in the box.

11. Save **4-RPBudget.xlsx**.

Check Your Work

Inserting a Background Picture

Quick Steps
Insert a Background Picture
1. Click Page Layout tab.
2. Click Background button.
3. Navigate to picture and double-click picture.

Background

Insert a picture as a background for a worksheet with the Background button in the Page Setup group on the Page Layout tab. The picture displays only on the screen and does not print. To insert a picture, click the Background button in the Page Setup group and then click the Browse button at the Insert Pictures window. At the Sheet Background dialog box, navigate to the folder containing the picture and then double-click the picture. To remove the picture from the worksheet, click the Delete Background button.

Project 1f   Inserting a Background Picture

Part 6 of 12

1. With **4-RPBudget.xlsx** open, insert a background picture by completing the following steps:
   a. Click the Background button in the Page Setup group on the Page Layout tab.
   b. At the Insert Pictures window, click the Browse button.
   c. At the Sheet Background dialog box, navigate to your EL1C4 folder and then double-click *Ship.jpg*.
   d. Scroll down the worksheet to display the ship.

2. Display the Print backstage area, notice that the picture does not display in the preview worksheet, and then return to the worksheet.

3. Remove the picture by clicking the Delete Background button in the Page Setup group on the Page Layout tab.

4. Save **4-RPBudget.xlsx**.

Check Your Work

Printing Gridlines and Row and Column Headings

Quick Steps

Print Gridlines and/or Row and Column Headings
1. Click Page Layout tab.
2. Click *Print* check boxes in *Gridlines* and/or *Headings* section in Sheet Options group.
OR
1. Click Page Layout tab.
2. Click Sheet Options dialog box launcher.
3. Click *Gridlines* and/or *Row and column headings* check boxes.
4. Click OK.

By default, the gridlines that create the cells in a worksheet and the row numbers and column letters that label the cells do not print. The Sheet Options group on the Page Layout tab contains check boxes for gridlines and headings. The *View* check boxes for gridlines and headings contain check marks. At these settings, gridlines and row and column headings display on the screen but do not print. To print gridlines and headings, insert check marks in the *Print* check boxes. Complex worksheets may be easier to read with the gridlines printed.

The display and printing of gridlines and headings can also be controlled with options at the Page Setup dialog box with the Sheet tab selected. Display this dialog box by clicking the Sheet Options group dialog box launcher. To print gridlines and headings, insert check marks in the check boxes in the *Print* section of the dialog box. The *Print* section contains two additional options: *Black and white* and *Draft quality*. When printing with a color printer, insert a check mark in the *Black and white* check box to print the worksheet in black and white. Insert a check mark in the *Draft quality* option to print a draft of the worksheet. With this option checked, some types of formatting, such as shading and fill, do not print.

Project 1g   Printing Gridlines and Row and Column Headings   Part 7 of 12

1. With **4-RPBudget.xlsx** open, click in the *Print* check box below *Gridlines* in the Sheet Options group on the Page Layout tab to insert a check mark.
2. Click in the *Print* check box below *Headings* in the Sheet Options group to insert a check mark.
3. Click the Margins button in the Page Setup group and then click *Custom Margins* at the drop-down list.
4. At the Page Setup dialog box with the Margins tab selected, click in the *Horizontally* check box to insert a check mark.
5. Click in the *Vertically* check box to insert a check mark.
6. Click OK to close the dialog box.
7. Save and then print **4-RPBudget.xlsx**.
8. Click in the *Print* check box below *Headings* in the Sheet Options group to remove the check mark.
9. Click in the *Print* check box below *Gridlines* in the Sheet Options group to remove the check mark.
10. Save **4-RPBudget.xlsx**.

Check Your Work

Printing a Specific Area of a Worksheet

Print Area

Use the Print Area button in the Page Setup group on the Page Layout tab to select and print specific areas of a worksheet. To do this, select the cells to print, click the Print Area button in the Page Setup group, and then click *Set Print Area* at the drop-down list. This inserts a border around the selected cells. Display the Print backstage area and click the Print button to print the cells within the border.

More than one print area can be specified in a worksheet. To do this, select the first group of cells, click the Print Area button in the Page Setup group, and then click *Set Print Area*. Select the next group of cells, click the Print Area button, and then click *Add to Print Area*. Clear a print area by clicking the Print Area button in the Page Setup group and then clicking *Clear Print Area* at the drop-down list.

Each area specified as a print area prints on a separate page. To print nonadjacent print areas on the same page, consider hiding columns and/or rows in the worksheet to bring the areas together.

Project 1h Printing Specific Areas

1. With **4-RPBudget.xlsx** open, print the first half of the year's income and expenses by completing the following steps:
   a. Select the range A3:G21.
   b. Click the Print Area button in the Page Setup group on the Page Layout tab and then click *Set Print Area* at the drop-down list.
   c. With the border surrounding the range A3:G21, click the File tab, click the *Print* option, and then click the Print button at the Print backstage area.
   d. Clear the print area by clicking the Print Area button in the Page Setup group and then clicking *Clear Print Area* at the drop-down list.

2. Suppose you want to print the income and expenses information as well as the totals for April. To do this, hide columns and select a print area by completing the following steps:
   a. Select columns B through D.
   b. Click the Home tab.
   c. Click the Format button in the Cells group, point to *Hide & Unhide*, and then click *Hide Columns*.
   d. Click the Page Layout tab.
   e. Select the range A3:E21. (Columns A and E are now adjacent.)
   f. Click the Print Area button in the Page Setup group and then click *Set Print Area* at the drop-down list.
3. Click the File tab, click the *Print* option, and then click the Print button.
4. Clear the print area by ensuring that the range A3:E21 is selected, clicking the Print Area button in the Page Setup group, and then clicking *Clear Print Area* at the drop-down list.
5. Unhide the columns by completing the following steps:
   a. Click the Home tab.
   b. Select columns A and E. (These columns are adjacent.)
   c. Click the Format button in the Cells group, point to *Hide & Unhide*, and then click *Unhide Columns*.
   d. Deselect the text by clicking in any cell containing data in the worksheet.
6. Save **4-RPBudget.xlsx**.

Check Your Work

Inserting Headers and Footers

Text that prints at the top of each worksheet page is called a *header* and text that prints at the bottom of each worksheet page is called a *footer*. Create a header and/or footer with the Header & Footer button in the Text group on the Insert tab in Page Layout view or with options at the Page Setup dialog box with the Header/Footer tab selected.

Header &
Footer

To create a header with the Header & Footer button, click the Insert tab and then click the Header & Footer button in the Text group. This displays the worksheet in Page Layout view and displays the Header & Footer Tools Design tab. Use buttons on this tab, shown in Figure 4.5, to insert predesigned headers and/or footers or to insert header and footer elements such as page numbers, date, time, path name, and file name. A different header or footer can be created on the first page of the worksheet or one header or footer can be created for even pages and another for odd pages.

Quick Steps

Insert a Header or Footer
1. Click Insert tab.
2. Click Header & Footer button.
3. Click Header button and then click predesigned header or click Footer button and then click predesigned footer.
OR
1. Click Insert tab.
2. Click Header & Footer button.
3. Click header or footer elements.

At the Print backstage area, preview headers and footers before printing. Click the File tab and then click the *Print* option to display the Print backstage area. A preview of the worksheet displays at the right side of the backstage area. If the worksheet will print on more than one page, view the different pages by clicking the Next Page button or the Previous Page button. These buttons are below and to the left of the preview worksheet at the Print backstage area. Two buttons display in the bottom right corner of the Print backstage area. Click the Zoom to Page button to zoom in or out of the preview of the worksheet. Click the Show Margins button to display margin guidelines and handles on the preview page. The handles, which display as black squares, can be used to increase or decrease the page margins and column widths. To do this, position the mouse pointer on the desired handle, click and hold down the left mouse button, drag to the new position, and then release the mouse button.

Figure 4.5 Header & Footer Tools Design Tab

Project 1i Inserting a Header in a Worksheet

1. With **4-RPBudget.xlsx** open, create a header by completing the following steps:
   a. Click the Insert tab.
   b. Click the Header & Footer button in the Text group.

c. Click the Header button at the left side of the Header & Footer Tools Design tab and then click *Page 1, 4-RPBudget.xlsx* at the drop-down list. (This inserts the page number in the middle header box and the workbook name in the right header box.)

2. Preview the worksheet by completing the following steps:
   a. Click the File tab and then click the *Print* option.
   b. At the Print backstage area, look at the preview worksheet at the right side of the backstage area.
   c. View the next page of the worksheet by clicking the Next Page button below and to the left of the preview worksheet.
   d. View the first page by clicking the Previous Page button left of the Next Page button.
   e. Click the Zoom to Page button in the lower right corner of the backstage area. (Notice that the preview page has zoomed in on the worksheet.)
   f. Click the Zoom to Page button again.
   g. Click the Page Margins button in the lower right corner of the backstage area. (Notice the guidelines and handles that display on the preview page.)
   h. Click the Page Margins button to remove the guidelines and handles.
   i. Click the Back button to return to the worksheet.
3. Save **4-RPBudget.xlsx**.

Check Your Work

A header and/or footer can also be inserted by working in Page Layout view. In Page Layout view, the top of the worksheet page displays the text *Add header*. Click this text and the insertion point is positioned in the middle header box. Type the header in this box or click in the left box or right box and then type the header. Create a footer in a similar manner. Scroll down the worksheet until the bottom of the page displays and then click the text *Add footer*. Type the footer in the center footer box or click the left box or right box and then type the footer.

1. With **4-RPBudget.xlsx** open, make sure the workbook displays in Page Layout view.
2. Scroll down the worksheet until the text *Add footer* displays and then click the text.

3. Type your first and last names.
4. Click in the left footer box, click the Header & Footer Tools Design tab, and then click the Current Date button in the Header & Footer Elements group. (This inserts a date code. The date will display when you click outside the footer box.)
5. Click in the right footer box and then click the Current Time button in the Header & Footer Elements group. (This inserts the time as a code. The time will display when you click outside the footer box.)
6. View the header and footer at the Print backstage area and then return to the worksheet.
7. Modify the header by completing the following steps:
   a. Scroll to the beginning of the worksheet and display the header text.
   b. Click the page number in the middle header box. (This displays the Header & Footer Tools Design tab, changes the header to a field, and selects the field.)
   c. Press the Delete key to delete the header.
   d. Click the header text in the right header box and then press the Delete key.
   e. With the insertion point positioned in the right header box, insert the page number by clicking the Header & Footer Tools Design tab and then clicking the Page Number button in the Header & Footer Elements group.
   f. Click in the left header box and then click the File Name button in the Header & Footer Elements group.

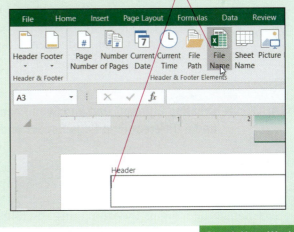

8. Click in any cell in the worksheet that contains data.
9. View the header and footer at the Print backstage area and then return to the worksheet.
10. Save **4-RPBudget.xlsx**.

Check Your Work

Headers and footers can also be inserted and customized using options at the Page Setup dialog box with the Header/Footer tab selected, as shown in Figure 4.6. Display this dialog box by clicking the Page Layout tab and then clicking the Page Setup group dialog box launcher. At the Page Setup dialog box, click the Header/Footer tab. If a worksheet contains headers or footers, they will display in the dialog box. Use the check box options in the lower left corner of the dialog box to

Figure 4.6 Page Setup Dialog Box with Header/Footer Tab Selected

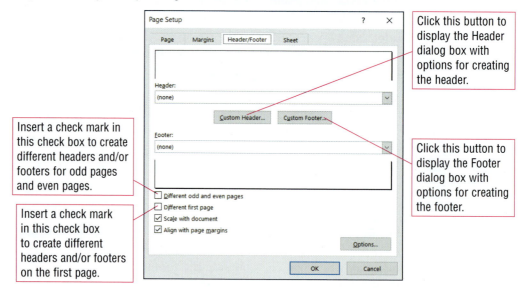

Click this button to display the Header dialog box with options for creating the header.

Insert a check mark in this check box to create different headers and/or footers for odd pages and even pages.

Insert a check mark in this check box to create different headers and/or footers on the first page.

Click this button to display the Footer dialog box with options for creating the footer.

insert different odd and even page headers and/or footers or to insert a different first page header and/or footer. The bottom two check box options are active by default. These defaults scale the header and footer text with the worksheet text and align the header and footer with the page margins.

To create different odd and even page headers, click the *Different odd and even pages* check box to insert a check mark and then click the Custom Header button. This displays the Header dialog box with the Odd Page Header tab selected. Type or insert the odd page header data in the *Left section*, *Center section*, or *Right section* text box and then click the Even Page Header tab. Type or insert the even page header data in the desired section text box and then click OK. Use the buttons that display above the section boxes to format the header text and insert information such as the page number, current date, current time, file name, worksheet name, and so on. Complete similar steps to create different odd and even page footers and a different first page header or footer.

Project 1k **Creating Different Odd and Even Page Headers and Footers and a Different First Page Header and Footer**

Part 11 of 12

1. With **4-RPBudget.xlsx** open, remove the page break by clicking the Page Layout tab, clicking the Breaks button in the Page Setup group, and then clicking *Reset All Page Breaks* at the drop-down list.
2. Change the margins by completing the following steps:
   a. Click the Margins button in the Page Setup group on the Page Layout tab and then click *Custom Margins* at the drop-down list.
   b. At the Page Setup dialog box with the Margins tab selected, select the current number in the *Left* measurement box and then type 3.
   c. Select the current number in the *Right* measurement box and then type 3.
   d. Click OK to close the dialog box.

3. Click the Page Setup group dialog box launcher on the Page Layout tab.
4. At the Page Setup dialog box, click the Header/Footer tab.
5. At the Page Setup dialog box with the Header/Footer tab selected, click the *Different odd and even pages* check box to insert a check mark and then click the Custom Header button.
6. At the Header dialog box with the Odd Page Header tab selected, click the Format Text button (above the *Left section* text box).
7. At the Font dialog box, click *12* in the *Size* list box and then click OK.
8. At the Header dialog box with the file name code (&[File]) highlighted, type Yearly Budget in the *Left section* text box.

9. Click the Even Page Header tab, click in the *Left section* text box, and then click the Insert Page Number button.
10. Click in the *Right section* text box and then type Yearly Budget.
11. Select the text *Yearly Budget*, click the Format Text button, click *12* in the *Size* list box, and then click OK.
12. Click OK to close the Header dialog box.
13. Click the Custom Footer button and, at the Footer dialog box with the Odd Page Footer tab selected, delete the data in the *Left section* text box and select and delete the data in the *Right section* text box. (The footer should contain only your name.)
14. Select your name, click the Format Text button, click *12* in the *Size* list box, and then click OK.
15. Click the Even Page Footer tab, type your name in the *Center section* text box, select your name, and then change the font size to 12 points.
16. Click OK to close the Footer dialog box and then click OK to close the Page Setup dialog box. (View the header and footer in the Print backstage area and then return to the worksheet.)
17. Click the Page Setup group dialog box launcher on the Page Layout tab.
18. At the Page Setup dialog box, click the Header/Footer tab.
19. At the Page Setup dialog box with the Header/Footer tab selected, click the *Different odd and even pages* check box to remove the check mark.
20. Click the *Different first page* check box to insert a check mark and then click the Custom Header button.

21. At the Header dialog box with the Header tab selected, click the First Page Header tab.
22. Click in the *Right section* text box and then click the Insert Page Number button.
23. Click OK to close the Header dialog box and then click OK to close the Page Setup dialog box.
24. View the header and footer in the Print backstage area and then return to the worksheet.
25. Save **4-RPBudget.xlsx**.

Check Your Work

Customizing Print Jobs

Use options in the *Settings* category at the Print backstage area to specify what to print. By default, the active worksheet prints. Change this by clicking the first gallery in the *Settings* category. At the drop-down list, specify if the entire workbook is to print (which is useful when a workbook contains multiple worksheets) or only selected cells. With the other galleries in the *Settings* category, specify if pages are to print on one side or both sides (this depends on the printer) and if they are to be collated. With other options, specify the worksheet orientation, size, and margins and whether the worksheet is to be scaled to fit all the columns or rows on one page.

With the *Pages* text boxes in the *Settings* category, specify the pages of the worksheet to be printed. For example, to print pages 2 and 3 of the active worksheet, type *2* in the *Pages* measurement box in the *Settings* category and then type *3* in the *to* measurement box. Or click the up- and down-pointing arrows to insert page numbers.

Project 1l Printing Specific Pages of a Worksheet

Part 12 of 12

1. With **4-RPBudget.xlsx** open, print the first two pages of the worksheet by completing the following steps:
    a. Click the File tab and then click the *Print* option.
    b. At the Print backstage area, click in the *Pages* measurement box below the first gallery in the *Settings* category and then type 1.
    c. Click in the *to* measurement box in the *Settings* category and then type 2.
    d. Click the Print button.

2. Print selected cells by completing the following steps:
   a. Display the worksheet in Normal view.
   b. Select the range A3:D11.
   c. Click the File tab and then click the *Print* option.
   d. At the Print backstage area, select and then delete the number in the *Pages* measurement box and the number in the *to* measurement box. (These are the numbers you inserted in Steps 1b and 1c.)
   e. Click the first gallery in the *Settings* category (displays with *Print Active Sheets*) and then click *Print Selection* at the drop-down list.
   f. Click the Print button.
3. Save and then close **4-RPBudget.xlsx**.

Check Your Work

Project 2 **Format a Sales and Commissions Worksheet**   **3 Parts**

You will format a sales commission worksheet by inserting a formula, completing a spelling check, and finding and replacing data and cell formatting.

Preview Finished Project

Tutorial

Checking Spelling

Checking Spelling

 Spelling

⏱ **Quick Steps**

Checking Spelling
1. Click Review tab.
2. Click Spelling button.
3. Replace or ignore selected words.

Excel provides a spelling check feature that verifies the spelling of text in a worksheet. The spelling check uses an electronic dictionary to identify misspelled words and suggest alternatives. Before checking the spelling in a worksheet, make the first cell active. The spelling check reviews the worksheet from the active cell to the last cell in the worksheet that contains data.

To use the spelling check, click the Review tab and then click the Spelling button. Figure 4.7 displays the Spelling dialog box. At this dialog box, tell Excel to ignore a word or to replace a misspelled word with a word from the *Suggestions* list box using one of the available buttons.

Tutorial

Using Undo and Redo

Using Undo and Redo

 Undo

Redo

Excel includes an Undo button on the Quick Access Toolbar that reverses certain commands or deletes the last data typed in a cell. For example, apply formatting to cells in a worksheet and then click the Undo button on the Quick Access Toolbar and the formatting is removed. To reapply the formatting, click the Redo button on the Quick Access Toolbar.

Figure 4.7 Spelling Dialog Box

A word in the worksheet not found in the spelling check dictionary displays here.

Suggested spellings display in the *Suggestions* list box.

Hint Ctrl + Z is the keyboard shortcut to undo a command.

Excel maintains actions in temporary memory. To undo an action, click the Undo button arrow and a drop-down list displays containing the actions performed on the worksheet. Click a specific action at the drop-down list and that action along with any preceding actions are undone. Click the Redo button and click a specific action at the drop-down list and that action along with any preceding actions are redone. Multiple actions must be undone or redone in sequence.

Project 2a Spell Checking and Formatting a Worksheet

Part 1 of 3

1. Open **MRSales.xlsx** and then save it with the name **4-MRSales**.
2. Complete a spelling check on the worksheet by completing the following steps:
   a. If necessary, make cell A1 active.
   b. Click the Review tab.
   c. Click the Spelling button in the Proofing group.
   d. Click the Change button as needed to correct misspelled words in the worksheet. (When the spelling check stops at the proper names *Pirozzi* and *Yonemoto*, click the Ignore All button.)
   e. At the message stating the spelling check is complete, click OK.
3. Insert a formula and then copy the formula without the formatting by completing the following steps:
   a. Make cell G4 active and then insert a formula that multiplies the sale price by the commission percentage.
   b. Copy the formula down into the range G5:G26.
   c. Some of the cells contain shading that you do not want removed, so click the Auto Fill Options button at the bottom right of the selected cells and then click the *Fill Without Formatting* option at the drop-down list.
4. Make cell G27 active and then insert the sum of the range G4:G26.
5. Apply the Accounting format with no digits displayed after the decimal point to cell G4 and cell G27.

6. Apply a theme by clicking the Page Layout tab, clicking the Themes button, and then clicking *Ion* at the drop-down gallery.

7. After looking at the worksheet with the Ion theme applied, you decide that you want to return to the original formatting. To do this, click the Undo button on the Quick Access Toolbar.

8. Save **4-MRSales.xlsx**.

Check Your Work

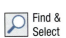

Tutorial

Finding Data

Tutorial

Replacing Data

Tutorial

Replacing Formatting

Quick Steps

Find Data
1. Click Find & Select button.
2. Click *Find*.
3. Type data in *Find what* text box.
4. Click Find Next button.

🔍 Find & Select

Finding and Replacing Data and Cell Formatting

Use Excel's find feature to look for specific data and either replace it with nothing or replace it with other data. This feature is particularly helpful for finding data quickly in a large worksheet. Excel also includes a find and replace feature. Use this feature to look for specific data in a worksheet and replace it with other data.

To find specific data in a worksheet, click the Find & Select button in the Editing group on the Home tab and then click *Find* at the drop-down list. This displays the Find and Replace dialog box with the Find tab selected, as shown in Figure 4.8. Type the find data in the *Find what* text box and then click the Find Next button. Continue clicking the Find Next button to move to the next occurrence of the data. If the Find and Replace dialog box obstructs the worksheet, use the mouse pointer on the title bar to drag the dialog box to a different location.

To find specific data in a worksheet and replace it with other data, click the Find & Select button in the Editing group on the Home tab and then click *Replace* at the drop-down list. This displays the Find and Replace dialog box with the

Figure 4.8 Find and Replace Dialog Box with Find Tab Selected

Type the data to be found in this text box.

Click this button to move to the next occurrence of the data.

Click this button to expand the dialog box.

Quick Steps

Find and Replace Data

1. Click Find & Select button.
2. Click *Replace*.
3. Type data in *Find what* text box.
4. Type data in *Replace with* text box.
5. Click Replace button or Replace All button.

Replace tab selected, as shown in Figure 4.9. Enter the find data in the *Find what* text box. Press the Tab key or click in the *Replace with* text box and then enter the replace data in the *Replace with* text box.

Click the Find Next button to find the next occurrence of the data. Click the Replace button to replace the data and find the next occurrence. To replace all the occurrences of the data in the *Find what* text box with the data in the *Replace with* text box, click the Replace All button. Click the Close button to close the Replace dialog box.

Display additional find and replace options by clicking the Options button. This expands the dialog box, as shown in Figure 4.10. By default, Excel will look for any data that contains the same characters as the data entered in the *Find what* text box, without concern for the characters before or after the entered data. For example, in Project 2b, you will look for sale prices of $450,000 and replace them with sale prices of $475,000. If you do not specify that you want to find only cells that contain *450000*, Excel will stop at any cell containing *450000*. For example, Excel will stop at a cell containing *$1,450,000* and a cell containing *$2,450,000*. To specify that the only data to be contained in the cell is what is entered in the *Find what* text box, click the Options button to expand the dialog box and then insert a check mark in the *Match entire cell contents* check box.

If the *Match case* option is active (contains a check mark), Excel will look for only that data that matches the case of the data entered in the *Find what* text box. Remove the check mark from this check box and Excel will find the data entered in the *Find what* text box in any case. By default, Excel will search in the current worksheet. If the workbook contains more than one worksheet, change the *Within* option to *Workbook*. By default, Excel searches by rows in a worksheet. This can be changed to by columns with the *Search* option.

Figure 4.9 Find and Replace Dialog Box with Replace Tab Selected

Type the data to be found in this text box.

Type the data to replace the found data in this text box.

Click this button to expand the dialog box.

Figure 4.10 Expanded Find and Replace Dialog Box

Search the active worksheet or the entire workbook with the *Within* option box.

Use this option to search by rows or by columns.

Use these two Format buttons to search for specific cell formatting and replace it with other cell formatting.

1. With **4-MRSales.xlsx** open, find all occurrences of *Land* in the worksheet and replace them with *Acreage* by completing the following steps:
   a. Click the Find & Select button in the Editing group on the Home tab and then click *Replace* at the drop-down list.
   b. At the Find and Replace dialog box with the Replace tab selected, type Land in the *Find what* text box.
   c. Press the Tab key. (This moves the insertion point to the *Replace with* text box.)
   d. Type Acreage.
   e. Click the Replace All button.
   f. At the message stating that four replacements were made, click OK.
   g. Click the Close button to close the Find and Replace dialog box.
2. Find all occurrences of *$450,000* and replace them with *$475,000* by completing the following steps:
   a. Click the Find & Select button in the Editing group and then click *Replace* at the drop-down list.
   b. At the Find and Replace dialog box with the Replace tab selected, select any text that displays in the *Find what* text box and then type 450000.
   c. Press the Tab key.
   d. Type 475000.
   e. Click the Options button to display additional options. (If additional options already display, skip this step.)
   f. Click the *Match entire cell contents* check box to insert a check mark.
   g. Click the Replace All button.
   h. At the message stating that two replacements were made, click OK.
   i. At the Find and Replace dialog box, click the *Match entire cell contents* check box to remove the check mark.
   j. Click the Close button to close the Find and Replace dialog box.
3. Save **4-MRSales.xlsx**.

Use the Format buttons at the expanded Find and Replace dialog box (see Figure 4.10) to search for specific cell formatting and replace it with other formatting. Click the Format button arrow and a drop-down list displays. Click the *Format* option and the Find Format dialog box displays with the Number, Alignment, Font, Border, Fill, and Protection tabs. Specify formatting at this dialog box. Click the *Choose Format From Cell* option from the Format button drop-down list or click the Choose Format From Cell button in the Find Format dialog box and the mouse pointer displays with a pointer tool attached. Click in the cell containing the desired formatting and the formatting displays in the *Preview* box left of the Format button. Click the *Clear Find Format* option at the Find button drop-down list and any formatting in the *Preview* box is removed.

Project 2c Finding and Replacing Cell Formatting

Part 3 of 3

1. With **4-MRSales.xlsx** open, search for a light-turquoise fill color and replace it with a light-green fill color by completing the following steps:

   a. Click the Find & Select button in the Editing group on the Home tab and then click *Replace* at the drop-down list.

   b. At the Find and Replace dialog box with the Replace tab selected, make sure the dialog box is expanded. (If not, click the Options button.)

   c. Select and then delete any text in the *Find what* text box.

   d. Select and then delete any text in the *Replace with* text box.

   e. Make sure the boxes immediately before the two Format buttons display with the text *No Format Set*. (If not, click the Format button arrow and then click the *Clear Find Format* option at the drop-down list. Do this for each Format button.)

   f. Click the top Format button.

   g. At the Find Format dialog box, click the Fill tab.

   h. Click the More Colors button.

   i. At the Colors dialog box with the Standard tab selected, click the light turquoise color, as shown at the right.

   j. Click OK to close the Colors dialog box.

   k. Click OK to close the Find Format dialog box.

   l. Click the bottom Format button.

   m. At the Replace Format dialog box with the Fill tab selected, click the light green color (last column, second row), as shown at the right.

   n. Click OK to close the dialog box.

   o. At the Find and Replace dialog box, click the Replace All button.

   p. At the message stating that 10 replacements were made, click OK.

2. Search for a light-gray fill color and replace it with a light-yellow fill color by completing the following steps:

   a. At the Find and Replace dialog box, click the top Format button.

   b. At the Find Format dialog box with the Fill tab selected, click the light gray color (fourth column, second row), as shown at the right.

   c. Click OK to close the Find Format dialog box.

   d. Click the bottom Format button.

   e. At the Replace Format dialog box with the Fill tab selected, click the yellow color (eighth column, second row), as shown below and to the right.

   f. Click OK to close the dialog box.

   g. At the Find and Replace dialog box, click the Replace All button.

   h. At the message stating that 78 replacements were made, click OK.

3. Search for 11-point Calibri formatting and replace it with 10-point Arial formatting by completing the following steps:

   a. With the Find and Replace dialog box open, clear formatting from the top Format button by clicking the top Format button arrow and then clicking the *Clear Find Format* option at the drop-down list.

   b. Clear formatting from the bottom Format button by clicking the bottom Format button arrow and then clicking *Clear Replace Format*.

   c. Click the top Format button.

   d. At the Find Format dialog box, click the Font tab.

   e. Scroll down the *Font* list box and then click *Calibri*.

   f. Click *11* in the *Size* list box.

   g. Click OK to close the dialog box.

   h. Click the bottom Format button.

   i. At the Replace Format dialog box with the Font tab selected, scroll down the *Font* list box and then click *Arial*.

   j. Click *10* in the *Size* list box.

   k. Click OK to close the dialog box.

   l. At the Find and Replace dialog box, click the Replace All button.

   m. At the message stating that 174 replacements were made, click OK.

   n. At the Find and Replace dialog box, remove formatting from both Format buttons.

   o. Click the Close button to close the Find and Replace dialog box.

4. Save, print, and then close **4-MRSales.xlsx**.

Check Your Work

Project 3   Insert a Formula and Sort and Filter Data in a Billing Worksheet   4 Parts

You will insert a formula in a weekly billing worksheet and then sort and filter specific data in the worksheet.

Preview Finished Project

Tutorial

Sorting Data

Sorting Data

Excel is primarily a spreadsheet program but it also includes some basic database functions, such as sorting data in alphabetic or numeric order. To sort data in a worksheet, use the Sort & Filter button in the Editing group on the Home tab.

 Sort & Filter

Quick Steps

Sort Data
1. Select cells.
2. Click Sort & Filter button.
3. Click sort option at drop-down list.

To sort data in a worksheet, select the cells containing the data to be sorted, click the Sort & Filter button in the Editing group, and then click the option representing the desired sort. The sort option names vary depending on the data in selected cells. For example, if the first column of selected cells contains text, the sort options in the drop-down list display as *Sort A to Z* and *Sort Z to A*. If the selected cells contain dates, the sort options in the drop-down list display as *Sort Oldest to Newest* and *Sort Newest to Oldest*. If the cells contain numbers or values, the sort options display as *Sort Smallest to Largest* and *Sort Largest to Smallest*. If more than one column is selected in a worksheet, Excel sorts the data in the first selected column.

Project 3a Sorting Data

Part 1 of 4

1. Open **APTBilling.xlsx** and then save it with the name **4-APTBilling**.
2. Insert a formula in cell F4 that multiplies the rate by the hours. Copy the formula down into the range F5:F29.
3. Sort the data in the first column in descending order by completing the following steps:
   a. Make cell A4 active.
   b. Click the Sort & Filter button in the Editing group on the Home tab.
   c. Click the *Sort Largest to Smallest* option at the drop-down list.
4. Sort in ascending order by clicking the Sort & Filter button and then clicking *Sort Smallest to Largest* at the drop-down list.
5. Save **4-APTBilling.xlsx**.

Check Your Work

Completing a Custom Sort

Quick Steps

Complete a Custom Sort
1. Select cells.
2. Click Sort & Filter button.
3. Click *Custom Sort* at drop-down list.
4. Specify options at Sort dialog box.
5. Click OK.

To sort data in a column other than the first column, use options at the Sort dialog box. Select one column in a worksheet, click the Sort & Filter button, and then click the desired sort option; only the data in that column is sorted. If this data is related to data to the left or right of the data in the sorted column, that relationship is broken. For example, after sorting the range C4:C29 in 4-APTBilling.xlsx, the client number, treatment, hours, and total no longer match the date.

Use options at the Sort dialog box to sort data and maintain the relationship among all the cells. To sort using the Sort dialog box, select the cells to be sorted, click the Sort & Filter button, and then click *Custom Sort*. This displays the Sort dialog box, shown in Figure 4.11.

Figure 4.11 Sort Dialog Box

Click this button to specify a second column for sorting.

Click this option box arrow and then specify if sorting on values, cell color, font color, or cell icon.

Click this option box arrow and then specify the sort order.

Click this down-pointing arrow and then click the desired column in the drop-down list.

The data displayed in the *Sort by* option box will vary depending on what is selected. Generally, the data that displays is the title of the first column of selected cells. If the selected cells do not have a title, the data may display as *Column A*. Use this option to specify what column is to be sorted. Using the Sort dialog box to sort data in a column maintains the relationship among the data.

Project 3b Sorting Data Using the Sort Dialog Box

Part 2 of 4

1. With **4-APTBilling.xlsx** open, sort the rates in the range E4:E29 in descending order and maintain the relationship to the other data by completing the following steps:
   a. Select the range A3:F29.
   b. Click the Sort & Filter button and then click *Custom Sort*.
   c. At the Sort dialog box, click the *Sort by* option box arrow and then click *Rate* at the drop-down list.
   d. Click the *Order* option box arrow and then click *Largest to Smallest* at the drop-down list.

   e. Click OK to close the Sort dialog box.
   f. Deselect the cells.
2. Sort the dates in ascending order (oldest to newest) by completing steps similar to those in Step 1.
3. Save and then print **4-APTBilling.xlsx**.

Check Your Work

Sorting More Than One Column

When sorting data in cells, data in more than one column can be sorted. For example, in Project 3c, you will sort the dates from oldest to newest and the client numbers from lowest to highest. In this sort, the dates are sorted first and then the client numbers are sorted in ascending order within the same date.

To sort data in more than one column, select all the columns in the worksheet that need to remain relative and then display the Sort dialog box. At the Sort dialog box, specify the first column to be sorted in the *Sort by* option box, click the *Add Level* button, and then specify the second column in the first *Then by* option box. To sort multiple columns, add additional *Then by* option boxes by clicking the *Add Level* button.

Project 3c Sorting Data in Two Columns   Part 3 of 4

1. With **4-APTBilling.xlsx** open, select the range A3:F29.
2. Click the Sort & Filter button and then click *Custom Sort*.
3. At the Sort dialog box, click the *Sort by* option box arrow and then click *Date* in the drop-down list. (Skip this step if *Date* already displays in the *Sort by* option box.)
4. Make sure *Oldest to Newest* displays in the *Order* option box.
5. Click the Add Level button.
6. Click the *Then by* option box arrow and then click *Client #* in the drop-down list.
7. Click OK to close the dialog box.
8. Deselect the cells.
9. Save and then print **4-APTBilling.xlsx**.

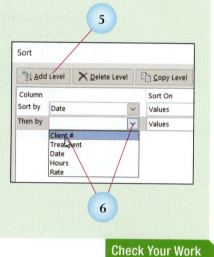

Check Your Work

Filtering Data

A restriction, called a *filter*, can be placed temporarily on data in a worksheet to isolate specific data. To turn on filtering, make a cell containing data active, click the Sort & Filter button in the Editing group on the Home tab, and then click *Filter* at the drop-down list. This turns on filtering and causes a filter arrow to appear with each column label in the worksheet, as shown in Figure 4.12. Data does not need to be selected before turning on filtering because Excel automatically searches for column labels in a worksheet.

Quick Steps

Filter a List
1. Select cells.
2. Click Sort & Filter button.
3. Click *Filter* at drop-down list.
4. Click filter arrow in heading to filter.
5. Click option at drop-down list.

To filter data in a worksheet, click the filter arrow in the heading to be filtered. This causes a drop-down list to display with options to filter all the records, create a custom filter, or select an entry that appears in one or more of the cells in the column. When data is filtered, the filter arrow changes to a funnel icon. The funnel icon indicates that rows in the worksheet have been filtered. To turn off filtering, click the Sort & Filter button and then click *Filter*.

If a column contains numbers, click the filter arrow and point to *Number Filters* and a side menu displays with options for filtering numbers. For example, numbers can be filtered that are equal to, greater than, or less than a specified number; the top 10 numbers can be filtered; and numbers can be filtered that are above or below a specified number.

Figure 4.12 Filtering Data

Turn on filtering and filter arrows display with column headings.

Click the filter arrow in the *Client #* heading, click the *(Select All)* check box to remove the check mark, and then click the *3102* check box to display only those rows containing client number 3102.

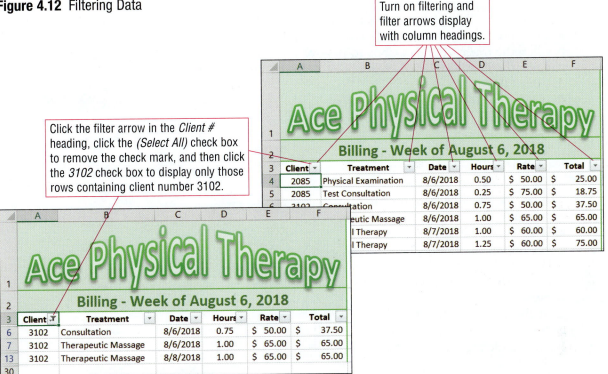

Project 3d Filtering Data

Part 4 of 4

1. With **4-APTBilling.xlsx** open, click in cell A4.
2. Turn on filtering by clicking the Sort & Filter button in the Editing group on the Home tab and then clicking *Filter* at the drop-down list.
3. Filter rows for client number 3102 by completing the following steps:
   a. Click the filter arrow in the *Client #* heading.
   b. Click the *(Select All)* check box to remove the check mark.
   c. Scroll down the list box and then click *3102* to insert a check mark in the check box.
   d. Click OK.
4. Redisplay all the rows containing data by completing the following steps:
   a. Click the funnel icon in the *Client #* heading.
   b. Click the *(Select All)* check box to insert a check mark. (This also inserts check marks for all the items in the list.)
   c. Click OK.

5. Filter a list of clients who receive physical therapy by completing the following steps:
   a. Click the filter arrow in the *Treatment* heading.
   b. Click the *(Select All)* check box to remove the check mark.
   c. Click the *Physical Therapy* check box to insert a check mark.
   d. Click OK.

6. Redisplay all the rows containing data by completing the following steps:
   a. Click the funnel icon in the *Treatment* heading.
   b. Click the *Clear Filter From "Treatment"* option.

7. Display the two highest rates by completing the following steps:
   a. Click the filter arrow in the *Rate* heading.
   b. Point to *Number Filters* and then click *Top 10* at the side menu.
   c. At the Top 10 AutoFilter dialog box, select the *10* in the middle measurement box and then type 2.
   d. Click OK to close the dialog box.

8. Redisplay all the rows that contain data by completing the following steps:
   a. Click the funnel icon in the *Rate* heading.
   b. Click the *Clear Filter From "Rate"* option.

9. Display totals greater than $60 by completing the following steps:
   a. Click the filter arrow in the *Total* heading.
   b. Point to *Number Filters* and then click *Greater Than*.
   c. At the Custom AutoFilter dialog box, type 60 and then click OK.

10. Print the worksheet by clicking the File tab, clicking the *Print* option, and then clicking the Print button.

11. Turn off the filtering feature by clicking the Sort & Filter button and then clicking *Filter* at the drop-down list.

12. Save and then close **4-APTBilling.xlsx**.

Check Your Work

Chapter Summary

- The Page Setup group on the Page Layout tab contains buttons for changing the margins and page orientation and size, as well as buttons for establishing the print area, inserting a page break, applying a picture background, and printing titles.

- The default left and right margins are 0.7 inch and the default top and bottom margins are 0.75 inch. Change these default margins with the Margins button in the Page Setup group on the Page Layout tab.

- Display the Page Setup dialog box with the Margins tab selected by clicking the Margins button in the Page Setup group on the Page Layout tab and then clicking *Custom Margins* at the drop-down list.

- Center a worksheet on the page with the *Horizontally* and *Vertically* check boxes at the Page Setup dialog box with the Margins tab selected.

- Click the Orientation button in the Page Setup group on the Page Layout tab to display the two orientation choices: *Portrait* and *Landscape*.

- Insert a page break by selecting the column or row, clicking the Breaks button in the Page Setup group on the Page Layout tab, and then clicking *Insert Page Break* at the drop-down list.

- To insert both horizontal and vertical page breaks at the same time, make a cell active, click the Breaks button, and then click *Insert Page Break* at the drop-down list.

- Preview the page breaks in a worksheet by clicking the Page Break Preview button in the view area on the Status bar or clicking the View tab and then clicking the Page Break Preview button in the Workbook Views group.

- Use options at the Page Setup dialog box with the Sheet tab selected to specify printing column and/or row titles on each page. Display this dialog box by clicking the Print Titles button in the Page Setup group on the Page Layout tab.

- Use options in the Scale to Fit group on the Page Layout tab to scale data to fit on a specific number of pages.

- Use the Background button in the Page Setup group on the Page Layout tab to insert a worksheet background picture. A background picture displays on the screen but does not print.

- Use options in the Sheet Options group on the Page Layout tab to specify whether to view and/or print gridlines and headings.

- Specify the print area by selecting cells, clicking the Print Area button in the Page Setup group on the Page Layout tab, and then clicking *Set Print Area* at the drop-down list. Add another print area by selecting the cells, clicking the Print Area button, and then clicking *Add to Print Area* at the drop-down list.

- Create a header and/or footer with the Header & Footer button in the Text group on the Insert tab, in Page Layout view, or with options at the Page Setup dialog box with the Header/Footer tab selected.

- Customize a print job with options at the Print backstage area.

- To check spelling in a worksheet, click the Review tab and then click the Spelling button.

- Click the Undo button on the Quick Access Toolbar to reverse the most recent action and click the Redo button to redo a previously reversed action.

- Use options at the Find and Replace dialog box with the Find tab selected to find specific data and/or formatting in a worksheet.
- Use options at the Find and Replace dialog box with the Replace tab selected to find specific data and/or formatting and replace it with other data and/or formatting.
- Sort data in a worksheet with options from the Sort & Filter button in the Editing group on the Home tab.
- Create a custom sort with options at the Sort dialog box. Display this dialog box by clicking the Sort & Filter button and then clicking *Custom Sort* at the drop-down list.
- Temporarily isolate data by filtering it. Turn on the filter feature by clicking the Sort & Filter button in the Editing group on the Home tab and then clicking *Filter* at the drop-down list. This inserts a filter arrow with each column label. Click a filter arrow and then use options at the drop-down list to specify the filter data.

Commands Review

FEATURE	RIBBON TAB, GROUP	BUTTON, OPTION	KEYBOARD SHORTCUT
background picture	Page Layout, Page Setup		
filter data	Home, Editing		
Find and Replace dialog box with Find tab selected	Home, Editing	, *Find*	Ctrl + F
Find and Replace dialog box with Replace tab selected	Home, Editing	, *Replace*	Ctrl + H
header and footer	Insert, Text		
insert page break	Page Layout, Page Setup	, *Insert Page Break*	
margins	Page Layout, Page Setup		
orientation	Page Layout, Page Setup		
Page Layout view	View, Workbook Views		
Page Setup dialog box with Margins tab selected	Page Layout, Page Setup	, *Custom Margins*	
Page Setup dialog box with Sheet tab selected	Page Layout, Page Setup		
preview page break	View, Workbook Views		
print area	Page Layout, Page Setup		
remove page break	Page Layout, Page Setup	, *Remove Page Break*	

FEATURE	RIBBON TAB, GROUP	BUTTON, OPTION	KEYBOARD SHORTCUT
scale height	Page Layout, Scale to Fit		
scale to fit	Page Layout, Scale to Fit		
scale width	Page Layout, Scale to Fit		
size	Page Layout, Page Setup		
sort data	Home, Editing		
spelling check	Review, Proofing		F7

Workbook

Chapter study tools and assessment activities are available in the *Workbook* ebook. These resources are designed to help you further develop and demonstrate mastery of the skills learned in this chapter.

Unit assessment activities are also available in the *Workbook*. These activities are designed to help you demonstrate mastery of the skills learned in this unit.

Unit 2

Enhancing the Display of Workbooks

Microsoft®

Excel®

Moving Data within and between Workbooks

Performance Objectives

Upon successful completion of Chapter 5, you will be able to:

1 Insert and delete worksheets

2 Move, copy, and paste cells within and between worksheets

3 Move, rename, format worksheet tabs

4 Hide/unhide worksheets

5 Print a workbook containing multiple worksheets

6 Change the zoom

7 Split a worksheet into windows and freeze/unfreeze panes

8 Name a range of cells and use a range in a formula

9 Open multiple workbooks

10 Arrange, size, and move workbooks

11 Copy and paste data between workbooks

12 Link data between worksheets

Precheck

Check your current skills to help focus your study.

Up to this point, the workbooks you have worked in have consisted of single worksheets. In this chapter, you will learn to create a workbook with several worksheets and complete tasks such as copying and pasting data within and between worksheets. Moving and pasting or copying and pasting selected cells within and between worksheets is useful for rearranging data and saving time. You will also work with multiple workbooks and complete tasks such as arranging, sizing, and moving workbooks and opening and closing multiple workbooks.

Data Files

Before beginning chapter work, copy the EL1C5 folder to your storage medium and then make EL1C5 the active folder.

SNAP

If you are a SNAP user, launch the Precheck and Tutorials from your Assignments page.

Project 1 **Manage Data in a Multiple-Worksheet Account Workbook** **7 Parts**

You will open an account workbook containing multiple worksheets and then insert and delete worksheets and move, copy, and paste data between worksheets. You will also hide and unhide worksheets and format and print multiple worksheets in the workbook.

Preview Finished Project

Creating a Workbook with Multiple Worksheets

Hint Creating multiple worksheets within a workbook is helpful for saving related data.

An Excel workbook contains one worksheet by default but additional worksheets can be added. Add additional worksheets to a workbook to store related data, such as a worksheet for expenses for individual salespeople in the company and another worksheet for the monthly payroll for all the departments within the company. Another example is to record quarterly sales statistics in individual worksheets within a workbook.

Tutorial

Inserting and Renaming Worksheets

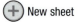 New sheet

Quick Steps

Insert a Worksheet
Click New sheet button.
OR
Press Shift + F11.

Delete a Worksheet
1. Click worksheet tab.
2. Click Delete button arrow.
3. Click *Delete Sheet*.
4. Click Delete button.

Inserting a New Worksheet

Insert a new worksheet in a workbook by clicking the New sheet button to the right of the Sheet1 tab at the bottom of the worksheet area. A new worksheet can also be inserted in a workbook with the keyboard shortcut Shift + F11. A new worksheet tab is inserted to the right of the active tab. To move between worksheets, click the desired tab. The active worksheet tab displays with a white background and the worksheet name displays in green. Any inactive tabs display with a light-gray background and gray text.

Deleting a Worksheet

If a worksheet is no longer needed in a workbook, delete it by clicking the worksheet tab, clicking the Delete button arrow in the Cells group on the Home tab, and then clicking *Delete Sheet* at the drop-down list. Another method for deleting a worksheet is to right-click the worksheet tab and then click *Delete* at the shortcut menu. When deleting a worksheet, Excel displays a deletion confirmation message. At this message, click the Delete button.

Selecting Multiple Worksheets

To work with more than one worksheet at a time, select the worksheets. With multiple worksheets selected, the same formatting can be applied to cells or the selected worksheets can be deleted. To select adjacent worksheet tabs, click the first tab, press and hold down the Shift key, click the last tab, and then release the Shift key. To select nonadjacent worksheet tabs, click the first tab, press and hold down the Ctrl key, click any other tabs to be selected, and then release the Ctrl key.

Tutorial

Copying and
Pasting Cells

 Copy

 Cut

Paste

Copying, Cutting, and Pasting Cells

Cells in a workbook may need to be copied or moved to different locations within a worksheet or to another worksheet in the workbook. Move or copy cells in a worksheet or between worksheets or workbooks by selecting the cells and then using the Cut, Copy, and/or Paste buttons in the Clipboard group on the Home tab.

Copying and Pasting Selected Cells

Copying selected cells can be useful in worksheets that contain repetitive data. To copy cells, select the cells and then click the Copy button in the Clipboard group on the Home tab. This causes a moving dashed line border (called a *marquee*) to display around the selected cells. To copy cells to another worksheet, click the worksheet tab, click in the cell where the first selected cell is to be pasted, and then click the Paste button in the Clipboard group. Remove the moving marquee from selected cells by pressing the Esc key or double-clicking in any cell.

Selected cells in the same worksheet can be copied using the mouse and the Ctrl key. To do this, select the cells to be copied and then position the mouse pointer on any border around the selected cells until the pointer turns into an arrow pointer. Press and hold down the Ctrl key, click and hold down the left mouse button, drag the outline of the selected cells to the new location, release the left mouse button, and then release the Ctrl key.

Quick Steps

Copy and Paste Cells
1. Select cells.
2. Click Copy button.
3. Click cell.
4. Click Paste button.

Hint Ctrl + C is the keyboard shortcut to copy selected data.

Project 1a **Inserting, Deleting, Selecting, Copying, Pasting, and Formatting Worksheets**

Part 1 of 7

1. Open **RPFacAccts.xlsx** and then save it with the name **5-RPFacAccts**.
2. Insert a new worksheet in the workbook by completing the following steps:
   a. Click the 2ndHalfSales worksheet tab to make it active.
   b. Click the New sheet button to the right of the 2ndHalfSales worksheet tab. (This inserts a new worksheet to the right of the 2ndHalfSales worksheet with the name Sheet4.)
3. Delete two worksheet tabs by completing the following steps:
   a. Click the 1stHalfSales worksheet tab.
   b. Press and hold down the Shift key, click the 2ndHalfSales worksheet tab, and then release the Shift key. (These tabs must be adjacent. If they are not, press and hold down the Ctrl key when clicking the 2ndHalfSales worksheet tab.)
   c. With the two worksheet tabs selected, click the Delete button arrow in the Cells group on the Home tab and then click *Delete Sheet* at the drop-down list.
   d. At the message stating that you cannot undo deleting sheets, click the Delete button.

4. Copy cells from Sheet1 to Sheet4 by completing the following steps:
   a. Click the Sheet1 tab to make it the active worksheet.
   b. Select the range A1:A3 (the first three rows of data).
   c. Click the Copy button in the Clipboard group on the Home tab.
   d. Click the Sheet4 tab to make it the active tab.
   e. With A1 the active cell, click the Paste button in the Clipboard group on the Home tab.

5. Make the following changes to the new worksheet:
   a. Click in cell A3 and then type First Quarter Summary 2018.
   b. Change the width of column A to 20.00 characters.
   c. Change the width of columns B, C, and D to 12.00 characters.
   d. Type the following text in the specified cells:
      B4: January
      C4: February
      D4: March
      A5: Checks amount
      A6: Deposit amount
      A7: End-of-month balance
   e. Select the range B4:D4, click the Bold button in the Font group on the Home tab, and then click the Center button in the Alignment group.
   f. Select the range B5:D7 and then apply the Comma format (using the Comma Style button in the Number group on the Home tab) with two digits after the decimal point.
6. Apply formatting to the cells in all four worksheets by completing the following steps:
   a. Click the Sheet1 tab to make it active and then click in cell A1 to make it the active cell.
   b. Press and hold down the Shift key, click the Sheet4 tab, and then release the Shift key. (This selects all four worksheets.)
   c. With cell A1 active, change the row height to 51.00 points.
   d. Click in cell A3.
   e. Change the font size to 14 points.
   f. Click each remaining worksheet tab (Sheet2, Sheet3, and Sheet4) and notice the formatting changes applied to all the cells.
7. Change column width for the three worksheets by completing the following steps:
   a. Click the Sheet1 tab to make it active.
   b. Press and hold down the Shift key, click the Sheet3 tab, and then release the Shift key.
   c. Select columns E, F, and G and then change the column width to 10.00 characters.
   d. Click the Sheet2 tab and then click the Sheet3 tab. Notice that the width of columns E, F, and G has changed to 10.00 characters. Click the Sheet4 tab and notice that the column width did not change.
8. Save 5-RPFacAccts.xlsx.

Check Your Work

Tutorial

Using Paste Options

Paste Options

Using Paste Options

When pasting cells in a worksheet, specify how the cells are pasted by clicking the Paste button arrow and then clicking a paste option button at the drop-down list. Click the Paste button (not the button arrow) and a Paste Options button displays in the lower right corner of the pasted cell(s). Display a list of paste options by clicking the button or pressing the Ctrl key. This causes a drop-down list to display, as shown in Figure 5.1. The same option buttons display when the

Figure 5.1 Paste Options Buttons

Use buttons in this section to specify how text and formulas are pasted in cells and whether to keep source column widths.

Use buttons in this section to specify how values are pasted in the worksheet.

Use buttons in this section to specify whether an image, such as a picture, is copied or linked to the worksheet.

Paste button arrow is clicked. Hover the mouse pointer over a button in the drop-down list and the descriptive name of the button displays along with the keyboard shortcut. Use buttons in this drop-down list to specify what is pasted.

Tutorial

Moving Selected Cells

Moving Cells

Selected cells and cell contents can be moved within and between worksheets. Move selected cells with the Cut and Paste buttons in the Clipboard group on the Home tab or by dragging with the mouse.

Quick Steps

Move and Paste Cells
1. Select cells.
2. Click Cut button.
3. Click cell.
4. Click Paste button.

To move selected cells with buttons on the Home tab, select the cells and then click the Cut button in the Clipboard group. Click in the cell where the first selected cell is to be inserted and then click the Paste button in the Clipboard group.

Hint Ctrl + X is the keyboard shortcut to cut selected data. Ctrl + V is the keyboard shortcut to paste data.

To move selected cells with the mouse, select the cells and then position the mouse pointer on any border of the selected cells until the pointer turns into an arrow pointer with a four-headed arrow attached. Click and hold down the left mouse button, drag the outline of the selected cells to the new location, and then release the mouse button.

Project 1b Copying and Moving Cells and Pasting Cells Using Paste Options   **Part 2 of 7**

1. With **5-RPFacAccts.xlsx** open, copy cells from Sheet2 to Sheet3 using the Paste Options button by completing the following steps:
   a. Click the Sheet2 tab to make it active.
   b. Select the range C7:E9.
   c. Click the Copy button in the Clipboard group.
   d. Click the Sheet3 tab.
   e. Click in cell C7.
   f. Click the Paste button in the Clipboard group.

g. Click the Paste Options button in the lower right corner of the pasted cells and then click the Keep Source Column Widths button at the drop-down list.

h. Make Sheet2 active and then press the Esc key to remove the moving marquee.

2. Click the Sheet1 tab.

3. You realize that the sublet rent deposit was recorded on the wrong day. The correct day is January 9. To move the cells containing information on the deposit, complete the following steps:

a. Click in cell A13 and then insert a row. (The new row should display above the row containing *Rainier Suppliers*.)

b. Select the range A7:F7.

c. Click the Cut button in the Clipboard group on the Home tab.

d. Click in cell A13.

e. Click the Paste button in the Clipboard group.

f. Change the date of the deposit from January 1 to January 9.

g. Select row 7 and then delete it.

4. Move cells using the mouse by completing the following steps:

a. Click the Sheet2 tab.

b. Click in cell A13 and then insert a new row.

c. Using the mouse, select the range A7:F7.

d. Position the mouse pointer on any boundary of the selected cells until it turns into an arrow pointer with a four-headed arrow attached. Click and hold down the left mouse button, drag the outline of the selected cells to row 13, and then release the mouse button.

12	12-Feb	518	Clear Source	Developer supplies	123.74
13					
14	-Feb	519	Rainier Suppliers	Camera supplies	119.62
15	17-Feb	520	A1 Wedding Supplies	Photo albums	323.58

4d

e. Change the date of the deposit to February 13.

f. Delete row 7.

5. Save **5-RPFacAccts.xlsx**.

Check Your Work

Copying and Pasting Using the Clipboard Task Pane

Quick Steps

Copy and Paste Multiple Items

1. Click Clipboard group task pane launcher.
2. Select cells.
3. Click Copy button.
4. Repeat Steps 2 and 3 as desired.
5. Make cell active.
6. Click item in Clipboard task pane to be inserted in worksheet.
7. Repeat Step 6 as desired.

Use the Clipboard task pane to copy and paste multiple items. To use the task pane, click the Clipboard group task pane launcher in the lower right corner of the Clipboard group on the Home tab. The Clipboard task pane displays at the left side of the screen similarly to what is shown in Figure 5.2.

Select data or an object to be copied and then click the Copy button in the Clipboard group. Continue selecting cells, text, or other items and clicking the Copy button. To paste an item into a worksheet, make the desired cell active and then click the item in the Clipboard task pane. If the copied item is text, the first 50 characters display in the task pane. To paste all the selected items into a single location, make the desired cell active and then click the Paste All button in the task pane. When all the items have been pasted into the worksheet, click the Clear All button to remove any remaining items from the task pane.

Figure 5.2 Clipboard Task Pane

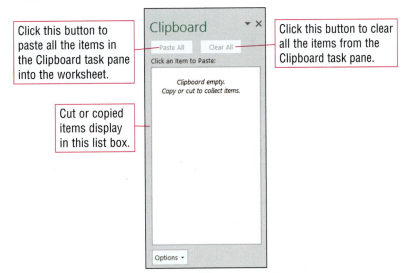

Click this button to paste all the items in the Clipboard task pane into the worksheet.

Click this button to clear all the items from the Clipboard task pane.

Cut or copied items display in this list box.

Project 1c Copying and Pasting Cells Using the Clipboard Task Pane

Part 3 of 7

1. With **5-RPFacAccts.xlsx** open, select cells for copying by completing the following steps:
   a. Display the Clipboard task pane by clicking the Clipboard group task pane launcher. (If the Clipboard task pane contains any copied data, click the Clear All button.)
   b. Click the Sheet1 tab.
   c. Select the range C15:E16.
   d. Click the Copy button in the Clipboard group.
   e. Select the range C19:E19.
   f. Click the Copy button in the Clipboard group.
2. Paste the copied cells by completing the following steps:
   a. Click the Sheet2 tab.
   b. Click in cell C15.
   c. Click the item in the Clipboard task pane representing *General Systems Developer*.
   d. Click the Sheet3 tab.
   e. Click in cell C15.
   f. Click the item in the Clipboard task pane representing *General Systems Developer*.
   g. Click in cell C19.
   h. Click the item in the Clipboard task pane representing *Parkland City Services*.
3. Click the Clear All button at the top of the Clipboard task pane.
4. Close the Clipboard task pane by clicking the Close button (contains an *X*) in the upper right corner of the task pane.
5. Save **5-RPFacAccts.xlsx**.

Check Your Work

Pasting Values Only

When pasting cells that contain a value and a formula, specify what is to be pasted using button options from the Paste button or Paste Options button drop-down list. Use the buttons in the *Paste Values* section of the drop-down list to insert only the value, the value with numbering formatting, or the value with source formatting.

Project 1d Copying and Pasting Values

Part 4 of 7

1. With **5-RPFacAccts.xlsx** open, make Sheet1 the active tab.
2. Click in cell G6, type the formula =(f6-e6)+g5, and then press the Enter key.
3. Copy the formula in cell G6 down into the range G7:G20.
4. Copy as a value (and not a formula) the final balance amount from Sheet1 to Sheet2 by completing the following steps:
   a. Click in cell G20.
   b. Click the Copy button in the Clipboard group.
   c. Click the Sheet2 tab.
   d. Click in cell G5 and then click the Paste button arrow.
   e. At the drop-down list, click the Values button in the *Paste Values* section of the drop-down list. (This inserts the value and not the formula.)

5. Click in cell G6, insert a formula that determines the balance (see Step 2), and then copy the formula down into the range G7:G20.
6. Copy the amount in cell G20 and then paste the value only in cell G5 in Sheet3. Apply to the cell the Accounting format with a dollar symbol and two digits past the decimal point.
7. With Sheet3 active, make cell G6 active, insert a formula that determines the balance (see Step 2), and then copy the formula down into the range G7:G20.
8. Insert formulas and apply formatting to cells in the three worksheets by completing the following steps:
   a. Click the Sheet1 tab.
   b. Press and hold down the Shift key, click the Sheet3 tab, and then release the Shift key.
   c. Click in cell D21, click the Bold button in the Font group on the Home tab, and then type Total.
   d. Click in cell E21 and then click the AutoSum button in the Editing group on the Home tab. (This inserts the formula =SUM(E13:E20).)
   e. Change the formula to =SUM(E7:E20) and then press the Enter key.
   f. Click in cell F21 and then click the AutoSum button. (This inserts the formula =SUM(F12:F20).)
   g. Change the formula to =SUM(F6:F20) and then press the Enter key.
   h. Select cells E21 and F21 and then click the Accounting Number Format button. Click in cell G5 and then click the Accounting Number Format button. (Cell G5 in Sheet1 already contains the Accounting format but cells G5 in Sheet2 and Sheet3 do not.)
   i. Click the Sheet2 tab and notice the text and formulas inserted in the worksheet, click the Sheet3 tab and notice the text and formulas, and then click the Sheet4 tab (to deselect the tabs).
9. Copy values from Sheet1 to Sheet4 by completing the following steps:
   a. Click the Sheet1 tab.
   b. Click in cell E21 and then click the Copy button in the Clipboard group.
   c. Click the Sheet4 tab.

d. Click in cell B5 and then click the Paste button in the Clipboard group.

e. Click the Paste Options button and then click the Values button in the *Paste Values* section of the drop-down list.

f. Click the Sheet1 tab.

g. Click in cell F21 and then click the Copy button.

h. Click the Sheet4 tab.

i. Click in cell B6, click the Paste button arrow, and then click the Values button at the drop-down list.

j. Click the Sheet1 tab.

k. Click in cell G20 and then click the Copy button.

l. Click the Sheet4 tab.

m. Click in cell B7, click the Paste button arrow, and then click the Values button at the drop-down list.

10. Complete steps similar to those in Step 9 to insert amounts and balances for February and March.

11. Select the range B5:D5 and then click the Accounting Number Format button.

12. Save **5-RPFacAccts.xlsx**.

Check Your Work

Tutorial

Moving, Copying, and Deleting a Worksheet

Quick Steps

Move or Copy a Worksheet
1. Right-click sheet tab.
2. Click *Move or Copy.*
3. At Move or Copy dialog box, click worksheet name in *Before sheet* list box.
4. Click OK.
OR
Drag worksheet tab to new position. (To copy, press and hold down Ctrl key while dragging.)

Managing Worksheets

Right-click a sheet tab and a shortcut menu displays with options for managing worksheets, as shown in Figure 5.3. For example, remove a worksheet by clicking the *Delete* option. Move or copy a worksheet by clicking the *Move or Copy* option. Clicking this option causes a Move or Copy dialog box to display with options for specifying where to move or copy the selected sheet. By default, Excel names worksheets in a workbook *Sheet1, Sheet2, Sheet3,* and so on. To rename a worksheet, click the *Rename* option (which selects the default sheet name) and then type the new name.

In addition to the shortcut menu options, the mouse can be used to move or copy worksheets. To move a worksheet, position the mouse pointer on the worksheet tab, click and hold down the left mouse button (a page icon displays next to the mouse pointer), drag the page icon to the new position, and then release the mouse button. For example, to move the Sheet2 tab after the Sheet3 tab, position the mouse pointer on the Sheet2 tab, click and hold down the left mouse button, drag the page icon after the Sheet3 tab, and then release the mouse button. To copy a worksheet, press and hold down the Ctrl key while dragging the sheet tab.

Figure 5.3 Sheet Tab Shortcut Menu

Quick Steps

Apply Color to a Sheet Tab
1. Right-click sheet tab.
2. Point to *Tab Color*.
3. Click color at color palette.

Use the *Tab Color* option at the shortcut menu to apply a color to a worksheet tab. Right-click a worksheet tab, point to *Tab Color* at the shortcut menu, and then click a color at the color palette.

Project 1e Selecting, Moving, Renaming, and Changing the Color of Worksheet Tabs   **Part 5 of 7**

1. With **5-RPFacAccts.xlsx** open, move Sheet4 by completing the following steps:
   a. Right-click the Sheet4 tab and then click *Move or Copy* at the shortcut menu.
   b. At the Move or Copy dialog box, make sure *Sheet1* is selected in the *Before sheet* list box and then click OK.

2. Rename Sheet4 by completing the following steps:
   a. Right-click the Sheet4 tab and then click *Rename*.
   b. Type Summary and then press the Enter key.
3. Complete steps similar to those in Step 2 to rename Sheet1 to *January*, Sheet2 to *February*, and Sheet3 to *March*.
4. Change the color of the Summary sheet tab by completing the following steps:
   a. Right-click the Summary sheet tab.
   b. Point to *Tab Color* at the shortcut menu.
   c. Click the *Red* color option (second option in the *Standard Colors* section).
5. Follow steps similar to those in Step 4 to change the January sheet tab to standard blue (eighth option in the *Standard Colors* section), the February sheet tab to standard purple (last option in the *Standard Colors* section), and the March sheet tab to standard green (sixth option in the *Standard Colors* section).
6. Save **5-RPFacAccts.xlsx**.

Check Your Work

Hiding a Worksheet in a Workbook

Format

Quick Steps

Hide a Worksheet
1. Click Format button.
2. Point to *Hide & Unhide*.
3. Click *Hide Sheet*.
OR
1. Right-click worksheet tab.
2. Click *Hide* at shortcut menu.

Unhide a Worksheet
1. Click Format button.
2. Point to *Hide & Unhide*.
3. Click *Unhide Sheet*.
4. Double-click hidden worksheet in Unhide dialog box.
OR
1. Right-click worksheet tab.
2. Click *Unhide* at shortcut menu.
3. Double-click hidden worksheet in Unhide dialog box.

In a workbook with multiple worksheets, a worksheet can be hidden that contains data that should not display or print with the workbook. To hide a worksheet in a workbook, click the Format button in the Cells group on the Home tab, point to *Hide & Unhide*, and then click *Hide Sheet*. A worksheet can also be hidden by right-clicking a worksheet tab and then clicking the *Hide* option at the shortcut menu.

To make a hidden worksheet visible, click the Format button in the Cells group, point to *Hide & Unhide* and then click *Unhide Sheet*, or right-click a worksheet tab and then click *Unhide* at the shortcut menu. At the Unhide dialog box, shown in Figure 5.4, double-click the name of the worksheet to be unhidden.

Figure 5.4 Unhide Dialog Box

The names of hidden worksheets display in this list box.

Project 1f **Hiding a Worksheet and Formatting Multiple Worksheets**   Part 6 of 7

1. With **5-RPFacAccts.xlsx** open, hide the Summary worksheet by completing the following steps:
   a. Click the Summary tab.
   b. Click the Format button in the Cells group on the Home tab, point to *Hide & Unhide*, and then click *Hide Sheet*.

2. Unhide the worksheet by completing the following steps:
   a. Click the Format button in the Cells group, point to *Hide & Unhide*, and then click *Unhide Sheet*.
   b. At the Unhide dialog box, make sure *Summary* is selected and then click OK.

3. Insert a header for each worksheet by completing the following steps:
   a. With the Summary tab active, press and hold down the Shift key, click the March tab, and then release the Shift key. (This selects all four tabs.)
   b. Click the Insert tab.
   c. Click the Header & Footer button in the Text group.
   d. Click the Header button in the Header & Footer group on the Header & Footer Tools Design tab and then click the option at the drop-down list that prints your name at the left side of the page (if a name other than your own displays at the left side of the page, select the name and then type your first and last names), the page number in the middle, and the date at the right side.
4. With all the sheet tabs selected, center each worksheet horizontally and vertically on the page. **Hint: Do this at the Page Setup dialog box with the Margins tab selected.**
5. With all the sheet tabs still selected, change to landscape orientation. **Hint: Do this with the Orientation button on the Page Layout tab.**
6. Save **5-RPFacAccts.xlsx**.

Check Your Work

Tutorial

Printing Multiple
Worksheets

Printing a Workbook Containing Multiple Worksheets

By default, Excel prints the currently displayed worksheet. To print all the worksheets in a workbook, display the Print backstage area, click the first gallery in the *Settings* category, click *Print Entire Workbook* at the drop-down list, and then click the Print button. Print specific worksheets in a workbook by selecting the tabs of the worksheets to be printed. With the worksheet tabs selected, display the Print backstage area and then click the Print button.

Quick Steps
Print All Worksheets in a Workbook
1. Click File tab.
2. Click *Print* option.
3. Click first gallery in *Settings* category.
4. Click *Print Entire Workbook*.
5. Click Print button.

1. With **5-RPFacAccts.xlsx** open, click the File tab and then click the *Print* option.
2. At the Print backstage area, click the first gallery in the *Settings* category and then click *Print Entire Workbook* at the drop-down list.
3. Click the Print button.
4. Save and then close **5-RPFacAccts.xlsx**.

Check Your Work

Project 2 Write Formulas Using Ranges in an Equipment Usage Workbook

2 Parts

You will open an equipment usage workbook, view the document at different zoom percentages, and then split the window and edit cells. You will also name ranges and then use the range names to write formulas in the workbook.

Preview Finished Project

Tutorial

Changing the Zoom

 Zoom

 100%

 Zoom to Selection

Changing the Zoom

The View tab contains a Zoom group with three buttons for changing zoom settings. Click the Zoom button in the Zoom group to open the Zoom dialog box, which contains options for changing the zoom percentage. Click the 100% button in the Zoom group to return the view to 100%, which is the default. Select a range of cells and then click the Zoom to Selection button to scale the zoom setting so the selected range fills the worksheet area.

Use the zoom slider bar at the right side of the Status bar to change the zoom percentage. Click the Zoom Out button (displays with a minus symbol [−]) to decrease the zoom percentage or click the Zoom In button (displays with a plus symbol [+]) to increase the zoom percentage. Another method for increasing or decreasing zoom percentage is to click and drag the zoom slider bar button on the slider bar.

Tutorial

Splitting a
Worksheet

Tutorial

Freezing and
Unfreezing Panes

Split

Quick Steps

Split a Worksheet
1. Click View tab.
2. Click Split button.

 Freeze Panes

Hint Remove a
split line by double-
clicking anywhere
on the split line that
divides the panes.

Splitting a Worksheet and Freezing and Unfreezing Panes

In some worksheets, not all the cells display at one time in the worksheet area (for example, the worksheet that will be used in Project 2a). When working in a worksheet with more cells than can display at one time, splitting the worksheet window into panes may be helpful. Split the worksheet window into panes with the Split button in the Window group on the View tab. Click the Split button and the worksheet splits into four window panes, as shown in Figure 5.5. The windows are split by thick light-gray lines called *split lines*. To remove split lines from a worksheet, click the Split button to deactivate it.

A window pane will display the active cell. As the insertion point is moved through the pane, another active cell may display. This additional active cell displays when the insertion point passes over one of the split lines that creates the pane. Move through a worksheet and both active cells may display. Make a change to one active cell and the change is made in the other as well. To display only one active cell, freeze the window panes by clicking the Freeze Panes button in the Window group on the View tab and then clicking *Freeze Panes* at the drop-down list. Maintain the display of column headings while editing or typing text in cells by clicking the Freeze Panes button and then clicking *Freeze Top Row*. Maintain the display of row headings by clicking the Freeze Panes button and then clicking *Freeze First Column*. Unfreeze window panes by clicking the Freeze Panes button and then clicking *Unfreeze Panes* at the drop-down list.

The split lines that divide the window can be moved using the mouse. To do this, position the mouse pointer on a split line until the pointer turns into a left-and-right-pointing arrow with a double line in the middle. Click and hold down the left mouse button, drag the outline of the split line to the desired location, and then release the mouse button. To move both the horizontal and vertical split lines at the same time, position the mouse pointer on the intersection of the split lines until the pointer turns into a four-headed arrow. Click and hold down the left mouse button, drag the split lines to the desired location, and then release the mouse button.

Figure 5.5 Split Window

split lines

Hours	January	February	March	April	May	June	July	August	September	October
Total hours available	2300	2430	2530	2400	2440	2240	2520	2520	2390	2540
Avoidable delays	19	12	16	20	14	15	9	8	12	7
Unavoidable delays	9	8	6	12	9	10	10	13	8	9
Repairs	5	7	12	9	10	6	7	8	10	13
Servicing	6	13	7	6	4	5	8	3	12	6
Unassigned	128	95	85	135	95	75	145	120	124	112
In use	2040	2105	2320	2180	2050	1995	2320	2250	2190	1945

Highland Construction
EQUIPMENT USAGE REPORT

1. Open **HCEqpRpt.xlsx** and then save it with the name **5-HCEqpRpt**.
2. Increase the Zoom percentage by clicking the Zoom In button at the right side of the zoom slider bar two times.
3. Select the range G3:I10, click the View tab, and then click the Zoom to Selection button in the Zoom group.
4. Click the Zoom button in the Zoom group, click the *75%* option at the Zoom dialog box, and then click OK.
5. Click the 100% button in the Zoom group.
6. Make cell A1 active and then split the window by clicking the Split button in the Window group on the View tab. (This splits the window into four panes.)
7. Drag the vertical split line by completing the following steps:
   a. Position the mouse pointer on the vertical split line until the pointer turns into a left-and-right-pointing arrow with a double line in the middle.
   b. Click and hold down the left mouse button, drag to the left until the vertical split line is immediately to the right of the first column, and then release the mouse button.

	A	B	C	D	E	F
1						Highland C
2						EQUIPMENT U
3	**Hours**	**January**	**February**	**March**	**April**	**May**
4	Total hours available	2300	2430	2530	2400	2440
5	Avoidable delays	19	12	16	20	14
6	Unavoidable delays	9	8	6	12	9
7	Repairs	5	7	12	9	10

8. Freeze the window panes by clicking the Freeze Panes button in the Window group on the View tab and then clicking *Freeze Panes* at the drop-down list.

9. Make cell L4 active and then type the following data in the specified cells:

L4	2310	M4	2210
L5	12	M5	5
L6	5	M6	7
L7	9	M7	8
L8	11	M8	12
L9	95	M9	120
L10	2005	M10	1830

10. Unfreeze the window panes by clicking the Freeze Panes button and then clicking *Unfreeze Panes* at the drop-down list.
11. Remove the panes by clicking the Split button in the Window group to deactivate it.
12. Save **5-HCEqpRpt.xlsx**.

Check Your Work

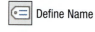
Naming and Using a Range

A selected group of cells is referred to as a *range*. A range of cells can be formatted, moved, copied, or deleted. A range can also be named and then the insertion point can be moved to the range or the named range can be used as part of a formula.

To name a range, select the cells and then click in the Name box at the left of the Formula bar. Type a name for the range (do not use a space) and then press the Enter key. To move the insertion point to a specific range and select the range, click the Name box arrow and then click the range name at the drop-down list.

A range can also be named using the Define Name button in the Defined Names group on the Formulas tab. Clicking the Define Name button displays the New Name dialog box. At the New Name dialog box, type a name for the range and then click OK.

A range name can be used in a formula. For example, to insert in a cell the average of all the cells in a range named *Profit*, make the cell active and then type the formula =AVERAGE(Profit). Use a named range in the current worksheet or in another worksheet within the workbook.

Quick Steps

Name a Range
1. Select cells.
2. Click in Name box.
3. Type range name.
4. Press Enter.

▦ Define Name

💡 **Hint** Another method for moving to a range is to click the Find & Select button in the Editing group on the Home tab and then click *Go To*. At the Go To dialog box, double-click the range name.

Project 2b Naming a Range and Using a Range in a Formula

Part 2 of 2

1. With **5-HCEqpRpt.xlsx** open, click the Sheet2 tab and then type the following text in the specified cells:

   A1   EQUIPMENT USAGE REPORT
   A2   Yearly hours
   A3   Avoidable delays
   A4   Unavoidable delays
   A5   Total delay hours
   A6   (leave blank)
   A7   Repairs
   A8   Servicing
   A9   Total repair/servicing hours

2. Make the following formatting changes to the worksheet:
   a. Automatically adjust the width of column A.
   b. Center and apply bold formatting to the text in cells A1 and A2.

3. Select a range of cells in Sheet1, name the range, and use it in a formula in Sheet2 by completing the following steps:
   a. Click the Sheet1 tab.
   b. Select the range B5:M5.
   c. Click in the Name box to the left of the Formula bar.
   d. Type adhours (for Avoidable Delays Hours) and then press the Enter key.
   e. Click the Sheet2 tab.
   f. Click in cell B3.
   g. Type the equation =sum(adhours) and then press the Enter key.

4. Click the Sheet1 tab and then complete the following steps:
   a. Select the range B6:M6.
   b. Click the Formulas tab.
   c. Click the Define Name button in the Defined Names group.
   d. At the New Name dialog box, type udhours and then click OK.
   e. Click the Sheet2 tab, make sure cell B4 is active, type the equation =sum(udhours), and then press the Enter key.

5. Click the Sheet1 tab and then complete the following steps:
   a. Select the range B7:M7 and then name the range *rhours*.
   b. Click the Sheet2 tab, make cell B7 active, type the equation =sum(rhours), and then press the Enter key.
   c. Click the Sheet1 tab.
   d. Select the range B8:M8 and then name the range *shours*.
   e. Click the Sheet2 tab, make sure cell B8 is active, type the equation =sum(shours), and then press the Enter key.
6. With Sheet2 still active, make the following changes:
   a. Make cell B5 active.
   b. Double-click the AutoSum button in the Editing group on the Home tab.
   c. Make cell B9 active.
   d. Double-click the AutoSum button in the Editing group.
7. Click the Sheet1 tab and then move to the adhours range by clicking the Name box arrow and then clicking *adhours* at the drop-down list.
8. Select both sheet tabs, change to landscape orientation, scale the contents to fit on one page (by changing the width to *1 page* on the Page Layout tab), and then insert a custom footer with your name, the page number, and the date.
9. With both worksheet tabs selected, print both worksheets in the workbook.
10. Save and then close **5-HCEqpRpt.xlsx**.

Check Your Work

Project 3 Arrange, Size, and Copy Data between Workbooks   3 Parts

You will open, arrange, hide, unhide, size, and move multiple workbooks. You will also copy cells from one workbook and paste them in another workbook.

Preview Finished Project

Tutorial

Working with Windows and Hiding and Unhiding Workbooks

Working with Windows

In Excel, multiple workbooks can be opened, a new window with the current workbook can be opened, and the open workbooks can be arranged in the Excel window. With multiple workbooks open, cell entries can be cut and pasted or copied and pasted from one workbook to another using the techniques discussed earlier in this chapter. The exception is that the destination workbook must be active before using the Paste command.

Opening Multiple Workbooks

With multiple workbooks or more than one version of the current workbook open, data can be moved or copied between workbooks and the contents of several workbooks can be compared. When a new workbook or a new window of the current workbook is opened, it is placed on top of the original workbook.

 New Window

Open a new window of the current workbook by clicking the View tab and then clicking the New Window button in the Window group. Excel adds a colon followed by the number *2* to the end of the workbook title and adds a colon followed by the number *1* to the end of the originating workbook name.

Open multiple workbooks at one time at the Open dialog box. Select adjacent workbooks by clicking the name of the first workbook to be opened, pressing and holding down the Shift key, clicking the name of the last workbook to be opened, releasing the Shift key, and then clicking the Open button. If the workbooks are nonadjacent, click the name of the first workbook to be opened, press and hold down the Ctrl key, and then click the names of any other workbooks to be opened.

 Switch Windows

To see what workbooks are currently open, click the View tab and then click the Switch Windows button in the Window group. The names of the open workbooks display in a drop-down list and the workbook name preceded by a check mark is the active workbook. To make another workbook active, click the workbook name at the drop-down list.

Another method for determining which workbooks are open is to hover the mouse over the Excel button on the taskbar. This causes a thumbnail to display of each open workbook. If more than one workbook is open, the Excel button on the taskbar displays additional layers in a cascaded manner. The layer behind the Excel button displays only a portion of the edge at the right side of the button. Hovering the mouse over the Excel button on the taskbar displays thumbnails of all the workbooks above the button. To make another workbook active, click the thumbnail that represents the workbook.

Arranging Workbooks

If more than one workbook is open, arrange the workbooks at the Arrange Windows dialog box, shown in Figure 5.6. To display this dialog box, click the Arrange All button in the Window group on the View tab. At the Arrange Windows dialog box, click *Tiled* to display a portion of each open workbook. Figure 5.7 displays four tiled workbooks.

Arrange All

Quick Steps

Arrange Workbooks
1. Click View tab.
2. Click Arrange All button.
3. At Arrange Windows dialog box, click arrangement.
4. Click OK.

Figure 5.6 Arrange Windows Dialog Box

 Use options at this dialog box to choose an arrange method.

Choose the *Horizontal* option at the Arrange Windows dialog box to display the open workbooks across the screen. Choose the *Vertical* option to display the open workbooks up and down the screen. Choose the last option, *Cascade*, to display the Title bar of each open workbook. Figure 5.8 shows four cascaded workbooks.

Select the arrange option for displaying multiple workbooks based on which parts of the workbooks are most important to view simultaneously. For example, the tiled workbooks in Figure 5.7 display the company names of each workbook.

Figure 5.7 Tiled Workbooks

Figure 5.8 Cascaded Workbooks

Hiding and Unhiding Workbooks

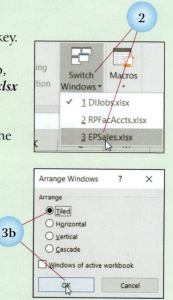

Hide

Unhide

Use the Hide button in the Window group on the View tab to hide the active workbook. If a workbook has been hidden, redisplay it by clicking the Unhide button in the Window group. At the Unhide dialog box, make sure the specific workbook is selected in the list box and then click OK.

Project 3a Opening, Arranging, and Hiding and Unhiding Workbooks

Part 1 of 3

1. Open several workbooks at the same time by completing the following steps:
   a. Display the Open dialog box with EL1C5 the active folder.
   b. Click the workbook named *DIJobs.xlsx*.
   c. Press and hold down the Ctrl key, click *EPSales.xlsx*, click *FinCon.xlsx*, click *RPFacAccts.xlsx*, and then release the Ctrl key.
   d. Click the Open button in the dialog box.
2. Make **DIJobs.xlsx** the active workbook by clicking the View tab, clicking the Switch Windows button, and then clicking **DIJobs.xlsx** at the drop-down list.
3. Tile the workbooks by completing the following steps:
   a. Click the View tab and then click the Arrange All button in the Window group.
   b. At the Arrange Windows dialog box, make sure *Tiled* is selected and then click OK.
4. Cascade the workbooks by completing the following steps:
   a. Click the Arrange All button in the **DIJobs.xlsx** workbook.
   b. At the Arrange Windows dialog box, click *Cascade* and then click OK.
5. Hide and unhide workbooks by completing the following steps:
   a. Make sure **DIJobs.xlsx** is the active workbook. (The file name displays on top of each workbook file.)
   b. Click the Hide button in the Window group on the View tab.
   c. Make sure **RPFacAccts.xlsx** is the active workbook. (The file name displays at the top of each workbook file.)
   d. Click the Hide button in the Window group on the View tab.
   e. At the active workbook, click the View tab and then click the Unhide button.
   f. At the Unhide dialog box, click *RPFacAccts.xlsx* in the list box and then click OK.
   g. Click the Unhide button.
   h. At the Unhide dialog box, make sure **DIJobs.xlsx** is selected in the list box and then click OK.

6. Close all the open workbooks (without saving changes) except **DIJobs.xlsx**.
7. Open a new window with the current workbook by clicking the New Window button in the Window group on the View tab. (Notice that the new window contains the workbook name followed by a colon and the number *2*.)
8. Switch back and forth between the two versions of the workbook.
9. Make **DIJobs.xlsx:2** the active window and then close the workbook.

Sizing and Moving Workbooks

Maximize

Minimize

Close

Restore Down

Change the size of the window using the Maximize and Minimize buttons in the upper right corner of the active workbook. The Maximize button is in the upper right corner of the active workbook immediately to the left of the Close button. (The Close button is the button containing the *X*.) The Minimize button is immediately to the left of the Maximize button.

If all the open workbooks are arranged, clicking the Maximize button causes the active workbook to expand to fill the screen. In addition, the Maximize button changes to the Restore Down button. To return the active workbook back to its original size, click the Restore Down button.

Click the Minimize button in the active workbook and the workbook is reduced and displays as a layer behind the Excel button on the taskbar. To maximize a workbook that has been minimized, click the Excel button on the taskbar and then click the thumbnail representing the workbook.

Project 3b Minimizing, Maximizing, and Restoring Workbooks   Part 2 of 3

1. Make sure **DIJobs.xlsx** is open.
2. Maximize **DIJobs.xlsx** by clicking the Maximize button in the upper right corner of the screen immediately left of the Close button.
3. Open **EPSales.xlsx** and **FinCon.xlsx**.
4. Make the following changes to the open workbooks:
   a. Tile the workbooks.
   b. Click the **DIJobs.xlsx** Title bar to make it the active workbook.
   c. Minimize **DIJobs.xlsx** by clicking the Minimize button at the right side of the Title bar.
   d. Make **EPSales.xlsx** the active workbook and then minimize it.
   e. Minimize **FinCon.xlsx**.
5. Click the Excel button on the taskbar, click the **DIJobs.xlsx** thumbnail, and then close the workbook without saving changes.
6. Complete steps similar to Step 5 to close the other two workbooks.

Moving, Linking, Copying, and Pasting Data between Workbooks

With more than one workbook open, data can be moved, linked, copied, and/or pasted from one workbook to another. To move, link, copy, and/or paste data between workbooks, use the cutting and pasting options discussed earlier in this chapter together with the information about windows.

Moving and Copying Data

Data can be moved or copied within a worksheet, between worksheets, and between workbooks and documents created in other programs, such as Word, PowerPoint, and Access. The Paste Options button provides a variety of options for pasting data in a worksheet, another workbook, or a document created in another program. In addition to being pasted, data can be linked and data can be pasted as an object or a picture object.

Project 3c **Copying Selected Cells from One Open Worksheet to Another**   Part 3 of 3

1. Open **DIFebJobs.xlsx**.
2. If you just completed Project 3b, click the Maximize button so the worksheet fills the entire worksheet window.
3. Save the workbook and name it **5-DIFebJobs**.
4. With **5-DIFebJobs.xlsx** open, open **DIJobs.xlsx**.
5. Select and then copy text from **DIJobs.xlsx** to **5-DIFebJobs.xlsx** by completing the following steps:
   a. With **DIJobs.xlsx** the active workbook, select the range A3:D10.
   b. Click the Copy button in the Clipboard group on the Home tab.
   c. Click the Excel button on the taskbar and then click the **5-DIFebJobs.xlsx** thumbnail.

   d. Make cell A8 active and then click the Paste button in the Clipboard group.
   e. Make cell E7 active and then drag the fill handle down into cell E15.
6. Print **5-DIFebJobs.xlsx** centered horizontally and vertically on the page.
7. Save and then close **5-DIFebJobs.xlsx**.
8. Close **DIJobs.xlsx**.

Check Your Work

Project 4 **Linking and Copying Data within and between Worksheets and Word**   2 Parts

You will open a workbook containing four worksheets with quarterly expenses data, copy and link cells between the worksheets, and then copy and paste the worksheets into Word as picture objects.

Preview Finished Project

Linking Data

In addition to being copied and pasted, data can be copied and then linked within or between worksheets or workbooks. Linking data is useful for maintaining consistency and control over critical data in worksheets or workbooks. When data is linked, a change made in a linked cell is automatically made to the other cells in the link. Links can be made with individual cells or with a range of cells. When linking data, the worksheet that contains the original data is called the *source worksheet* and the worksheet that relies on the source worksheet for the data in the link is called the *dependent worksheet*.

To create a link, make active the cell containing the data to be linked (or select the cells) and then click the Copy button in the Clipboard group on the Home tab. Make active the worksheet where the cells are to be linked, click the Paste button arrow, and then click the Paste Link button in the *Other Paste Options* section in the drop-down list. Another method for creating a link is to click the Paste button, click the Paste Options button, and then click the Paste Link button in the *Other Paste Options* section in the drop-down list.

Quick Steps

Link Data between Worksheets
1. Select cells.
2. Click Copy button.
3. Click worksheet tab.
4. Click in cell.
5. Click Paste button arrow.
6. Click *Paste Link.*

Project 4a Linking Cells between Worksheets

Part 1 of 2

1. Open **DWQtrlyExp.xlsx** and then save it with the name **5-DWQtrlyExp**.
2. Link cells in the first-quarter worksheet to the other three worksheets by completing the following steps:
   a. With the 1st Qtr tab active, select the range C4:C10.
   b. Click the Copy button in the Clipboard group on the Home tab.
   c. Click the 2nd Qtr tab.
   d. Make cell C4 active.
   e. Click the Paste button arrow and then click the Paste Link button in the *Other Paste Options* section in the drop-down list.
   f. Click the 3rd Qtr tab and then make cell C4 active.
   g. Click the Paste button arrow and then click the Paste Link button.
   h. Click the 4th Qtr tab and then make cell C4 active.
   i. Click the Paste button.
   j. Click the Paste Options button and then click the Paste Link button in the *Other Paste Options* section in the drop-down list.

3. Click the 1st Qtr tab and then press the Esc key to remove the moving marquee.

4. Insert a formula in each worksheet that subtracts the budget amount from the variance amount by completing the following steps:
   a. Make sure the first-quarter worksheet displays.
   b. Press and hold down the Shift key, click the 4th Qtr tab. (This selects all four tabs.)
   c. Make cell D4 active, type the formula =c4-b4, and then press the Enter key.
   d. Copy the formula in cell D4 down into the range D5:D10.
   e. Make cell D4 active and then apply the Accounting format with two digits after the decimal point and a dollar symbol.
   f. Click the 2nd Qtr tab and notice that the formula was inserted and copied in this worksheet.
   g. Click the other worksheet tabs and notice the amounts in column D.
   h. Click the 1st Qtr tab.

uarter	
Budget	Variance
$ 126,000.00	4,000.00
54,500.00	(3,500.00)
10,100.00	1,850.00
6,000.00	(350.00)
4,500.00	360.00
2,200.00	(230.00)
1,500.00	50.00

4d

5. With the first-quarter worksheet active, make the following changes to the specified linked cells:

   C4: Change *$126,000 to $128,000*

   C5: Change *54,500 to 56,000*

   C9: Change *2,200 to 2,400*

6. Click the 2nd Qtr tab and notice that the values in cells C4, C5, and C9 automatically changed (because they were linked to the first-quarter worksheet).
7. Click the other tabs and notice that the values changed.
8. Save **5-DWQtrlyExp.xlsx** and then print all four worksheets in the workbook.

Check Your Work

Tutorial

Copying and Pasting Data between Programs

Copying and Pasting Data between Programs

Microsoft Office is a suite that allows *integration*, which is the combining of data from files created by two or more programs into one file. Integration can occur by copying and pasting data between files created in different programs. For example, a worksheet can be created in Excel and specific data can be selected in the worksheet and then copied to a Word document. When pasting Excel data in a Word document, choose from among these formatting options: keep the source formatting, use destination styles, link the data, insert the data as a picture, or keep the text only.

Project 4b Copying and Pasting Excel Data into a Word Document   Part 2 of 2

1. With **5-DWQtrlyExp.xlsx** open, open the Word program.
2. In Word, open the document named **DWQtrlyRpt.docx** in the EL1C5 folder on your storage medium.
3. Save the Word document with the name **5-DWQtrlyRpt**.
4. Click the Excel button on the taskbar.
5. Copy the first-quarter data into the Word document by completing the following steps:
   a. Click the 1st Qtr tab.
   b. Select the range A2:D10.
   c. Click the Copy button in the Clipboard group on the Home tab.
   d. Click the Word button on the taskbar.

e. In the **5-DWQtrlyRpt.docx** document, press Ctrl + End to move the insertion point below the heading.

f. Click the Paste button arrow. (This displays a drop-down list of paste option buttons.)

g. Move the mouse over the various buttons in the drop-down list to see how each option inserts the data in the document.

h. Click the Picture button. (This inserts the data as a picture object.)

i. Press Ctrl + End and then press the Enter key two times. (This moves the insertion point below the data.)

j. Click the Excel button on the taskbar.

6. Click the 2nd Qtr tab and then complete steps similar to those in Step 5 to copy and paste the second-quarter data into the Word document.

7. Click the 3rd Qtr tab and then complete steps similar to those in Step 5 to copy and paste the third-quarter data to the Word document.

8. Click the 4th Qtr tab and then complete steps similar to those in Step 5 to copy and paste the fourth-quarter data to the Word document. (The data will display on two pages.)

9. Print the document by clicking the File tab, clicking the *Print* option, and then clicking the Print button at the Print backstage area.

10. Save and close **5-DWQtrlyRpt.docx** and then close Word.

11. In Excel, press the Esc key to remove the moving marquee and then make cell A1 active.

12. Save and then close **5-DWQtrlyExp.xlsx**.

Check Your Work

Chapter Summary

- By default, an Excel workbook contains one worksheet. Add a new worksheet to a workbook by clicking the New sheet button or using the keyboard shortcut Shift + F11.

- Delete a worksheet with the Delete button in the Cells group on the Home tab or by right-clicking a worksheet tab and then clicking *Delete* at the shortcut menu.

- To manage more than one worksheet at a time, first select the worksheets. Use the mouse together with the Shift key to select adjacent worksheet tabs and use the mouse together with the Ctrl key to select nonadjacent worksheet tabs.

- Copy or move selected cells and cell contents in and between worksheets using the Cut, Copy, and Paste buttons in the Clipboard group on the Home tab or by dragging with the mouse.

- Move selected cells with the mouse by dragging the outline of the selected cells to the new position.

- Copy selected cells with the mouse by pressing and holding down the Ctrl key while dragging the cells to the new position.

- When pasting data, specify how cells are to be pasted by clicking the Paste button arrow or pasting the cells and then clicking the Paste Options button. Clicking either button displays a drop-down list of paste option buttons. Click a button at the drop-down list.

- Use the Clipboard task pane to copy and paste data within and between worksheets and workbooks. Display the Clipboard task pane by clicking the Clipboard group task pane launcher.

- Perform maintenance activities, such as deleting and renaming, on worksheets within a workbook by right-clicking a worksheet tab and then clicking an option at the shortcut menu.

- The mouse can be used to move or copy worksheets. To move a worksheet, drag the worksheet tab with the mouse. To copy a worksheet, press and hold down the Ctrl key and then drag the worksheet tab with the mouse.

- Use the *Tab Color* option at the worksheet tab shortcut menu to apply a color to a worksheet tab.

- Hide and unhide a worksheet by clicking the Format button in the Cells group and then clicking the desired option at the drop-down list or by right-clicking the worksheet tab and then clicking the desired option at the shortcut menu.

- To print all the worksheets in a workbook, display the Print backstage area, click the first gallery in the *Settings* category, and then click *Print Entire Workbook* at the drop-down list. Print specific worksheets by selecting their tabs.

- Use buttons in the Zoom group on the View tab or the zoom slider bar at the right side of the Status bar to change the display zoom percentage.

- Split the worksheet window into panes with the Split button in the Window group on the View tab. To remove a split from a worksheet, click the Split button to deactivate it.

- Freeze window panes by clicking the Freeze Panes button in the Window group on the View tab and then clicking *Freeze Panes* at the drop-down list. Unfreeze window panes by clicking the Freeze Panes button and then clicking *Unfreeze Panes* at the drop-down list.

- A selected group of cells is referred to as a *range*. A range can be named and used in a formula. Name a range by typing the name in the Name box to the left of the Formula bar or at the New Name dialog box.

- To open multiple workbooks that are adjacent, display the Open dialog box, click the first workbook, press and hold down the Shift key, click the last workbook, release the Shift key, and then click the Open button. To open workbooks that are nonadjacent, click the first workbook, press and hold down the Ctrl key, click the desired workbooks, release the Ctrl key, and then click the Open button.

- To see a list of open workbooks, click the View tab and then click the Switch Windows button in the Window group.

- Arrange multiple workbooks in a window with options at the Arrange Windows dialog box.

- Hide the active workbook by clicking the Hide button and unhide a workbook by clicking the Unhide button in the Window group on the View tab.

- Click the Maximize button in the upper right corner of the active workbook to make the workbook fill the entire window area. Click the Minimize button to shrink the active workbook to a button on the taskbar. Click the Restore Down button to return the workbook to its previous size.

- Data can be moved, copied, linked, and/or pasted between workbooks. Also, a workbook can be pasted as a link in a different Microsoft Office application, such a Word or PowerPoint. Changing the data in one application will change linked data that exists in a different application.

Commands Review

FEATURE	RIBBON TAB, GROUP	BUTTON, OPTION	KEYBOARD SHORTCUT
Arrange Windows dialog box	View, Window		
Clipboard task pane	Home, Clipboard		
copy selected cells	Home, Clipboard		Ctrl + C
cut selected cells	Home, Clipboard		Ctrl + X
freeze window panes	View, Window	, *Freeze Panes*	
hide worksheet	Home, Cells	, *Hide & Unhide, Hide Sheet*	
insert new worksheet			Shift + F11
maximize window			
minimize window			
New Name dialog box	Formulas, Defined Names		
paste selected cells	Home, Clipboard		Ctrl + V
restore down			
split window into panes	View, Window		
unfreeze window panes	View, Window	, *Unfreeze Panes*	
unhide worksheet	Home, Cells	, *Hide & Unhide, Unhide Sheet*	

> ### Workbook
>
> Chapter study tools and assessment activities are available in the *Workbook* ebook. These resources are designed to help you further develop and demonstrate mastery of the skills learned in this chapter.

Microsoft® Excel®

CHAPTER 6

Maintaining Workbooks

Performance Objectives

Upon successful completion of Chapter 6, you will be able to:

1 Create and rename a folder

2 Delete workbooks and folders

3 Copy and move workbooks within and between folders

4 Copy and move worksheets between workbooks

5 Maintain consistent formatting with cell styles

6 Insert, modify, and remove hyperlinks

7 Create financial forms using templates

Precheck

Check your current skills to help focus your study.

After you have worked with Excel for a period of time, you will have accumulated several workbook files. You should organize your workbooks into folders to facilitate the fast retrieval of information. Occasionally, you should perform file maintenance tasks, such as copying, moving, renaming, and deleting workbooks, to ensure the workbook lists in your folders are manageable. You will learn these tasks in this chapter, along with how to create and apply styles to a workbook, insert hyperlinks in a workbook, and use an Excel template to create a workbook.

Data Files

Before beginning the projects, copy the EL1C6 folder to your storage medium and then make EL1C6 the active folder.

SNAP

If you are a SNAP user, launch the Precheck and Tutorials from your Assignments page.

You will perform a variety of file management tasks, including creating and renaming a folder; selecting and then deleting, copying, cutting, pasting, and renaming a workbook; deleting a folder; and opening, printing, and closing a workbook.

Maintaining Workbooks

Many workbook management tasks can be completed at the Open dialog box and Save As dialog box. These tasks include copying, moving, printing, and renaming workbooks; opening multiple workbooks; and creating and renaming new folders. Perform some file maintenance tasks, such as creating a folder and deleting files, with options from the Organize button drop-down list or the shortcut menu and navigate to folders using the Address bar. The elements of the Open dialog box are identified in Figure 6.1.

Figure 6.1 Open Dialog Box

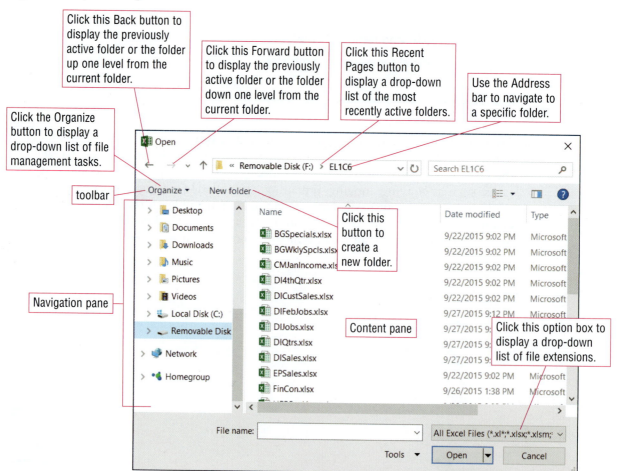

Click this Back button to display the previously active folder or the folder up one level from the current folder.

Click this Forward button to display the previously active folder or the folder down one level from the current folder.

Click this Recent Pages button to display a drop-down list of the most recently active folders.

Use the Address bar to navigate to a specific folder.

Click the Organize button to display a drop-down list of file management tasks.

toolbar

Navigation pane

Click this button to create a new folder.

Content pane

Click this option box to display a drop-down list of file extensions.

Hint Change the default folder with the *Default local file location* option at the Excel Options dialog box with *Save* selected.

Tutorial

Managing Folders

Quick Steps

Create a Folder
1. Press Ctrl + F12.
2. Click New folder button.
3. Type folder name.
4. Press Enter.

New folder

New folder

Creating a Folder

Directions and projects in this chapter assume that you are managing workbooks and folders on a USB flash drive or your computer's hard drive. If you are using your OneDrive account, some of the workbook and folder management tasks may vary.

In Excel, workbooks should be grouped logically and stored in folders. For example, all the workbooks related to one department can be stored in one folder that is named the department name. A folder can also be created within a folder (called a *subfolder*). The main folder on a disk or drive is called the *root folder*. Additional folders can be created as branches of this root folder.

At the Open dialog box and Save As dialog box, workbook file names display in the Content pane preceded by workbook icons and folder names display preceded by folder icons. Create a new folder by clicking the New folder button on the toolbar at the Open dialog box or Save As dialog box. This inserts a new folder in the Content pane. Type the name for the folder and then press the Enter key.

A folder name can contain a maximum of 255 characters. The characters can include numbers, spaces, and symbols, except those symbols identified in the Saving a Workbook section in Chapter 1.

Project 1a Creating a Folder   **Part 1 of 8**

1. With Excel open, create a folder named *Payroll* on your storage medium by completing the following steps:
   a. Press Ctrl + F12 to display the Open dialog box.
   b. At the Open dialog box, navigate to your storage medium.
   c. Click the View button arrow on the toolbar.
   d. Click the *Details* option in the drop-down list.
2. Double-click the *EL1C6* folder name to make it the active folder.
3. Click the New folder button on the toolbar.
4. Type *Payroll* and then press the Enter key.
5. Close the Open dialog box.

Renaming a Folder

Managing folders may include renaming them. Rename a folder using the Organize button in the Open dialog box or using the shortcut menu. To rename a folder using the Organize button, display the Open dialog box, click in the Content pane the folder to be renamed, click the Organize button on the toolbar, and then click *Rename* at the drop-down list. This selects the folder name and inserts a border around it. Type the new name for the folder and then press the Enter key. To rename a folder using the shortcut menu, display the Open dialog box, right-click the folder name in the Content pane, and then click *Rename* at the shortcut menu. Type a new name for the folder and then press the Enter key.

When organizing files and folders, make sure the computer is set to display all the files in a particular folder and not just the Excel files, for example. Display all the files in a folder in the Open dialog box by clicking the button to the right of the *File name* text box and then clicking *All Files (*.*)* at the drop-down list.

Project 1b **Renaming a Folder**   Part 2 of 8

1. Press Ctrl + F12 to display the Open dialog box and make sure EL1C6 is the active folder.
2. Right-click the *Payroll* folder name in the Content pane.
3. Click *Rename* at the shortcut menu.
4. Type Finances and then press the Enter key.

Selecting Workbooks

Complete workbook management tasks on one workbook or selected workbooks. To select one workbook, display the Open dialog box and then click the workbook name. To select several adjacent workbooks, click the first workbook name, press and hold down the Shift key, click the last workbook name, and then release the Shift key. To select workbooks that are not adjacent, click the first workbook name, press and hold down the Ctrl key, click any other workbook names, and then release the Ctrl key.

Deleting Workbooks and Folders

Quick Steps

Delete a Workbook or Folder
1. Display Open dialog box.
2. Right-click workbook or folder name.
3. Click *Delete*.
4. If deleting from a removable drive, click Yes.

At some point, certain workbooks may need to be deleted from a storage medium or any other drive or folder in which workbooks are located. To delete a workbook, display the Open dialog box or the Save As dialog box, click the workbook name in the Content pane, click the Organize button, and then click *Delete* at the drop-down list. If the workbook is being deleted from a removable storage medium, such as a USB drive, a message will display asking to confirm the deletion. At this message, click Yes. To delete a workbook using the shortcut menu, display the Open dialog box, right-click the workbook name in the Content pane, and then click *Delete* at the shortcut menu.

Deleting to the Recycle Bin

Workbooks deleted from a removable drive are deleted permanently while workbooks deleted from the hard drive are automatically sent to the Windows Recycle Bin. A deleted workbook can be restored from the Recycle Bin. To free space on the drive, empty the Recycle Bin on a periodic basis. Restore a workbook from or empty the contents of the Recycle Bin at the Windows desktop (not in Excel). To display the Recycle Bin, minimize the Excel window and then double-click the Recycle Bin icon on the Windows desktop. At the Recycle Bin, restore file(s) and empty the Recycle Bin.

Project 1c   Selecting and Deleting Workbooks   **Part 3 of 8**

1. At the Open dialog box, open **RPFacAccts.xlsx** and then save it with the name **6-RPFacAccts**.
2. Close **6-RPFacAccts.xlsx**.
3. Delete **6-RPFacAccts.xlsx** by completing the following steps:
   a. Display the Open dialog box with EL1C6 the active folder.
   b. Click *6-RPFacAccts.xlsx* to select it.
   c. Click the Organize button and then click *Delete* at the drop-down list.

   d. If a message displays asking if you are sure you want to delete the worksheet, click Yes.

---

4. Delete selected workbooks by completing the following steps:
   a. Click **DICustSales.xlsx** in the Content pane.
   b. Press and hold down the Shift key, click **DIJobs.xlsx**, and then release the Shift key.
   c. Position the mouse pointer on one of the selected workbook names and then click the right mouse button.
   d. At the shortcut menu that displays, click *Delete*.
   e. If a message displays asking if you are sure you want to delete the items, click Yes.
5. Close the Open dialog box.

Name
CMJanIncome.xlsx
DI4thQtr.xlsx
DICustSales.xlsx
DIFebJo...
DIJobs.x...
DIQtrs.x...
DISales.
EPSales.
FinCon.x
HERBac
HEREqu
HEREqu

Select

Open
New
Print

Send to   >

Cut
Copy

Create shortcut
Delete
Rename

Properties

4d

ne: "DICustSale

Copying Workbooks

In previous chapters, a workbook has been opened and then saved with a new name in the same location. This makes an exact copy of the workbook, preserving the original file. A workbook can also be copied into another folder.

Project 1d **Saving a Copy of an Open Workbook to Another Folder**   **Part 4 of 8**

1. Open **EPSales.xlsx**.
2. Save the workbook with Save As and name it **TotalSales**. (Make sure EL1C6 is the active folder.)
3. Save a copy of **TotalSales.xlsx** in the Finances folder you created in Project 1a (and renamed in Project 1b) by completing the following steps:
   a. With **TotalSales.xlsx** open, press the F12 function key to display the Save As dialog box.
   b. At the Save As dialog box, change to the Finances folder. To do this, double-click *Finances* at the beginning of the Content pane. (Folders are listed before workbooks.)
   c. Click the Save button in the lower right corner of the dialog box.
4. Close **TotalSales.xlsx**.
5. Change back to the EL1C6 folder by completing the following steps:
   a. Press Ctrl + F12 to display the Open dialog box.
   b. Click *EL1C6* that displays in the Address bar.
6. Close the Open dialog box.

5b

Save As

← → ∨ ↑ ⬛ « EL1C6 > Finances

Organize ▾   New folder

	Name
This PC	
Desktop	TotalSales.xlsx

Quick Steps

Copy a Workbook
1. Display Open or Save As dialog box.
2. Right-click workbook name.
3. Click *Copy.*
4. Navigate to folder.
5. Right-click blank area in Content pane.
6. Click *Paste.*

A workbook can be copied to another folder without opening the workbook first. To do this, use the *Copy* and *Paste* options from the shortcut menu at the Open dialog box or the Save As dialog box. A workbook or selected workbooks can also be copied into the same folder. When copied into the same folder, Excel adds a hyphen followed by the word *Copy* to the end of the workbook name.

To move or copy files or folders in your OneDrive account, go to onedrive.com, make sure you are logged into your account, and then use the onedrive.com toolbar to move a workbook or folder to another location. Or copy and then move a workbook or folder to another location.

Project 1e   Copying a Workbook at the Open Dialog Box   Part 5 of 8

Note: If you are using your OneDrive account, the steps for copying, cutting, and pasting workbooks will vary from the steps in Project 1e and 1f. Please check with your instructor.

1. Copy **CMJanIncome.xlsx** to the Finances folder. To begin, display the Open dialog box with the EL1C6 folder active.
2. Position the mouse pointer on **CMJanIncome.xlsx**, click the right mouse button, and then click *Copy* at the shortcut menu.
3. Change to the Finances folder by double-clicking *Finances* at the beginning of the Content pane.
4. Position the mouse pointer in any blank area in the Content pane, click the right mouse button, and then click *Paste* at the shortcut menu.
5. Change back to the EL1C6 folder by clicking *EL1C6* in the Address bar.
6. Close the Open dialog box.

Sending Workbooks to a Different Drive or Folder

Quick Steps

Move a Workbook
1. Display Open dialog box.
2. Right-click workbook name.
3. Click *Cut.*
4. Navigate to folder.
5. Right-click in blank area in Content pane.
6. Click *Paste.*

Use the *Send to* option to copy a workbook to another folder or drive without having to navigate to the new location. To use this option, position the mouse pointer on the name of the workbook to be copied, click the right mouse button, point to *Send to* (which causes a side menu to display), and then click the specific drive or folder.

Cutting and Pasting a Workbook

Remove a workbook from one folder and insert it in another folder using the *Cut* and *Paste* options from the shortcut menu at the Open dialog box. To do this, display the Open dialog box, position the mouse pointer on the workbook to be removed (cut), click the right mouse button, and then click *Cut* at the shortcut menu. Change to the specific folder or drive, position the mouse pointer in any blank area in the Content pane, click the right mouse button, and then click *Paste* at the shortcut menu.

1. Display the Open dialog box with the EL1C6 folder active.
2. Position the mouse pointer on **FinCon.xlsx**, click the right mouse button, and then click *Cut* at the shortcut menu.
3. Double-click *Finances* to make it the active folder.
4. Position the mouse pointer in any blank area in the Content pane, click the right mouse button, and then click *Paste* at the shortcut menu.
5. Click *EL1C6* in the Address bar.

Quick Steps

Rename a Workbook
1. Display Open dialog box.
2. Click workbook.
3. Click Organize button.
4. Click *Rename*.
5. Type new name.
6. Press Enter.
OR
1. Display Open dialog box.
2. Right-click workbook name.
3. Click *Rename*.
4. Type new name.
5. Press Enter.

Renaming Workbooks

At the Open dialog box, use the *Rename* option from the Organize button drop-down list or the shortcut menu to give a workbook a different name. The *Rename* option changes the name of the workbook and keeps the workbook in the same folder. To use *Rename*, display the Open dialog box, click the workbook to be renamed, click the Organize button, and then click *Rename* at the drop-down list. This puts a thin black border around the workbook name and selects the name. Type the new name and then press the Enter key.

Another method for renaming a workbook is to right-click the workbook name at the Open dialog box and then click *Rename* at the shortcut menu. Type the new name for the workbook and then press the Enter key.

1. Make sure the Open dialog box displays with EL1C6 the active folder.
2. Double-click *Finances* to make it the active folder.
3. Click **FinCon.xlsx** to select it.
4. Click the Organize button on the toolbar.
5. Click *Rename* at the drop-down list.
6. Type Analysis and then press the Enter key.

7. Complete steps similar to those in Steps 3 through 6 to rename **CMJanIncome.xlsx** to **CMJanProfits**.
8. Click the Back button (displays as *Back to EL1C6*) at the left side of the Address bar.

Deleting a Folder and Its Contents

As explained earlier in this chapter, a workbook or selected workbooks can be deleted. In addition, a folder and all of its contents can be deleted. Delete a folder in the same manner as a workbook.

Project 1h Deleting a Folder and Its Contents   **Part 8 of 8**

1. Make sure the Open dialog box displays with the EL1C6 folder active.
2. Right-click *Finances* in the Content pane.
3. Click *Delete* at the shortcut menu.
4. If you are deleting the folder from a removable drive, click Yes at the message that displays asking if you want to delete the folder.
5. Close the Open dialog box.

Project 2 **Copy and Move Worksheets into an Equipment Rental Workbook**   **3 Parts**

You will manage workbooks at the Open backstage area and then open multiple workbooks and copy and move worksheets between the workbooks.

Preview Finished Project

Tutorial

Managing the *Recent* Option List

Managing the *Recent* Option List

As workbooks are opened and closed, Excel keeps a list of the most recently opened workbooks. To view this list, click the File tab and then click the *Open* option. This displays the Open backstage area, similar to what is shown in Figure 6.2. (The workbook names you see may vary from those in the figure.) Generally, the names of the 25 most recently opened workbooks display in the *Recent* option list and are organized in categories such as *Today*, *Yesterday*, and *Last Week*. To open a workbook, scroll down the list and then click the workbook name. The Excel 2016 opening screen also displays a list of the most recently opened workbooks. The workbook names in the Recent list are the same as those in the *Recent* option list at the Open backstage area.

Figure 6.2 Open Backstage Area

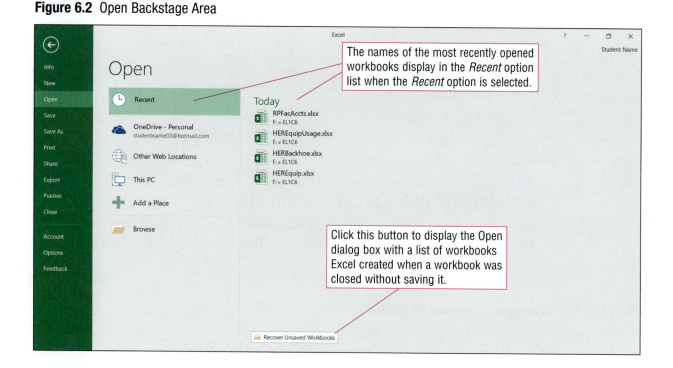

The names of the most recently opened workbooks display in the *Recent* option list when the *Recent* option is selected.

Click this button to display the Open dialog box with a list of workbooks Excel created when a workbook was closed without saving it.

Pinning and Unpinning a Workbook

A workbook that is opened on a regular basis can be pinned to the *Recent* option list. To pin a workbook to the *Recent* option list at the Open backstage area, hover the mouse pointer over the workbook name and then click the small left-pointing push pin to the right of the workbook name. The left-pointing push pin changes to a down-pointing push pin and the pinned workbook is inserted into a new category named *Pinned*. The *Pinned* category displays at the top of the *Recent* option list. The next time the Open backstage area displays, the pinned workbook displays in the *Pinned* category at the top of the *Recent* option list. A workbook can also be pinned to the Recent list at the Excel 2016 opening screen. When a workbook is pinned, it displays at the tops of both the Recent list and the *Recent* option list at the Open backstage area.

To "unpin" a workbook from the Recent list or the *Recent* option list, click the push pin to change it from a down-pointing pin to a left-pointing pin. More than one workbook can be pinned to a list. Another method for pinning and unpinning a workbook is to use the shortcut menu. Right-click a workbook name and then click the *Pin to list* or *Unpin from list* option.

Like workbooks, folders can be pinned to a list at the Save As backstage area. The third panel in the Save As backstage area displays a list of the most recently opened folders and organizes them into categories such as *Today*, *Yesterday*, and *Last Week*. Pin a folder or folders to the list and a *Pinned* category is created and the folder names display in the category.

Recovering an Unsaved Workbook

If a workbook is closed without saving it, it can be recovered with the Recover Unsaved Workbooks button below the *Recent* option list. Click this button and the Open dialog box displays with the names of the workbooks that Excel automatically saved. At this dialog box, double-click the workbook name to open it.

Clearing the *Recent* Option List and the Recent List

Clear the contents (except pinned workbooks) of the *Recent* option list or Recent list by right-clicking a workbook name in the list and then clicking *Clear unpinned Workbooks* at the shortcut menu. At the message asking to confirm removal of the items, click Yes. To clear a folder from the Save As backstage area, right-click a folder in the list and then click *Remove from list* at the shortcut menu.

Project 2a **Managing Workbooks at the Open Backstage Area**   **Part 1 of 3**

1. Close any open workbooks.
2. Click the File tab and then click the *Open* option.
3. Make sure the *Recent* option below the heading *Open* is selected. Notice the workbook names that display in the *Recent* option list.
4. Navigate to the EL1C6 folder on your storage medium, open **HEREquip.xlsx**, and then save it with the name **6-HEREquip**.
5. Close **6-HEREquip.xlsx**.
6. Open **HEREquipUsage.xlsx** and then close it.
7. Open **HERBackhoe.xlsx** and then close it.
8. Pin the three workbooks to the *Recent* option list (you will use them in Project 2b) by completing the following steps:
   a. Click the File tab and then make sure the *Open* option is selected. (This displays the Open backstage area with the *Recent* option selected.)
   b. Click the left-pointing push pin at the right side of **6-HEREquip.xlsx**. (This changes the pin from left pointing to down pointing.)

   c. Click the left-pointing push pin at the right side of **HEREquipUsage.xlsx**.

---

d. Right-click **HERBackhoe.xlsx** and then click *Pin to list* at the shortcut menu.

e. Click the Back button to exit the Open backstage area.

9. Open **6-HEREquip.xlsx** by clicking the File tab and then clicking **6-HEREquip.xlsx** in the *Recent* option list. (After clicking the File tab, make sure the *Open* option is selected. This displays the Open backstage area with the *Recent* option selected.)

Managing Worksheets

Quick Steps

Copy a Worksheet to Another Workbook
1. Right-click sheet tab.
2. Click *Move or Copy*.
3. Select destination workbook.
4. Select worksheet location.
5. Click *Create a copy* check box.
6. Click OK.

Individual worksheets can be moved or copied within the same workbook or to another existing workbook. Exercise caution when moving sheets, because the calculations and charts based on the data in a worksheet might become inaccurate. To duplicate a worksheet in the same workbook, press and hold down the Ctrl key, click the worksheet tab and hold down the left mouse button, drag to the new location, and then release the mouse button and the Ctrl key.

Copying a Worksheet to Another Workbook

To copy a worksheet to another workbook, open both the source and the destination workbooks. Right-click the worksheet tab and then click *Move or Copy* at the shortcut menu. At the Move or Copy dialog box, shown in Figure 6.3, select the name of the destination workbook in the *To book* option drop-down list, select the name of the worksheet the copied worksheet will be placed before in the *Before sheet* list box, click the *Create a copy* check box, and then click OK.

Figure 6.3 Move or Copy Dialog Box

1. With **6-HEREquip.xlsx** open, open **HEREquipUsage.xlsx**.
2. Copy the Front Loader worksheet by completing the following steps:
   a. With **HEREquipUsage.xlsx** the active workbook, right-click the Front Loader tab and then click *Move or Copy* at the shortcut menu.
   b. Click the *To book* option box arrow and then click **6-HEREquip.xlsx** at the drop-down list.
   c. Click *(move to end)* in the *Before sheet* list box.
   d. Click the *Create a copy* check box to insert a check mark.
   e. Click OK. (Excel switches to the **6-HEREquip.xlsx** workbook and inserts the copied Front Loader worksheet after Sheet1.)
3. Complete steps similar to those in Step 2 to copy the Tractor worksheet to the **6-HEREquip.xlsx** workbook.
4. Complete steps similar to those in Step 2 to copy the Forklift worksheet to the **6-HEREquip.xlsx** workbook and insert the Forklift worksheet before the Tractor worksheet.
5. Save **6-HEREquip.xlsx**.
6. Make **HEREquipUsage.xlsx** the active workbook and then close it.

Check Your Work

Moving a Worksheet to Another Workbook

To move a worksheet to another workbook, open both the source and the destination workbooks. Make active the worksheet to be moved in the source workbook, right-click the worksheet tab, and then click *Move or Copy* at the shortcut menu. At the Move or Copy dialog box, shown in Figure 6.3, select the name of the destination workbook in the *To book* drop-down list, select the name of the worksheet the moved worksheet will be placed before in the *Before sheet* list box, and then click OK. To reposition a worksheet tab, drag the tab to the new position.

Be careful when moving a worksheet to another workbook file. If formulas in the source workbook depend on the contents of the cells in the worksheet that is moved, they will no longer work properly.

1. With **6-HEREquip.xlsx** open, open **HERBackhoe.xlsx**.
2. Move Sheet1 from **HERBackhoe.xlsx** to **6-HEREquip.xlsx** by completing the following steps:
   a. With **HERBackhoe.xlsx** the active workbook, right-click the Sheet1 tab and then click *Move or Copy* at the shortcut menu.
   b. Click the *To book* option box arrow and then click **6-HEREquip.xlsx** at the drop-down list.
   c. Click *(move to end)* in the *Before sheet* list box.
   d. Click OK.
3. With **6-HEREquip.xlsx** open, make the following changes:
   a. Rename Sheet1 as *Equipment Hours*.
   b. Rename Sheet1 (2) as *Backhoe*.
4. Create a range for the front loader total hours available by completing the following steps:
   a. Click the Front Loader tab.
   b. Select the range B4:E4.
   c. Click in the Name box.
   d. Type FrontLoaderHours.
   e. Press the Enter key.
5. Complete steps similar to those in Step 4 to create the following ranges:
   a. In the Front Loader worksheet, select the range B10:E10 and name it *FrontLoaderHoursInUse*.
   b. Click the Forklift tab and then select the range B4:E4 and name it *ForkliftHours*. Also select the range B10:E10 and name it *ForkliftHoursInUse*.
   c. Click the Tractor tab and then select the range B4:E4 and name it *TractorHours*. Also select the range B10:E10 and name it *TractorHoursInUse*.
   d. Click the Backhoe tab and then select the range B4:E4 and name it *BackhoeHours*. Also select the range B10:E10 and name it *BackhoeHoursInUse*.
6. Click the Equipment Hours tab to make it the active worksheet and then insert a formula that calculates the total hours for the front loader by completing the following steps:
   a. Make cell C4 active.
   b. Type =sum(Fr.
   c. When you type *Fr*, a drop-down list displays with the front loader ranges. Double-click *FrontLoaderHours*.
   d. Type) (the closing parenthesis).
   e. Press the Enter key.

7. Complete steps similar to those in Step 6 to insert ranges in the following cells:
   a. Make cell C5 active and then insert a formula that calculates the total in-use hours for the front loader.
   b. Make cell C8 active and then insert a formula that calculates the total hours available for the forklift.
   c. Make cell C9 active and then insert a formula that calculates the total in-use hours for the forklift.
   d. Make cell C12 active and then insert a formula that calculates the total hours available for the tractor.
   e. Make cell C13 active and then insert a formula that calculates the total in-use hours for the tractor.
   f. Make cell C16 active and then insert a formula that calculates the total hours available for the backhoe.
   g. Make cell C17 active and then insert a formula that calculates the total in-use hours for the backhoe.
8. Make the following changes to specific worksheets:
   a. Click the Front Loader tab and then change the number in cell E4 from *415* to *426* and the number in cell C6 from *6* to *14*.
   b. Click the Forklift tab and then change the number in cell E4 from *415* to *426* and the number in cell D8 from *4* to *12*.
9. Select all the worksheet tabs and then create a header that prints your name at the left side of each worksheet, the page number in the middle, and the current date at the right side.
10. Save and then print all the worksheets in **6-HEREquip.xlsx**.
11. Close the workbook. (Make sure all the workbooks are closed.)
12. Make the following changes to the Open backstage area:
    a. Click the File tab.
    b. Make sure the *Open* option is selected and the *Recent* option is selected.
    c. Unpin **6-HEREquip.xlsx** from the *Recent* option list by clicking the down-pointing push pin at the right side of **6-HEREquip.xlsx**. (This changes the down-pointing push pin to a left-pointing push pin and moves the workbook down the list.)
    d. Unpin **HERBackhoe.xlsx** and **HEREquipUsage.xlsx**.
13. Click the Back button to exit the Open backstage area.

Check Your Work ▶

Project 3 Create and Apply Styles to a Payroll Workbook   5 Parts

You will open a payroll workbook, define and apply styles, and then modify the styles. You will also copy the styles to another workbook and then apply the styles in that new workbook.

Preview Finished Project ▶

Formatting with Cell Styles

Formatting can be applied in a worksheet to highlight or accentuate certain cells. Apply formatting to a cell or selected cells with a cell style, which is a predefined set of formatting attributes, such as font, font size, alignment, borders, shading, and so forth. Excel provides predesigned styles at the Cell Styles drop-down gallery.

Tutorial

Applying Cell Styles

Applying a Cell Style

To apply a style, select the cell(s), click the Cell Styles button in the Styles group on the Home tab, and then click the style at the drop-down gallery, shown in Figure 6.4. Hover the mouse pointer over a style in the drop-down gallery and the cell or selected cells display with the formatting applied.

Quick Steps

Apply a Cell Style
1. Select cell(s).
2. Click Cell Styles button.
3. Click style.

Cell Styles

Figure 6.4 Cell Styles Drop-Down Gallery

Choose an option at this drop-down gallery to apply a predesigned style to a cell or selected cells in the worksheet.

Project 3a Formatting with Cell Styles   Part 1 of 5

1. Open **OEPayroll.xlsx** and then save it with the name **6-OEPayroll**.
2. With Sheet1 the active worksheet, insert the necessary formulas to calculate gross pay, withholding tax amount, social security tax amount, and net pay. *Hint: Refer to Project 3c in Chapter 2 for assistance.* Select the range D4:G4 and then click the Accounting Number Format button to insert dollar symbols.
3. Make Sheet2 active and then insert a formula that calculates the amount due. *Hint: The formula in cell F4 will be =D4*(1+E4).* Make cell F4 active and then click the Accounting Number Format button to insert a dollar symbol.

4. Make Sheet3 active and then insert a formula in the *Due Date* column that calculates the purchase date plus the number of days in the *Terms* column. **Hint: The formula in cell F4 will be =D4+E4.**

5. Apply cell styles to cells by completing the following steps:
   a. Make Sheet1 active and then select cells A11 and A12.
   b. Click the Cell Styles button in the Styles group on the Home tab.
   c. At the drop-down gallery, hover the mouse pointer over different styles to see how the formatting affects the selected cells.
   d. Click the *Check Cell* option (second column, first row in the *Data and Model* section).

6. Select cells B11 and B12, click the Cell Styles button, and then click the *Output* option (first column, second row in the *Data and Model* section).

7. Save **6-OEPayroll.xlsx**.

Check Your Work

Defining a Cell Style

Apply a style from the Cell Styles drop-down gallery or create a new style. Using a style to apply formatting has several advantages. One key advantage is that it helps to ensure consistent formatting from one worksheet to another. To change the formatting, change the style and all the cells formatted with that style automatically reflect the change.

Two basic methods are available for defining a cell style. Define a style with formats already applied to a cell or display the Style dialog box, click the Format button, and then choose formatting options at the Format Cells dialog box. New styles are available only in the workbook in which they are created.

To define a style with existing formatting, select the cell or cells containing the formatting, click the Cell Styles button in the Styles group on the Home tab, and then click the *New Cell Style* option at the bottom of the drop-down gallery. At the Style dialog box, shown in Figure 6.5, type a name for the new style in the *Style name* text box and then click OK to close the dialog box. Custom styles display at the top of the Cell Styles button drop-down gallery in the *Custom* section.

Figure 6.5 Style Dialog Box

Check boxes identify options set by current styles.

Project 3b Defining and Applying a Cell Style

1. With **6-OEPayroll.xlsx** open, define a style named *C06Title* with the formatting in cell A1 by completing the following steps:
   a. Make sure Sheet1 is active and then make cell A1 active.
   b. Click the Cell Styles button in the Styles group on the Home tab and then click the *New Cell Style* option at the bottom of the drop-down gallery.
   c. At the Style dialog box, type C06Title in the *Style name* text box.
   d. Click OK.

2. Even though cell A1 is already formatted, the style has not been applied to it. (Later, you will modify the style and the style must be applied to the cell for the change to affect it.) Apply the C06Title style to cell A1 by completing the following steps:
   a. Make sure cell A1 is the active cell.

b. Click the Cell Styles button in the Styles group on the Home tab.

c. Click the *C06Title* style in the *Custom* section at the top of the drop-down gallery.

3. Apply the C06Title style to other cells by completing the following steps:

a. Click the Sheet2 tab.

b. Make cell A1 active.

c. Click the Cell Styles button in the Styles group and then click the *C06Title* style at the drop-down gallery. (Notice that the style does not apply row height formatting. The style applies only cell formatting.)

d. Click the Sheet3 tab.

e. Make cell A1 active.

f. Click the Cell Styles button and then click the *C06Title* style at the drop-down gallery.

g. Click the Sheet1 tab.

4. Save **6-OEPayroll.xlsx**.

Check Your Work

Quick Steps

Define a Cell Style
1. Click in blank cell.
2. Click Cell Styles button.
3. Click *New Cell Style*.
4. Type style name.
5. Click Format button.
6. Choose formatting options.
7. Click OK.

In addition to defining a style based on cell formatting, a custom style can be defined without first applying the formatting. To do this, display the Style dialog box, type a name for the custom style, and then click the Format button. At the Format Cells dialog box, apply the formatting and then click OK to close the dialog box. At the Style dialog box, remove the check mark from any formatting that should not be included in the style and then click OK to close the Style dialog box.

Project 3c Defining a Cell Style without First Applying Formatting

Part 3 of 5

1. With **6-OEPayroll.xlsx** open, define a custom style named *C06Subtitle* without first applying the formatting by completing the following steps:

a. With Sheet1 active, click in any empty cell.

b. Click the Cell Styles button in the Styles group and then click *New Cell Style* at the drop-down gallery.

c. At the Style dialog box, type C06Subtitle in the *Style name* text box.

d. Click the Format button in the Style dialog box.

e. At the Format Cells dialog box, click the Font tab.

f. At the Format Cells dialog box with the Font tab selected, change the font to Candara, the font style to bold, the size to 12 points, and the color to White, Background 1.

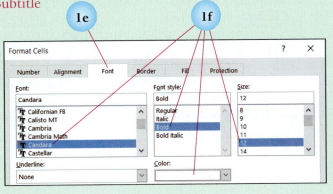

g. Click the Fill tab.

h. Click the green color shown at the right (last column, fifth row).

i. Click the Alignment tab.

j. Change the horizontal alignment to center alignment.

k. Click OK to close the Format Cells dialog box.

l. Click OK to close the Style dialog box.

2. Apply the C06Subtitle custom style by completing the following steps:

a. Make cell A2 active.

b. Click the Cell Styles button and then click the *C06Subtitle* style in the *Custom* section at the top of the drop-down gallery.

c. Click the Sheet2 tab.

d. Make cell A2 active.

e. Click the Cell Styles button and then click the *C06Subtitle* style.

f. Click the Sheet3 tab.

g. Make cell A2 active.

h. Click the Cell Styles button and then click the *C06Subtitle* style.

i. Click the Sheet1 tab.

3. Apply the following predesigned cell styles:

a. With Sheet1 the active tab, select the range A3:G3.

b. Click the Cell Styles button and then click the *Heading 3* style in the *Titles and Headings* section at the drop-down gallery.

c. Select the range A5:G5.

d. Click the Cell Styles button and then click the *20% - Accent3* style.

e. Apply the 20% - Accent3 style to the range A7:G7 and the range A9:G9.

f. Click the Sheet2 tab.

g. Select the range A3:F3 and then apply the Heading 3 style.

h. Select the range A5:F5 and then apply the 20% - Accent3 style.

i. Apply the 20% - Accent3 style to every other row of cells (the range A7:F7, A9:F9, and so on, finishing with the range A17:F17).

j. Click the Sheet3 tab.

k. Select the range A3:F3 and then apply the Heading 3 style.

l. Apply the 20% - Accent3 style to the ranges A5:F5, A7:F7, and A9:F9.

4. With Sheet3 active, change the height of row 1 to 36.00 points.

5. Make Sheet2 active and then change the height of row 1 to 36.00 points.

6. Make Sheet1 active.

7. Save **6-OEPayroll.xlsx** and then print only the first worksheet.

Check Your Work

Modifying a Cell Style

One of the advantages to formatting cells with a style is that the formatting can be modified and all the cells formatted with that style update automatically. Modify a predesigned style and only the style in the current workbook is affected. Open a blank workbook and the cell styles available are the default styles.

To modify a style, click the Cell Styles button in the Styles group on the Home tab and then right-click the style at the drop-down gallery. At the shortcut menu that displays, click *Modify*. At the Style dialog box, click the Format button. Make the formatting changes at the Format Cells dialog box and then click OK. Click OK to close the Style dialog box and any cells formatted with the style are automatically updated.

Quick Steps

Modify a Cell Style
1. Click Cell Styles button.
2. Right-click style.
3. Click *Modify*.
4. Click Format button.
5. Make formatting changes.
6. Click OK.
7. Click OK.

Project 3d   Modifying Cell Styles

1. With **6-OEPayroll.xlsx** open, modify the C06Title custom style by completing the following steps:
   a. Click in any empty cell.
   b. Click the Cell Styles button in the Styles group.
   c. At the drop-down gallery, right-click the *C06Title* style in the *Custom* section and then click *Modify* at the drop-down gallery.
   d. At the Style dialog box, click the Format button.
   e. At the Format Cells dialog box, click the Font tab and then change the font to Candara.
   f. Click the Alignment tab.
   g. Click the *Vertical* option box arrow and then click *Center* at the drop-down list.
   h. Click the Fill tab.
   i. Click the light blue fill color (fifth column, third row) as shown at the right.
   j. Click OK to close the Format Cells dialog box.
   k. Click OK to close the Style dialog box.

2. Modify the C06Subtitle style by completing the following steps:
   a. Click in any empty cell.
   b. Click the Cell Styles button in the Styles group.
   c. At the drop-down gallery, right-click the *C06Subtitle* style in the *Custom* section and then click *Modify*.
   d. At the Style dialog box, click the Format button.
   e. At the Format Cells dialog box, click the Font tab and then change the font to Calibri.
   f. Click the Fill tab.
   g. Click the dark blue fill color as shown at the right (fifth column, sixth row).
   h. Click OK to close the Format Cells dialog box.
   i. Click OK to close the Style dialog box.

3. Modify the predefined 20% - Accent3 style by completing the following steps:
   a. Click the Cell Styles button in the Styles group.
   b. At the drop-down gallery, right-click the *20% - Accent3* style and then click *Modify*.
   c. At the Style dialog box, click the Format button.
   d. At the Format Cells dialog box, make sure the Fill tab is active.
   e. Click the light blue fill color as shown at the right (fifth column, second row).
   f. Click OK to close the Format Cells dialog box.
   g. Click OK to close the Style dialog box.

4. Click each worksheet tab and notice the formatting changes made by the modified styles.
5. Change the name of Sheet1 to *Weekly Payroll*, the name of Sheet2 to *Invoices*, and the name of Sheet3 to *Overdue Accounts*.
6. Apply a different color to each of the three worksheet tabs.
7. Save and then print all the worksheets in **6-OEPayroll.xlsx**.

Check Your Work

Copying Cell Styles to Another Workbook

Quick Steps
Copy Cell Styles to Another Workbook
1. Open workbook containing styles.
2. Open workbook to be modified.
3. Click Cell Styles button.
4. Click *Merge Styles* option.
5. Double-click name of workbook that contains styles.

Custom styles are saved with the workbook they are created in. However, styles can be copied from one workbook to another. To do this, open the workbook containing the styles and open the workbook the styles will be copied into. Click the Cell Styles button in the Styles group on the Home tab and then click the *Merge Styles* option at the bottom of the drop-down gallery. At the Merge Styles dialog box, shown in Figure 6.6, double-click the name of the workbook that contains the styles to be copied.

Figure 6.6 Merge Styles Dialog Box

Hint The Undo command will not reverse the merging of styles at the Merge Styles dialog box.

Double-click the name of the workbook containing the styles to be copied.

Removing a Cell Style

Quick Steps

Remove a Cell Style
1. Select cells formatted with style to be removed.
2. Click Cell Styles button.
3. Click *Normal*.

Delete a Cell Style
1. Click Cell Styles button.
2. Right-click style.
3. Click *Delete*.

Remove formatting applied by a style by applying the Normal style, which is the default. To do this, select the cells, click the Cell Styles button, and then click *Normal* at the drop-down gallery.

Deleting a Cell Style

To delete a style, click the Cell Styles button in the Styles group on the Home tab. At the drop-down gallery that displays, right-click the style to be deleted and then click *Delete* at the shortcut menu. Formatting applied by the deleted style is removed from cells in the workbook. The Normal cell style cannot be deleted.

Project 3e Copying Cell Styles to Another Workbook   **Part 5 of 5**

1. With **6-OEPayroll.xlsx** open, open **OEPlans.xlsx**.
2. Save the workbook and name it **6-OEPlans**.
3. Copy the styles in **6-OEPayroll.xlsx** into **6-OEPlans.xlsx** by completing the following steps:
   a. Click the Cell Styles button in the Styles group on the Home tab.
   b. Click the *Merge Styles* option at the bottom of the drop-down gallery.
   c. At the Merge Styles dialog box, double-click **6-OEPayroll.xlsx** in the *Merge styles from* list box.
   d. At the message that displays asking if you want to merge styles that have the same names, click Yes.
4. Apply the C06Title custom style to cell A1 and the C06Subtitle custom style to cell A2.
5. Increase the height of row 1 to 36.00 points.
6. Save, print, and then close **6-OEPlans.xlsx**.
7. Close **6-OEPayroll.xlsx**.

Check Your Work

Project 4 Insert, Modify, and Remove Hyperlinks

3 Parts

You will open a facilities account workbook and then insert hyperlinks to a website, to cells in other worksheets in the workbook, and to another workbook. You will modify and edit hyperlinks and then remove a hyperlink from the workbook.

Preview Finished Project

Inserting Hyperlinks

A hyperlink can serve a number of purposes in a workbook: Click it to navigate to a web page on the Internet or a specific location in the workbook, to display a different workbook, to open a file in a different program, to create a new document, or to link to an email address. Create a customized hyperlink by clicking in a cell in a workbook, clicking the Insert tab, and then clicking the Hyperlink button in the Links group. This displays the Insert Hyperlink dialog box, shown in Figure 6.7. At this dialog box, identify what is to be linked and the location of the link. Click the ScreenTip button to customize the hyperlink ScreenTip.

Linking to an Existing Web Page or File

Link to a web page on the Internet by typing a web address or by using the Existing File or Web Page button in the *Link to* section. To link to an existing web page, type the address of the web page, such as *www.paradigmcollege.com*.

By default, the automatic formatting of hyperlinks is turned on and the web address is formatted as a hyperlink. (The text is underlined and the color changes to blue.) Turn off the automatic formatting of hyperlinks at the AutoCorrect dialog box. Display this dialog box by clicking the File tab, clicking *Options*, and then clicking *Proofing* in the left panel of the Excel Options dialog box. Click the AutoCorrect Options button to display the AutoCorrect dialog box. At this dialog

Figure 6.7 Insert Hyperlink Dialog Box

Type the text to display in the hyperlink.

Click this button to edit the hyperlink ScreenTip.

Click a button in this section to indicate the hyperlink location.

Type a web address in this text box.

box, click the AutoFormat As You Type tab and then remove the check mark from the *Internet and network paths with hyperlinks* check box.

A hyperlink can be inserted that links to any of several sources, such as another Excel workbook, a Word document, or a PowerPoint presentation. To link an Excel workbook to a workbook or file in another application, display the Insert Hyperlink dialog box and then click the Existing File or Web Page button in the *Link to* section. Use buttons in the *Look in* section to navigate to the folder containing the file and then click the file name. Make other changes in the Insert Hyperlink dialog box as needed and then click OK.

Navigating Using Hyperlinks

Navigate to a hyperlinked location by clicking the hyperlink in the worksheet. Hover the mouse pointer over the hyperlink and a ScreenTip displays with the address of the hyperlinked location. To display specific information in the ScreenTip, click the ScreenTip button at the Insert Hyperlink dialog box, type the text in the Set Hyperlink ScreenTip dialog box, and then click OK.

Project 4a Linking to a Website and Another Workbook   **Part 1 of 3**

1. Open **PSAccts.xlsx** and then save it with the name **6-PSAccts**.
2. Insert a hyperlink to information about Pyramid Sales, a fictitious company (the hyperlink will connect to the publishing company website), by completing the following steps:
   a. Make cell A13 active.
   b. Click the Insert tab and then click the Hyperlink button in the Links group.
   c. At the Insert Hyperlink dialog box, if necessary, click the Existing File or Web Page button in the *Link to* section.
   d. Type www.paradigmcollege.com in the *Address* text box.
   e. Select the text that displays in the *Text to display* text box and then type Company information.
   f. Click the ScreenTip button in the upper right corner of the dialog box.

g. At the Set Hyperlink ScreenTip dialog box, type View the company website. and then click OK.

h. Click OK to close the Insert Hyperlink dialog box.

3. Navigate to the company website (in this case, the publishing company website) by clicking the <u>Company information</u> hyperlink in cell A13.

4. Close the web browser.

5. Create a link to another workbook by completing the following steps:

a. Make cell A11 active, type Semiannual sales, and then press the Enter key.

b. Make cell A11 active and then click the Hyperlink button in the Links group on the Insert tab.

c. At the Insert Hyperlink dialog box, make sure the Existing File or Web Page button is selected.

d. If necessary, click the *Look in* option box arrow and then navigate to the EL1C6 folder on your storage medium.

e. Double-click *PSSalesAnalysis.xlsx*.

6. Click the <u>Semiannual sales</u> hyperlink to open **PSSalesAnalysis.xlsx**.

7. Look at the information in the workbook and then close it.

8. Save **6-PSAccts.xlsx**.

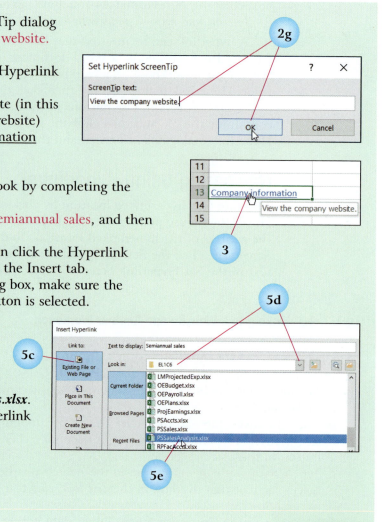

Check Your Work

Linking to a Place in the Workbook

To create a hyperlink to another location in the workbook, click the Place in This Document button in the *Link to* section in the Edit Hyperlink dialog box. To link to a cell within the same worksheet, type the cell name in the *Type the cell reference* text box. To link to another worksheet in the workbook, click the worksheet name in the *Or select a place in this document* list box.

Linking to a New Workbook

In addition to linking to an existing workbook, a hyperlink can be inserted that links to a new workbook. To do this, display the Insert Hyperlink dialog box and then click the Create New Document button in the *Link to* section. Type a name for the new workbook in the *Name of new document* text box and then specify if the workbook will be edited now or later.

Linking Using a Graphic

A graphic—such as a clip art image, picture, or text box—can be used to create a hyperlink to a file or website. To create a hyperlink with a graphic, select the graphic, click the Insert tab, and then click the Hyperlink button. Or right-click the graphic and then click *Hyperlink* at the shortcut menu. At the Insert Hyperlink dialog box, specify the location to be linked to and the text to display in the hyperlink.

Linking to an Email Address

At the Insert Hyperlink dialog box, a hyperlink can be inserted that links to an email address. To do this, click the E-mail Address button in the *Link to* section, type the address in the *E-mail address* text box, and then type a subject for the email in the *Subject* text box. Click in the *Text to display* text box and then type the text to display in the worksheet.

Project 4b **Linking to a Place in a Workbook, to Another Workbook, and Using a Graphic**   **Part 2 of 3**

1. With **6-PSAccts.xlsx** open, create a link from the balance in cell B8 to the balance in cell G20 in the January worksheet by completing the following steps:
   a. Make cell B8 active.
   b. Click the Hyperlink button in the Links group on the Insert tab.
   c. At the Insert Hyperlink dialog box, click the Place in This Document button in the *Link to* section.
   d. Select the text in the *Type the cell reference* text box and then type g20.
   e. Click *January* in the *Or select a place in this document* list box.
   f. Click OK to close the Insert Hyperlink dialog box.

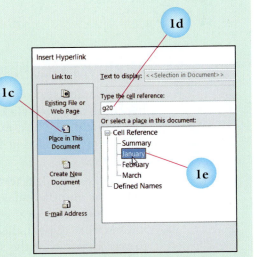

2. Make cell C8 active and then complete steps similar to those in Steps 1b through 1f except click *February* in the *Or select a place in this document* list box.
3. Make cell D8 active and then complete steps similar to those in Steps 1b through 1f except click *March* in the *Or select a place in this document* list box.
4. Click the hyperlinked amount in cell B8. (This makes cell G20 active in the January worksheet.)
5. Click the Summary worksheet tab.
6. Click the hyperlinked amount in cell C8. (This makes cell G20 active in the February worksheet.)
7. Click the Summary worksheet tab.
8. Click the hyperlinked amount in cell D8. (This makes cell G20 active in the March worksheet.)
9. Click the Summary worksheet tab.

10. Use the first pyramid graphic image in cell A1 to create a link to the company web page by completing the following steps:
   a. Right-click the first pyramid graphic image in cell A1 and then click *Hyperlink* at the shortcut menu.
   b. At the Insert Hyperlink dialog box, if necessary, click the Existing File or Web Page button in the *Link to* section.
   c. Type www.paradigmcollege.com in the *Address* text box.
   d. Click the ScreenTip button in the upper right corner of the dialog box.
   e. At the Set Hyperlink ScreenTip dialog box, type View the company website. and then click OK.
   f. Click OK to close the Insert Hyperlink dialog box.
11. Make cell A5 active.
12. Navigate to the company website (the publishing company website) by clicking the first pyramid graphic image.
13. Close the Web browser.
14. Save **6-PSAccts.xlsx**.

10a

> Check Your Work

Modifying, Editing, and Removing a Hyperlink

The hyperlink text or destination can be modified. To do this, right-click the hyperlink and then click *Edit Hyperlink* at the shortcut menu. At the Edit Hyperlink dialog box, make changes and then close the dialog box. The same options are provided at the Edit Hyperlink dialog box as the Insert Hyperlink dialog box.

The hyperlinked text in a cell can also be modified. To do this, make the cell active and then make the changes, such as applying a different font or font size, changing the text color, and adding a text effect. Remove a hyperlink from a workbook by right-clicking the cell containing the hyperlink and then clicking *Remove Hyperlink* at the shortcut menu.

Project 4c   Modifying, Editing, and Removing a Hyperlink   Part 3 of 3

1. With **6-PSAccts.xlsx** open, modify the <u>Semiannual sales</u> hyperlink by completing the following steps:
   a. Position the mouse pointer on the <u>Semiannual sales</u> hyperlink in cell A11, click the right mouse button, and then click *Edit Hyperlink* at the shortcut menu.
   b. At the Edit Hyperlink dialog box, select the text *Semiannual sales* in the *Text to display* text box and then type Customer sales analysis.

Edit Hyperlink

Link to: Text to display: Customer sales analysis

Existing File or Web Page

Look in: EL1C6

6-OEPayroll.xlsx
Current Folder   6-OEPlans.xlsx

1b

c. Click the ScreenTip button in the upper right corner of the dialog box.

d. At the Set Hyperlink ScreenTip dialog box, type Click this hyperlink to display the workbook containing customer sales analysis.

e. Click OK to close the Set Hyperlink ScreenTip dialog box.

f. Click OK to close the Edit Hyperlink dialog box.

2. Click the <u>Customer sales analysis</u> hyperlink.

3. After looking at the **PSSalesAnalysis.xlsx** workbook, close it.

4. With cell A11 active, edit the <u>Customer sales analysis</u> hyperlink text by completing the following steps:

a. Click the Home tab.

b. Click the Font Color button arrow in the Font group and then click the *Dark Red* color option (first option in the *Standard Colors* section).

c. Click the Bold button.

d. Click the Underline button. (This removes underlining from the text.)

5. Remove the <u>Company information</u> hyperlink by right-clicking in cell A13 and then clicking *Remove Hyperlink* at the shortcut menu.

6. Press the Delete key to remove the contents of cell A13.

7. Save, print only the first worksheet (the Summary worksheet), and then close **6-PSAccts.xlsx**.

Check Your Work

Project 5 Create a Billing Statement Workbook Using a Template   **1 Part**

You will open a Billing Statement template provided by Excel, add data, save the template as an Excel workbook, and then print the workbook.

Preview Finished Project

Tutorial

Using Templates

Using Excel Templates

Excel provides a number of template worksheet forms for specific uses. Use Excel templates to create a variety of worksheets with specialized formatting, such as balance sheets, billing statements, loan amortizations, sales invoices, and time cards. Display installed templates by clicking the File tab and then clicking the *New* option. This displays the New backstage area, as shown in Figure 6.8.

Quick Steps

Use an Excel Template
1. Click File tab.
2. Click *New* option.
3. Double-click template.

Click a template in the New backstage area and a preview of the template displays in a window. Click the Create button in the template window and a workbook based on the template opens and displays on the screen.

Locations for personalized text display in placeholders in the worksheet. To enter information in the worksheet, position the mouse pointer (white plus symbol) in the location the data is to be typed and then click the left mouse button. After typing the data, click the next location. The insertion point can also be moved to another cell using the commands learned in Chapter 1. For example, press the Tab key to make the next cell active or press Shift + Tab to make the previous cell active. If the computer is connected to the Internet, a number of templates offered by Microsoft can be downloaded.

Figure 6.8 New Backstage Area

Use this option to search for templates online.

The templates that display in this section of the New backstage area will vary from what is shown in this figure.

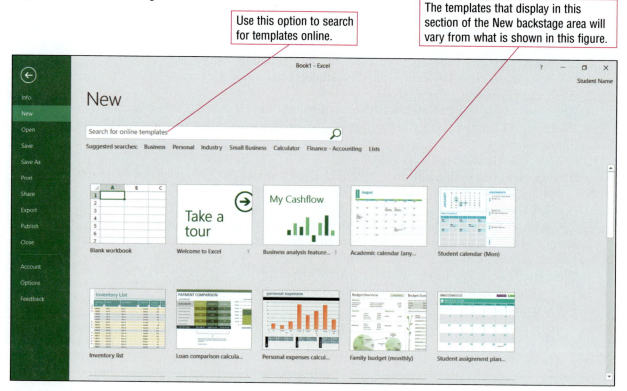

Project 5 Preparing a Billing Statement Using a Template

Part 1 of 1

1. Click the File tab and then click the *New* option.
2. At the New backstage area, click in the search text box, type billing statement, and then press the Enter key.
3. Double-click the *Billing statement* template (see image below).

4. Click the Normal button in the view area on the Status bar.
5. With cell B1 active, type IN-FLOW SYSTEMS.
6. Click the text *Street Address* (cell B2) and then type 320 Milander Way.

7. Click in each specified location (cell) and then type the text indicated:

Address 2 (cell B3): P.O. Box 2300
City, ST ZIP Code (cell B4): Boston, MA 02188
Phone (cell F2): (617) 555-3900
Fax (cell F3): (617) 555-3945
E-mail (cell F3): inflow@emcp.net
Statement # (cell C8): 5432
Customer ID (cell C10): 25-345
Name (cell F8): Aidan Mackenzie
Company Name (cell F9): Stanfield Enterprises
Street Address (cell F10): 9921 South 42nd Avenue
Address 2 (cell F11): P.O. Box 5540
City, ST ZIP Code (cell F12): Boston, MA 02193
Date (cell B15): (insert current date in numbers as ##/##/#### and if necessary, adjust the width of the column)
Type (cell C15): System Unit
Invoice # (cell D15): 7452
Description (cell E15): Calibration Unit
Amount (cell F15): 950
Payment (cell G15): 200
Customer Name (cell C21): Stanfield Enterprises
Amount Enclosed (cell C26): 750

8. Save the completed invoice and name it **6-Billing**.
9. Print and then close **6-Billing.xlsx**.

Check Your Work

Chapter Summary

- Perform file management tasks—such as copying, moving, printing, and renaming workbooks and creating and renaming folders—at the Open dialog box or Save As dialog box.

- Create a new folder by clicking the New folder button on the toolbar at the Open dialog box or Save As dialog box.

- Rename a folder with the *Rename* option from the Organize button drop-down list or with the shortcut menu.

- Use the Shift key to select adjacent workbooks in the Open dialog box and use the Ctrl key to select nonadjacent workbooks.

- To delete a workbook, use the *Delete* option from the Organize button drop-down list or use the *Delete* option at the shortcut menu. Workbooks deleted from the hard drive are automatically sent to the Windows Recycle Bin, where they can be restored or permanently deleted.

- Use the *Copy* and *Paste* options from the shortcut menu at the Open dialog box or Save As dialog box to copy a workbook from one folder to another folder or drive.

- Use the *Send to* option from the shortcut menu to send a copy of a workbook to another drive or folder.

- Remove a workbook from a folder or drive and insert it in another folder or drive using the *Cut* and *Paste* options from the shortcut menu.

- Use the *Rename* option from the Organize button drop-down list or the shortcut menu to give a workbook a different name.

- To move or copy a worksheet to another existing workbook, open both the source workbook and the destination workbook and then open the Move or Copy dialog box.

- Use options from the Cell Styles button drop-down gallery to apply predesigned styles to a cell or selected cells.

- Automate the formatting of cells in a workbook by defining and then applying styles. A style is a predefined set of formatting attributes.

- Define a style with formats already applied to a cell or display the Style dialog box, click the Format button, and then choose formatting options at the Format Cells dialog box.

- To apply a style, select the desired cell or cells, click the Cell Styles button in the Styles group on the Home tab, and then click the style at the drop-down gallery.

- Modify a style and all the cells to which it is applied update automatically. To modify a style, click the Cell Styles button in the Styles group on the Home tab, right-click the style, and then click *Modify* at the shortcut menu.

- Styles are saved in the workbook they are created in but can be copied to another workbook. Do this with options at the Merge Styles dialog box.

- With options at the Insert Hyperlink dialog box, create a hyperlink to a web page, another workbook, a location within a workbook, a new workbook, or an email address. Or create a hyperlink using a graphic.

- Hyperlinks can be modified, edited, and removed.

- Excel provides templates for creating forms. Search for and download templates at the New backstage area.

- Templates contain unique areas where information is entered at the keyboard. These areas vary depending on the template.

Commands Review

FEATURE	RIBBON TAB, GROUP/OPTION	BUTTON, OPTION	KEYBOARD SHORTCUT
cell styles	Home, Styles		
Insert Hyperlink dialog box	Insert, Links		Ctrl + K
Merge Styles dialog box	Home, Styles	, *Merge Styles*	
New backstage area	File, *New*		
new folder	File, *Open, Browse*	New folder	
Open backstage area	File, *Open*		Ctrl + O
Open dialog box	File, *Open, Browse*		Ctrl + F12
Save As backstage area	File, *Save As*		Ctrl + S
Save As dialog box	File, *Save As, Browse*		F12
Style dialog box	Home, Styles	, *New Cell Style*	

Workbook

Chapter study tools and assessment activities are available in the *Workbook* ebook. These resources are designed to help you further develop and demonstrate mastery of the skills learned in this chapter.

Microsoft®

Excel®

Creating Charts and Inserting Formulas

Performance Objectives

Upon successful completion of Chapter 7, you will be able to:

1 Create a chart with data in an Excel worksheet

2 Size, move, edit, format, and delete charts

3 Print a selected chart and print a worksheet containing a chart

4 Change a chart location

5 Insert, move, size, and delete chart elements and shapes

6 Using the Quick Analysis feature

7 Write formulas with the PMT and FV financial functions

8 Write formulas with the IF logical function

Precheck

Check your current skills to help focus your study.

In the previous Excel chapters, you learned how to create data in worksheets. While a worksheet does an adequate job of representing data, some data are better represented visually with a chart. A chart, which is sometimes referred to as a *graph*, is a picture of numeric data. In this chapter, you will learn to create and customize charts in Excel. You will also learn how to write formulas using financial and logical functions.

SNAP

If you are a SNAP user, launch the Precheck and Tutorials from your Assignments page.

Data Files

Before beginning the projects, copy the EL1C7 folder to your storage medium and then make EL1C7 the active folder.

Preview Finished Project

Creating a Chart

To provide a visual representation of data, consider inserting data in a chart. Use buttons in the Charts group on the Insert tab to create a variety of charts, such as a column chart, line chart, pie chart, and much more. Excel provides 15 basic chart types, as described in Table 7.1.

Table 7.1 Types of Charts

Chart	Description
Area	Emphasizes the magnitude of change rather than time and the rate of change. Also shows the relationship of the parts to the whole by displaying the sum of the plotted values.
Bar	Shows individual figures at a specific time or shows variations between components but not in relationship to the whole.
Box & Whisker	Displays medians, quartiles, and extremes of a data set on a number line to show the distribution of data. Lines extending vertically are called whiskers and indicate variability outside the upper and lower quartiles.
Column	Compares separate (noncontinuous) items as they vary over time.
Combo	Combines two or more chart types to make data easy to understand.
Histogram	Condenses a data series into a visual representation by grouping data points into logical ranges called *bins*.
Line	Shows trends and overall change across time at even intervals. Emphasizes the rate of change across time rather than the magnitude of change.
Pie	Shows proportions and the relationship of the parts to the whole.
Radar	Emphasizes differences and amounts of change over time as well as variations and trends. Each category has a value axis radiating from the center point. Lines connect all values in the same series.
Stock	Shows four values for a stock: open, high, low, and close.
Sunburst	Displays hierarchical data. Each level is represented by one ring, with the innermost ring as the top of the hierarchy.
Surface	Shows trends in values across two dimensions in a continuous curve.
Treemap	Provides a hierarchical view of data and compares proportions within the hierarchy.

continues

Table 7.1 Types of Charts—*Continued*

Chart	Description
X Y (Scatter)	Shows the relationships among numeric values in several data series or plots the interception points between *x* and *y* values. Shows uneven intervals of data and is commonly used for scientific data.
Waterfall	Determines how an initial value is affected by a series of positive and negative values.

To create a chart, select the cells in the worksheet to be charted, click the Insert tab, and then click a specific chart button in the Charts group. At the drop-down gallery that displays, click a specific chart style. Excel will make a recommendation on the type of chart that will best illustrate the data. To let Excel recommend a chart, select the data, click the Insert tab, and then click the Recommended Charts button. This displays the data in a chart in the Insert Chart dialog box. Customize the recommended chart with options in the left panel of the dialog box. Click the OK button to insert the recommended chart in the worksheet. Another method for inserting a recommended chart is to use the keyboard shortcut Alt + F1.

Recommended Charts

Sizing and Moving a Chart

Hint Hide rows or columns you do not want to chart.

By default, a chart is inserted in the same worksheet as the selected cells. Figure 7.1 displays the worksheet and chart that will be created in Project 1a. The chart is inserted in a box, which can be sized or moved within the worksheet.

Change the size of the chart using the sizing handles (white circles) on the chart borders. Drag the top-middle and bottom-middle sizing handles to increase or decrease the height of the chart; use the left-middle and right-middle sizing

Figure 7.1 Project 1a Chart

handles to increase or decrease the width; and use the corner sizing handles to increase or decrease the height and width at the same time. To increase or decrease the size of the chart but maintain its proportions, press and hold down the Shift key while dragging one of the chart's corner borders.

To move the chart, make sure it is selected (a border with sizing handles displays around the chart), position the mouse pointer on a border until the pointer displays with a four-headed arrow attached, click and hold down the left mouse button, drag to the new position, and then release the mouse button.

Tutorial

Editing Chart Data

Editing Data and Adding a Data Series

The cells selected to create a chart are linked to it. To change the data for a chart, edit the data in the specific cells and the corresponding sections of the chart will update automatically. If data is added to cells within the range of cells used for the chart, called the *source data*, the new data will be included in the chart. If a data series is added in cells next to or below the source data, click in the chart to display the source data with sizing handles and then drag with a sizing handle to include the new data.

Project 1a Creating a Chart

Part 1 of 3

1. Open **SalesChart.xlsx** and then save it with the name **7-SalesChart**.
2. Select the range A1:E4.
3. Let Excel recommend a chart type by completing the following steps:
   a. Click the Insert tab.
   b. Click the Recommended Charts button in the Charts group.

   c. At the Insert Chart dialog box, look at the options that display in the left panel and then click OK.
4. Slightly increase the size of the chart and maintain its proportions by completing the following steps:
   a. Position the mouse pointer on the sizing handle in the lower right corner of the chart border until the pointer turns into a two-headed arrow pointing diagonally.

b. Press and hold down the Shift key and then click and hold down the left mouse button.

c. Drag out approximately 0.5 inch. Release the mouse button and then release the Shift key.

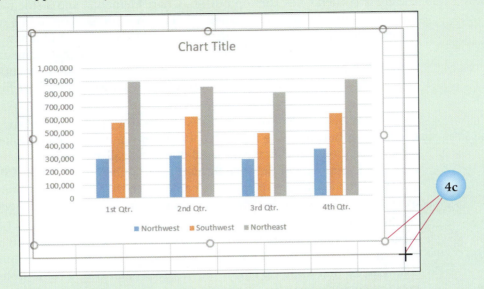

5. Move the chart below the cells containing data by completing the following steps:

a. Make sure the chart is selected. (When the chart is selected, the border surrounding it displays with sizing handles.)

b. Position the mouse pointer on the chart border until the pointer displays with a four-headed arrow attached.

c. Click and hold down the left mouse button, drag the chart to row 6 below the cells containing data, and then release the mouse button.

6. Make the following changes to the specified cells:

a. Make cell B2 active and then change *300,560* to *421,720*.

b. Make cell D2 active and then change *287,460* to *397,460*.

7. Add a new data series by typing data in the following cells:

A5	Southeast
B5	290,450
C5	320,765
D5	270,450
E5	300,455

8. Add the new data series to the chart by completing the following steps:

a. Click in the chart. (This selects the data source, which is the range A1:E4.)

b. Position the mouse pointer on the sizing handle in the lower right corner of cell E4 until the pointer displays as a two-headed diagonally pointing arrow.

c. Click and hold down the left mouse button, drag down into cell E5, and then release the mouse button. (This incorporates data row 5 in the chart.)

9. Save **7-SalesChart.xlsx**.

Check Your Work

Tutorial

Formatting with
Chart Buttons

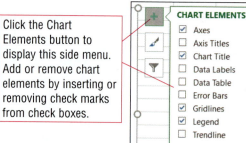

Chart
Elements

Chart Styles

Chart Filters

Formatting with Chart Buttons

When a chart is inserted in a worksheet, three buttons display at the right side of the chart border. Click the top button, Chart Elements, and a side menu displays chart elements, as shown in Figure 7.2. The check boxes containing check marks indicate the elements that are currently part of the chart. Add a new element to the chart by inserting a check mark in the check box for that element and remove an element by removing the check mark. Remove the Chart Elements side menu by clicking one of the other chart buttons or by clicking the Chart Elements button.

Excel offers a variety of chart styles that can be applied to a chart. Click the Chart Styles button at the right side of the chart and a side menu gallery of styles displays, as shown in Figure 7.3. Scroll down the gallery, hover the mouse pointer over a style option, and the style formatting is applied to the chart. Click the chart style that applies the desired formatting. Remove the Chart Styles side menu gallery by clicking one of the other chart buttons or by clicking the Chart Styles button.

In addition to offering a variety of chart styles, the Chart Styles button side menu gallery offers a variety of chart colors. Click the Chart Styles button and then click the Color tab to the right of the Style tab. Click a color option at the color palette that displays. Hover the mouse pointer over a color option to view how the color change affects the elements in the chart.

Use the bottom button, Chart Filters, to isolate specific data in the chart. Click the button and a side menu displays, as shown in Figure 7.4. Specify the series or categories to display in the chart. To do this, remove the check marks from those elements that should not appear in the chart. After removing the specific check marks, click the Apply button at the bottom of the side menu. Click the Names tab at the Chart Filters button side menu and options display for turning on/off the display of column and row names.

Figure 7.2 Chart Elements Button Side Menu

Click the Chart
Elements button to
display this side menu.
Add or remove chart
elements by inserting or
removing check marks
from check boxes.

CHART ELEMENTS
- ☑ Axes
- ☐ Axis Titles
- ☑ Chart Title
- ☐ Data Labels
- ☐ Data Table
- ☐ Error Bars
- ☑ Gridlines
- ☑ Legend
- ☐ Trendline

Figure 7.3 Chart Styles Button Side Menu Gallery

Click the Chart
Styles button
to display this
side menu
gallery of chart
style options.

Figure 7.4 Chart Filters Button Side Menu

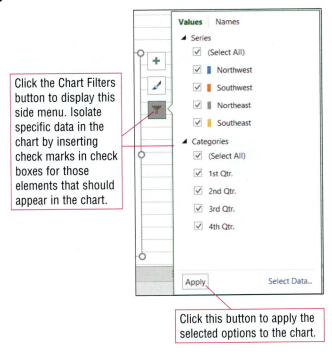

Click the Chart Filters button to display this side menu. Isolate specific data in the chart by inserting check marks in check boxes for those elements that should appear in the chart.

Click this button to apply the selected options to the chart.

Project 1b Formatting with Chart Buttons

Part 2 of 3

1. With **7-SalesChart.xlsx** open, make the chart active by clicking inside it but outside any elements.
2. Insert and remove chart elements by completing the following steps:
   a. Click the Chart Elements button outside the upper right side of the chart.
   b. At the side menu that displays, click the *Chart Title* check box to remove the check mark.
   c. Click the *Data Table* check box to insert a check mark.
   d. Hover the mouse pointer over *Gridlines* in the Chart Elements button side menu and then click the right-pointing triangle that displays.
   e. At the side menu that displays, click the *Primary Major Vertical* check box to insert a check mark.

   f. Click the *Legend* check box to remove the check mark.

3. Apply a different chart style by completing the following steps:
   a. Click the Chart Styles button outside the upper right side of the chart (immediately below the Chart Elements button). (Clicking the Chart Styles button removes the Chart Elements button side menu.)
   b. At the side menu gallery, click the *Style 3* option (third option in the gallery).
4. Display only the first-quarter and second-quarter sales by completing the following steps:
   a. Click the Chart Filters button outside the upper right corner of the chart (immediately below the Chart Styles button). (Clicking the Chart Filters button removes the Chart Styles side menu gallery.)
   b. Click the *3rd Qtr.* check box in the *Categories* section to remove the check mark.
   c. Click the *4th Qtr.* check box in the *Categories* section to remove the check mark.
   d. Click the Apply button at the bottom of the side menu.
   e. Click the Chart Filters button to remove the side menu.

5. Save **7-SalesChart.xlsx**.

Check Your Work

Printing a Chart

In a worksheet containing data in cells and in a chart, print only the chart by selecting it, displaying the Print backstage area, and then clicking the Print button. With the chart selected, the first gallery in the *Settings* category automatically changes to *Print Selected Chart*. A preview of the chart displays at the right side of the Print backstage area.

Project 1c Printing a Chart

1. With **7-SalesChart.xlsx** open, make sure the chart is selected.
2. Click the File tab and then click the *Print* option.
3. At the Print backstage area, look at the preview of the chart in the preview area and notice that the first gallery in the *Settings* category is set to *Print Selected Chart*.
4. Click the Print button.
5. Save and then close **7-SalesChart.xlsx**.

Check Your Work

Project 2 Create a Department Expenditures Bar Chart and Column Chart

2 Parts

You will open a workbook containing expenditure data by department and then create a bar chart with the data. You will then change the chart type, layout, and style; add chart elements; and move the chart to a new worksheet.

Preview Finished Project

Tutorial

Changing Chart Design

Changing the Chart Design

Along with the buttons outside the upper right side of the chart, buttons and options on the Chart Tools Design tab can be used to apply formatting to change the chart design. This tab, shown in Figure 7.5, displays when a chart is inserted in a worksheet or a chart is selected. Use buttons and options on the tab to add chart elements, change the chart type, specify a different layout or style for the chart, and change the location of the chart so it displays in a separate worksheet.

Figure 7.5 Chart Tools Design Tab

Changing the Chart Style

Quick Steps

Change the Chart Type and Style
1. Make chart active.
2. Click Chart Tools Design tab.
3. Click Change Chart Type button.
4. Click chart type.
5. Click chart style.
6. Click OK.

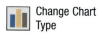

Change Chart Type

Excel offers a variety of preformatted custom charts and varying styles for each chart type. A chart style was applied to a chart in Project 1b using the Chart Styles button outside the right border of the chart. A chart style can also be applied to a chart with options in the Chart Styles group on the Chart Tools Design tab. To do this, click a chart style in the Chart Styles group or click the More Chart Styles button and then click the desired chart style.

Another method for applying a chart style is to use options at the Change Chart Type dialog box. Display this dialog box by clicking the Change Chart Type button in the Type group. The dialog box displays with the All Charts tab selected, as shown in Figure 7.6. Click a chart type in the left panel of the dialog box, click the chart style in the row of options at the top right, and then click a specific chart layout below the row of styles. Click the Recommended Charts tab to display chart styles recommended for the data by Excel.

Switching Rows and Columns

Switch Row/Column

Quick Steps

Switch Rows and Columns
1. Make chart active.
2. Click Chart Tools Design tab.
3. Click Switch Row/Column button.

When creating a chart, Excel uses row headings for grouping data along the bottom of the chart (the horizontal axis) and column headings for the legend (the area of a chart that identifies the data in the chart). Change this order by clicking the Switch Row/Column button in the Data group on the Chart Tools Design tab. Click this button and Excel uses the column headings to group data along the horizontal axis and the row headings for the legend.

Figure 7.6 Change Chart Type Dialog Box

1. Open **DIDeptExp.xlsx** and then save it with the name **7-DIDeptExp**.
2. Create a bar chart by completing the following steps:
   a. Select the range A3:G9.
   b. Click the Insert tab.
   c. Click the Insert Column or Bar Chart button in the Charts group.
   d. Click the *3-D Clustered Bar* option (first option in the *3-D Bar* section).
3. With the Chart Tools Design tab active, change the chart type by completing the following steps:
   a. Click the Change Chart Type button in the Type group.
   b. At the Change Chart Type dialog box, click the *Column* option in the left panel.
   c. Click the *3-D Clustered Column* option in the top row (fourth option from left).
   d. Click OK to close the Change Chart Type dialog box.
4. With the chart selected and the Chart Tools Design tab active, click the Switch Row/Column button in the Data group.

5. Save **7-DIDeptExp.xlsx**.

Check Your Work

Changing Chart Layout and Colors

 Quick Layout

Change Colors

The Chart Tools Design tab contains options for changing the chart layout and chart colors. Click the Quick Layout button in the Chart Layouts group and a drop-down gallery of layout options displays. Hover the mouse pointer over a layout option and the chart reflects the layout. Change the colors used in the chart by clicking the Change Colors button in the Chart Styles group and then clicking a color option at the drop-down gallery.

Changing the Chart Location

Quick Steps

Change the Chart Location
1. Make chart active.
2. Click Chart Tools Design tab.
3. Click Move Chart button.
4. Click *New Sheet* option.
5. Click OK.

Move Chart

Create a chart and it is inserted in the currently open worksheet as an embedded object. Change the location of a chart with the Move Chart button in the Location group on the Chart Tools Design tab. Click this button and the Move Chart dialog box displays, as shown in Figure 7.7. To move the chart to a new sheet in the workbook, click the *New sheet* option; Excel automatically names the new sheet *Chart1*. As explained earlier in the chapter, pressing Alt + F1 will insert a recommended chart in the active worksheet. To insert a recommended chart into a separate worksheet, press the F11 function key.

A chart that is moved to a separate sheet can be moved back to the original sheet or to a different sheet within the workbook. To move a chart to a different sheet, click the Move Chart button in the Location group. At the Move Chart dialog box, click the *Object in* option box arrow and then click the sheet at the drop-down list. Click OK and the chart is inserted in the specified sheet as an object that can be moved, sized, and formatted.

Adding, Moving, and Deleting Chart Elements

Add Chart Element

In addition to adding chart elements with the Chart Elements button at the right side of a selected chart, chart elements can be added with the Add Chart Element button on the Chart Tools Design tab. Click this button and a drop-down list of elements displays. Point to a category of elements and then click the desired element at the side menu.

Quick Steps

Delete a Chart Element
1. Click chart element.
2. Press Delete key.
OR
1. Right-click chart element.
2. Click *Delete*.

A chart element can be moved and/or sized. To move a chart element, click the element to select it and then move the mouse pointer over the border until the pointer turns into a four-headed arrow. Click and hold down the left mouse button, drag the element to the new location, and then release the mouse button. To size a chart element, click to select the element and then use the sizing handles to increase or decrease the size. To delete a chart element, click the element to select it and then press the Delete key. A chart element can also be deleted by right-clicking it and then clicking *Delete* at the shortcut menu.

Figure 7.7 Move Chart Dialog Box

1. With **7-DIDeptExp.xlsx** open, make sure the Chart Tools Design tab is active. (If it is not, make sure the chart is selected and then click the Chart Tools Design tab.)
2. Change the chart style by clicking the *Style 5* option in the Chart Styles group (fifth option from the left).

3. Change the chart colors by clicking the Change Colors button in the Chart Styles group and then clicking the *Color 3* option (third row in the *Colorful* group).
4. Change the chart layout by clicking the Quick Layout button in the Chart Layouts group and then clicking the *Layout 1* option (first option in the drop-down gallery).
5. Add axis titles by completing the following steps:
   a. Click the Add Chart Element button in the Chart Layouts group on the Chart Tools Design tab.
   b. Point to *Axis Titles* and then click *Primary Horizontal* at the side menu.
   c. Type Department and then press the Enter key. (The word *Department* will display in the Formula bar.)
   d. Click the Add Chart Element button, point to *Axis Titles*, and then click *Primary Vertical* at the side menu.
   e. Type Expenditure Amounts and then press the Enter key.
6. Click in the *Chart Title* placeholder text at the top of the chart, type Half-Yearly Expenditures, and then press the Enter key.
7. Delete the *Expenditure Amounts* axis title by clicking anywhere in it and then pressing the Delete key.
8. Move the legend by completing the following steps:
   a. Click in the legend to select it.
   b. Move the mouse pointer over the border until the pointer turns into a four-headed arrow.
   c. Click and hold down the left mouse button, drag up until the top border of the legend aligns with the top gridline in the chart, and then release the mouse button.

9. Move the chart to a new location by completing the following steps:
   a. Click the Move Chart button in the Location group.
   b. At the Move Chart dialog box, click the *New sheet* option and then click OK. (The chart is inserted in a worksheet named *Chart1*.)
10. Save **7-DIDeptExp.xlsx**.
11. Print the Chart1 worksheet.
12. Move the chart from Chart1 to Sheet2 by completing the following steps:
    a. Make sure that Chart1 is the active worksheet and that the chart is selected (not just an element in the chart).
    b. Make sure the Chart Tools Design tab is active.
    c. Click the Move Chart button in the Location group.
    d. At the Move Chart dialog box, click the *Object in* option box arrow and then click *Sheet2* at the drop-down list.
    e. Click OK.
13. Change the amounts in Sheet1 by completing the following steps:
    a. Click the Sheet1 tab.
    b. Make cell B7 active and then change the amount from *10,540* to *19,750*.
    c. Make cell D8 active and then change the amount from *78,320* to *63,320*.
    d. Make cell G8 active and then change the amount from *60,570* to *75,570*.
    e. Make cell A2 active.
    f. Click the Sheet2 tab and notice that the chart displays the updated amounts.
14. Click outside the chart to deselect it.
15. Insert a header in the Sheet2 worksheet that prints your name at the left side, the current date in the middle, and the workbook file name at the right side.
16. Display the worksheet at the Print backstage area and make sure it will print on one page. If the chart does not fit on the page, return to the worksheet and then move and/or decrease the size of the chart until it fits on one page.
17. Print the active worksheet (Sheet2).
18. Save and then close **7-DIDeptExp.xlsx**.

Check Your Work

Project 3 Create a Population Comparison Line Chart   2 Parts

You will open a workbook containing population comparison data for Seattle and Portland and then create a line chart with the data. You will move the chart to a new worksheet, format the chart elements, and insert a shape in the chart.

Preview Finished Project

Changing Chart Formatting

Customize the formatting of a chart and its elements with options on the Chart Tools Format tab, as shown in Figure 7.8. Use buttons in the Current Selection group to identify specific elements in the chart and then apply formatting. Insert a shape in a chart with options in the Insert Shapes group and format shapes with options in the Shape Styles group. Apply WordArt formatting to data in a chart with options in the WordArt Styles group. Arrange, align, and size a chart with options in the Arrange and Size groups.

Formatting a Selection

Identify a specific element in a chart for formatting by clicking the *Chart Elements* option box arrow in the Current Selection group on the Chart Tools Format tab and then clicking the element at the drop-down list. This selects the specific element in the chart. Click the Reset to Match Style button to return the formatting of the element back to the original style. Use buttons in the Shapes Styles group to apply formatting to a selected object and use buttons in the WordArt Styles group to apply formatting to selected data.

Figure 7.8 Chart Tools Format Tab

Project 3a Creating and Formatting a Line Chart

Part 1 of 2

1. Open **PopComp.xlsx** and then save it with the name **7-PopComp**.
2. Create a line chart and add a chart element by completing the following steps:
   a. Select the range A2:I4.
   b. Click the Insert tab.
   c. Click the Insert Line or Area Chart button in the Charts group.
   d. Click the *Line with Markers* option at the drop-down list (fourth column, first row in the *2-D Line* section).
   e. Click the Chart Elements button outside the upper right side of the chart.
   f. Hover the mouse pointer over the *Data Table* option at the side menu, click the right-pointing triangle, and then click *No Legend Keys* at the side menu.
   g. Click the Chart Elements button to remove the side menu.
3. Move the chart to a new sheet by completing the following steps:
   a. Click the Move Chart button in the Location group on the Chart Tools Design tab.
   b. At the Move Chart dialog box, click the *New sheet* option.
   c. Click OK.
4. Format the *Portland* line by completing the following steps:
   a. Click the Chart Tools Format tab.

b. Click the *Chart Elements* option box arrow in the Current Selection group and then click *Series "Portland"* at the drop-down list.

c. Click the Shape Fill button arrow in the Shape Styles group and then click the *Green* color (sixth color in the *Standard Colors* section).

d. Click the Shape Outline button arrow in the Shape Styles group and then click the *Green* color.

5. Type a title for the chart and format the title by completing the following steps:

a. Click the *Chart Elements* option box arrow in the Current Selection group and then click *Chart Title* at the drop-down list.

b. Type Population Comparison between Seattle and Portland and then press the Enter key.

c. Click the *Fill - Black, Text 1, Shadow* WordArt style in the WordArt Styles group (first style in the WordArt Styles gallery).

6. Format the legend by completing the following steps:

a. Click the *Chart Elements* option box arrow in the Current Selection group and then click *Legend* at the drop-down list.

b. Click the *Colored Outline - Blue, Accent 1* shape style in the Shape Styles group (second shape style).

7. Save **7-PopComp.xlsx**.

Check Your Work

Inserting a Shape

Quick Steps

Insert a Shape
1. Make chart active.
2. Click Chart Tools Format tab.
3. Click More Shapes button.
4. Click shape at drop-down list.
5. Click or drag to create shape.

The Insert Shapes group on the Chart Tools Format tab contains options for inserting shapes in a chart. Click a shape option and the mouse pointer turns into crosshairs (thin black plus symbol). Click in the chart or drag with the mouse to create the shape in the chart. The shape is inserted in the chart and the Drawing Tools Format tab is active. This tab contains many of the same options as the Chart Tools Format tab. For example, a shape style or WordArt style can be applied to the shape and the shape can be arranged and sized. Size a shape by clicking the up and down arrows at the right sides of the *Shape Height* and *Shape Width* measurement boxes in the Size group on the Drawing Tools Format tab. Or select the current measurement in the *Shape Height* or *Shape Width* measurement box and then type a specific measurement.

Project 3b Inserting and Customizing a Shape

1. With **7-PopComp.xlsx** open, create a shape similar to the one shown in Figure 7.9 by completing the following steps:

   a. Click the More Shapes button in the Insert Shapes group on the Chart Tools Format tab.

   b. Click the *Up Arrow Callout* shape (last column, second row in the *Block Arrows* section).

   c. Click in the chart to insert the shape.

   d. Click in the *Shape Height* measurement box in the Size group on the Drawing Tools Format tab, type 1.5, and then press the Enter key.

   e. Click in the *Shape Width* measurement box, type 1.5, and then press the Enter key.

   f. Apply a shape style by clicking the More Shape Styles button in the Shape Styles group and then clicking the *Subtle Effect - Blue, Accent 1* option (second column, fourth row in the *Theme Styles* section).

   g. Type Largest disparity in the shape, press the Enter key, and then type (184,411).

   h. Select the text you just typed.

   i. Click the Home tab.

   j. Click the Bold button in the Font group.

   k. Click the *Font Size* option box arrow and then click *14*.

   l. Click the Center button in the Alignment group.

2. With the shape selected, drag the shape so it is positioned as shown in Figure 7.9.

3. Save **7-PopComp.xlsx**, print the Chart1 worksheet, and then close the workbook.

Check Your Work

Figure 7.9 Project 3 Chart

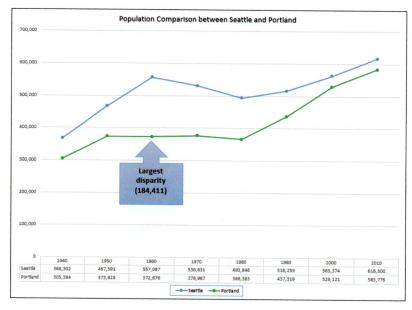

Project 4 Create a Costs Percentage Pie Chart   2 Parts

You will create a pie chart, add data labels, apply a style, format chart elements, and then size and move the pie chart.

Preview Finished Project

Using the Quick Analysis Feature

A variety of methods are available for adding visual elements to a worksheet, including charts, sparklines, and conditional formatting. The Quick Analysis feature consists of a toolbar that has buttons and options for inserting all of these visual elements plus common formulas in one location. When a range is selected, Excel determines how the data in the range can be analyzed and then provides buttons and options for inserting relevant visual elements or formulas. When a range of data that is used to create a pie chart is selected, the Quick Analysis Toolbar provides buttons and options for inserting many different visual elements or formulas, but also specifically including a pie chart.

A Quick Analysis button appears at the bottom right corner of the selected range and when clicked, displays the Quick Analysis Toolbar as shown in Figure 7.10. The Quick Analysis Toolbar includes the *Formatting, Charts, Totals, Tables,* and *Sparklines* options. Each option displays buttons that relate to how the data can be analyzed. Click a button to insert an element or formula into the worksheet.

Figure 7.10 Quick Analysis Toolbar

Applying Formatting at a Task Pane

To view and apply more formatting options for charts, display the formatting task pane by clicking the Format Selection button in the Current Selection group on the Chart Tools Format tab. The task pane displays at the right side of the screen and the name of and contents in the task pane vary depending on what is selected. If the entire chart is selected, the Format Chart Area task pane displays, as shown in Figure 7.11. Format the chart by clicking formatting options in the task pane. Display additional formatting options by clicking the icons toward the top of the task pane. For example, click the Effects icon in the Format Chart Area task pane and options display for applying shadow, glow, soft edges, and three-dimensional formatting.

Click a chart element and then click the Format Selection button and the task pane name and options change. Another method for displaying the task pane is to right-click a chart or chart element and then click the format option at the shortcut menu. The name of the format option varies depending on the selected element.

Quick Steps

Display a Task Pane
1. Select chart or specific element.
2. Click Chart Tools Format tab.
3. Click Format Selection button.

Format Selection

Figure 7.11 Format Chart Area Task Pane

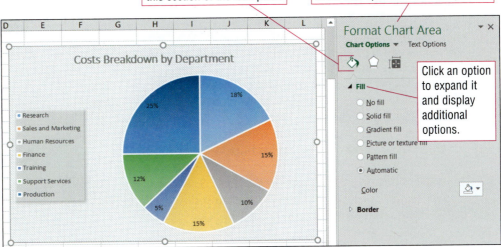

Changing Chart Height and Width Measurements

Quick Steps

Change Chart Height and/or Width
1. Make chart active.
2. Click Chart Tools Format tab.
3. Insert height and/or width with *Shape Height* and/or *Shape Width* measurement boxes.

A chart that is inserted into the current worksheet (not a separate new worksheet) can be sized by selecting it and dragging a sizing handle. A chart can also be sized with the *Shape Height* and *Shape Width* measurement boxes in the Size group on the Chart Tools Format tab. Click the up or down arrow at the right side of the measurement box to increase or decrease the size or click in the measurement box and then type a specific measurement. Another method for changing a chart size is to use options at the Format Chart Area task pane. Display this task pane by clicking the Size group task pane launcher on the Chart Tools Format tab.

Project 4a   Deleting a Chart and Creating and Formatting a Pie Chart

Part 1 of 2

1. Open **DIDeptCosts.xlsx** and then save it with the name **7-DIDeptCosts**.
2. Create the pie chart shown in Figure 7.11 by completing the following steps:
   a. Select the range A3:B10.
   b. Click the Quick Analysis button below and to the right of the selected range.
   c. Click the *Charts* option.
   d. Click the Pie button.
3. Insert data labels in the chart by completing the following steps:
   a. Click the Chart Elements button outside the upper right border of the chart.
   b. Hover the mouse pointer over the *Data Labels* option and then click the right-pointing triangle that displays.
   c. Click *Inside End* at the side menu.
   d. Click the Chart Elements button to hide the side menu.
4. Click the *Style 6* option in the Chart Styles group on the Chart Tools Design tab.
5. Type a title and then apply a WordArt style to it by completing the following steps:
   a. Click the Chart Tools Format tab.
   b. Click the *Chart Elements* option box arrow in the Current Selection group.
   c. Click *Chart Title* at the drop-down list.
   d. Type **C** and Excel's AutoComplete feature inserts the entire title, *Costs Breakdown by Department*, in the Formula bar. Accept this name by pressing the Enter key.
   e. Click the More WordArt Styles button in the WordArt Styles group.
   f. Click the *Pattern Fill - Gray-50%, Accent 3, Narrow Horizontal, Inner Shadow* style at the drop-down gallery (second column, fourth row).

6. Use the Format Legend task pane to apply formatting to the legend by completing the following steps:

a. Click the *Chart Elements* option box arrow and then click *Legend* at the drop-down list.

b. Click the Format Selection button in the Current Selection group.

c. At the Format Legend task pane, click the *Left* option in the *Legend Options* section to select it.

d. Click the Effects icon in the task pane. (This changes the options in the task pane.)

e. Click *Shadow* to expand the shadow options in the task pane.

f. Click the Shadow button to the right of *Presets* and then click the *Offset Diagonal Bottom Right* option (first option in the *Outer* section).

g. Click the Fill & Line icon in the task pane.

h. Click *Fill* to expand the fill options in the task pane.

i. Click the *Gradient fill* option.

j. Close the task pane by clicking the Close button in the upper right corner of the task pane.

7. Use the Format Chart Area task pane to apply formatting to the chart by completing the following steps:
   a. Click inside the chart but outside any chart elements.
   b. Click the Format Selection button in the Current Selection group.
   c. Make sure the Fill & Line icon in the Format Chart Area task pane is selected. (If not, click the icon.)
   d. Make sure the *Fill* option is expanded. (If not, click *Fill*.)
   e. Click the *Gradient fill* option.
   f. Click the Size & Properties icon in the task pane.
   g. Click *Size* to expand the size options in the task pane.
   h. Select the current measurement in the *Height* measurement box, type 3.5, and then press the Enter key.
   i. Select the current measurement in the *Width* measurement box, type 5.5, and then press the Enter key.

   j. Close the task pane.
8. Save **7-DIDeptCosts.xlsx** and then print only the chart.
9. Change the chart style by completing the following steps:
   a. Click the Chart Tools Design tab.
   b. Click the More Chart Styles button in the Chart Styles group.
   c. Click the *Style 9* option at the drop-down gallery.
10. Move the chart so it is positioned below the cells containing data.
11. Click outside the chart to deselect it.
12. Display the Print backstage area, make sure the chart fits on one page with the data, and then click the Print button.
13. Save **7-DIDeptCosts.xlsx**.

Check Your Work

Deleting a Chart

Quick Steps
Delete a Chart
1. Click chart.
2. Press Delete key.
OR
1. Right-click chart tab.
2. Click *Delete*.

Delete a chart created in Excel by clicking the chart to select it and then pressing the Delete key. If a chart has been moved to a different worksheet in the workbook, deleting the chart will delete the chart but not the worksheet. To delete the worksheet and the chart, position the mouse pointer on the sheet tab, click the right mouse button, and then click *Delete* at the shortcut menu. At the message box indicating that the selected sheet will be permanently deleted, click the Delete button.

1. With **7-DIDeptCosts.xlsx** open, click the Sheet2 tab.
2. Delete the column chart by completing the following steps:
   a. Click the column chart to select it. (Make sure the chart is selected, not a specific element in the chart.)
   b. Press the Delete key.
3. Create a treemap chart by completing the following steps:
   a. Select the range A2:C8.
   b. Click the Insert tab.
   c. Click the Insert Hierarchy Chart button.
   d. Click the *Treemap* option (first option).
4. Click the *Style 4* option in the Chart Styles group on the Chart Tools Design tab.
5. Click the Change Colors button in the Chart Styles group and then click the *Color 3* option in the *Colorful* section of the drop-down gallery.
6. Click the Add Chart Element button, position the mouse pointer over the *Legend* option, click the right-pointing triangle that displays, and then click the *None* option.
7. Click in the *Chart Title* placeholder text and then type Proportionate Departmental Expenses.
8. Change the chart height and width by completing the following steps:
   a. Make the entire chart active and then click the Chart Tools Format tab.
   b. Click in the *Shape Height* measurement box, type 5, and then press the Enter key.
   c. Click in the *Shape Width* measurement box, type 4, and then press the Enter key.
9. Move the chart so it is positioned below the cells containing data.
10. Click outside the chart to deselect it.
11. Center the worksheet horizontally and vertically.
12. Save, print, and then close **7-DIDeptCosts.xlsx**.

Check Your Work

You will use the PMT financial function to calculate payments and the FV financial function to find the future value of an investment.

Preview Finished Project

Tutorial

Using Financial Functions

Writing Formulas with Financial Functions

Excel provides a number of financial functions that can be used in formulas. Use financial functions to determine different aspects of a financial loan or investment, such as the payment amount, present value, future value, interest rate, and number of payment periods. Each financial function requires some of the variables listed below to return a result. Two such financial functions are the PMT function and FV function. The PMT function calculates the payment for a loan based on constant payments and a constant interest rate. The FV function calculates the future value of an investment. Financial functions use some of the following arguments:

- **Rate:** The rate is the interest rate for a payment period. The rate may need to be modified for the function to display the desired results. For example, most rate values are given as an APR (annual percentage rate), which is the percentage rate for one year, not a payment period. So a percentage rate may be given as 12% APR but if the payment period is a month, then the percentage rate for the function is 1%, not 12%. If a worksheet contains the annual percentage rate, enter the cell reference in the function argument and specify that it should be divided by 12 months. For example, if cell B6 contains the annual interest rate, enter *b6/12* as the Rate argument.

- **Nper:** The Nper is the number of payment periods in an investment. The Nper may also need to be modified depending on what information is provided. For example, if a loan duration is expressed in years but the payments are made each month, the Nper value needs to be adjusted accordingly. A five-year loan has an Nper of 60 (five years times 12 months in each year).

- **Pmt:** The Pmt is the payment amount for each period. This argument describes the payment amount for a period and is commonly expressed as a negative value because it is an outflow of cash. However, the Pmt value can be entered as a positive value if the present value (Pv) or future value (Fv) is entered as a negative value. Whether the Pmt value is positive or negative depends on who created the workbook. For example, a home owner lists the variable as outflow, while the lending institution lists it as inflow.

- **Pv:** The Pv is the present value of an investment, expressed in a lump sum. The Pv argument is generally the initial loan amount. For example, if a person is purchasing a new home, the Pv is the amount of money he or she borrowed to buy the home. Pv can be expressed as a negative value, which denotes it as an investment instead of a loan. For example, if a bank issues a loan to a home buyer, it enters the Pv value as negative because it is an outflow of cash.

- **Fv:** The Fv is the future value of an investment, expressed in a lump sum amount. The Fv argument is generally the loan amount plus the amount of interest paid during the loan. In the example of a home buyer, the Fv is the sum of payments, which includes both the principle and interest paid on the loan. In the example of a bank, the Fv is the total amount received after a loan has been paid off. Fv can also be expressed as either a positive or negative value depending on which side of the transaction is being reviewed.

Finding the Periodic Payments for a Loan

The PMT function finds the payment for a loan based on constant payments and a constant interest rate. In Project 5a, the PMT function will be used to determine monthly payments for equipment and a used van as well as monthly income from selling equipment. The formulas created with the PMT function will include Rate, Nper, and Pv arguments. The Nper argument is the number of payments that will be made on the loan or investment, Pv is the current value of amounts to be received or paid in the future, and Fv is the value of the loan or investment at the end of all periods.

Financial

To write the PMT function, click the Formulas tab, click the Financial button in the Function Library group, and then click the PMT function at the drop-down list. This displays the Function Arguments dialog box with options for inserting cell designations for Rate, Nper, and Pv. (These are the arguments displayed in bold formatting in the Function Arguments dialog box. The dialog box also contains the Fv and Type functions, which are dimmed.)

Project 5a Calculating Payments   **Part 1 of 2**

1. Open **RPReports.xlsx** and then save it with the name **7-RPReports**.
2. The owner of Real Photography is interested in purchasing a new developer and needs to determine monthly payments on three different models. Insert a formula that calculates monthly payments and then copy that formula by completing the following steps:
   a. Make cell E5 active.
   b. Click the Formulas tab.
   c. Click the Financial button in the Function Library group, scroll down the drop-down list, and then click *PMT*.

---

d. At the Function Arguments dialog box, type c5/12 in the *Rate* text box. (This tells Excel to divide the interest rate by 12 months.)

e. Press the Tab key. (This moves the insertion point to the *Nper* text box.)

f. Type d5. (This is the total number of months for the investment.)

g. Press the Tab key. (This moves the insertion point to the *Pv* text box.)

h. Type b5. (This is the purchase price of the developer.)

i. Click OK. (This closes the dialog box and inserts the monthly payment of *($316.98)* in cell E5. Excel displays the result of the PMT function as a negative number since the loan represents money going out of the company—a negative cash flow.)

j. Copy the formula in cell E5 down into cells E6 and E7.

3. The owner is interested in purchasing a used van for the company and wants an idea of what monthly payments would be at various terms and rates. Insert a formula that calculates monthly payments for a three-year loan at 5% interest by completing the following steps:

a. Make cell E12 active.

b. Make sure the Formulas tab is active.

c. Click the Financial button in the Function Library group, scroll down the drop-down list, and then click *PMT*.

d. At the Function Arguments dialog box, type c12/12 in the *Rate* text box. (This tells Excel to divide the interest rate by 12 months.)

e. Press the Tab key.

f. Type d12 in the *Nper* text box. (This is the total number of months for the investment.)

g. Press the Tab key.

h. Type b12 in the *Pv* text box.

i. Click OK. (This closes the dialog box and inserts the monthly payment of *($299.71)* in cell E12.)

j. Copy the formula in cell E12 down into the range E13:E15.

4. The owner has discovered that the interest rate for a used van will be 6.25% instead of 5%. Change the percentages in the range C12:C15 to 6.25%.

Term in Months	Monthly Payments
36	($299.71)
36	($449.56)
36	($599.42)
36	($749.27)

5. The owner is selling a camera and wants to determine the monthly payments for a two-year loan at 4.5% interest. Determine monthly payments on the camera (income to Real Photography) by completing the following steps:

   a. Make cell E20 active.

   b. Make sure the Formulas tab is active.

   c. Click the Financial button in the Function Library group, scroll down the drop-down list, and then click *PMT*.

   d. At the Function Arguments dialog box, type c20/12 in the *Rate* text box.

   e. Press the Tab key.

   f. Type d20 in the *Nper* text box.

   g. Press the Tab key.

   h. Type -b20 in the *Pv* text box. (Enter the *Pv* cell reference preceded by a hyphen because the sale of the camera represents an outflow of an asset. Excel displays the result of the PMT function as a positive number since the camera payments represent a positive cash inflow.)

   i. Click OK. (This closes the dialog box and inserts the monthly income of *$185.92* in cell E20.)

6. Save, print, and then close **7-RPReports.xlsx**.

Check Your Work

Finding the Future Value of a Series of Payments

The FV function calculates the future value of a series of equal payments or an annuity. Use this function to determine information such as how much money can be earned in an investment account with a specific interest rate and over a specific period of time.

Project 5b Finding the Future Value of an Investment   **Part 2 of 2**

1. Open **RPInvest.xlsx** and then save it with the name **7-RPInvest**.

2. The owner of Real Photography has decided to save the money needed to purchase a new developer and wants to compute how much money can be earned by investing in an investment account that returns 7.5% annual interest. The owner determines that $1,200 per month can be invested in the account for three years. Complete the following steps to determine the future value of the investment account:

   a. Make cell B6 active.

   b. Make sure the Formulas tab is active.

   c. Click the Financial button in the Function Library group.

   d. At the drop-down list that displays, scroll down the list and then click *FV*.

   e. At the Function Arguments dialog box, type b3/12 in the *Rate* text box.

   f. Press the Tab key.

   g. Type b4 in the *Nper* text box.

   h. Press the Tab key.

   i. Type b5 in the *Pmt* text box.

   j. Click OK. (This closes the dialog box and also inserts the future value of *$48,277.66* in cell B6.)

3. Save and then print **7-RPInvest.xlsx**.

4. The owner decides to determine the future return after two years. To do this, change the amount in cell B4 from *36* to *24* and then press the Enter key. (This recalculates the future investment amount in cell B6.)

5. Save, print, and then close **7-RPInvest.xlsx**.

Check Your Work

You will use the IF logical function to calculate sales bonuses, determine pass/fail grades based on averages, and identify discounts and discount amounts.

Preview Finished Project

Tutorial

Using Logical IF Functions

Writing Formulas with the Logical IF Function

A question that can be answered true or false is considered a *logical test*. The **IF function** can be used to create a logical test that performs a particular action if the answer is true (condition met) and another action if the answer is false (condition not met).

For example, an IF function can be used to write a formula that calculates a salesperson's bonus as 10% if he or she sells more than $99,999 worth of product and 0% if he or she does not sell more than $99,999 worth of product. When writing a formula with an IF function, think about the words *if* and *then*. For example, the formula written out for the bonus example would look like this:

> *If* the salesperson sells more than $99,999 of product, *then* the salesperson receives a bonus of 10%.

> *If* the salesperson does not sell more than $99,999 of product, *then* the salesperson receives a bonus of 0%.

When writing a formula with an IF function, use commas to separate the condition and the action. The formula for the bonus example would look like this: *=IF(sales>99999,sales*0.1,0)*. The formula contains three parts:

- the condition or logical test: *IF(sales>99999*
- the action taken if the condition or logical test is true: *sales*0.1*
- the action taken if the condition or logical test is false: *0*

In Project 6a, you will write a formula with cell references rather than cell data. You will write a formula with an IF function that determines the following:

> *If* the sales amount is greater than the quota amount, *then* the salesperson will receive a 15% bonus.

> *If* the sales amount is not greater than the quota amount, *then* the salesperson will not receive a bonus.

Written with cell references in the project, the formula looks like this: *=IF(C4>B4,C4*0.15,0)*. In this formula, the condition or logical test is whether the number in cell C4 is greater than the number in cell B4. If the condition is true and the number is greater, then the number in cell C4 is multiplied by 0.15 (providing a 15% bonus). If the condition is false and the number in cell C4 is less than the number in cell B4, then nothing happens (no bonus). Notice how commas are used to separate the logical test from the action.

1. Open **CMPReports.xlsx** and then save it with the name **7-CMPReports**.
2. Write a formula with the IF function that determines if a sales quota has been met and if it has, inserts the bonus of 15% of actual sales. (If the quota has not been met, the formula will insert a 0.) Write the formula by completing the following steps:
   a. Make cell D4 active.
   b. Type =if(c4>b4,c4*0.15,0) and then press the Enter key.

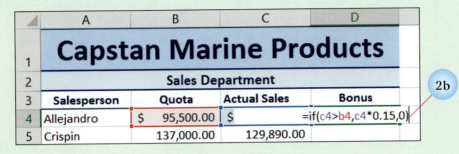

   c. Make cell D4 active and then use the fill handle to copy the formula into the range D5:D9.
3. Print the worksheet.
4. Revise the formula so it inserts a 20% bonus if the quota has been met by completing the following steps:
   a. Make cell D4 active.
   b. Click in the Formula bar, edit the formula so it displays as *=IF(C4>B4,C4*0.2,0)*, and then click the Enter button on the Formula bar.
   c. Copy the formula in cell D4 down into the range D5:D9.
   d. Make cell D4 active and then apply the Accounting format with a dollar symbol and two digits after the decimal point.
5. Save **7-CMPReports.xlsx**.

Check Your Work

Writing Formulas with an IF Function Using the Function Arguments Dialog Box

Logical

A formula containing an IF function can be typed directly into a cell or the Function Arguments dialog box can be used to help write the formula. To use the Function Arguments dialog box to write a formula with the IF function, click the Formulas tab, click the Logical button in the Function Library group, and then click *IF* at the drop-down list. This displays the Function Arguments dialog box, shown in Figure 7.12. The Function Arguments dialog box displays the information you will type in the three argument text boxes for Project 6b.

At the Function Arguments dialog box, click in the *Logical_test* text box and information about the Logical_test argument displays in the dialog box. In this text box, type the cell designation followed by what is evaluated. In the figure, the *Logical_test* text box contains *b14>599*, indicating that what is being evaluated is whether the amount in cell B14 is greater than $599. The *Value_if_true* text box contains *b14*0.95*, indicating that if the logical test is true, then the amount in cell B14 is multiplied by 0.95. (The discount for any product price greater than $599

Figure 7.12 Function Arguments Dialog Box

Insert in this text box the logical test (what is being evaluated).

Insert in this text box the action that will occur if the logical test is true.

Insert in this text box the action that will occur if the logical test is false.

is 5% and multiplying the product price by 0.95 determines the price after the 5% discount is applied.) The *Value_if_false* text box contains *b14*, indicating that if the logical test is false (the product price is not greater than $599), then the amount from cell B14 is simply inserted.

Project 6b   Writing a Formula with an IF Function Using the Function Arguments Dialog Box

Part 2 of 3

1. With **7-CMPReports.xlsx** open, insert a formula with an IF function using the Function Arguments dialog box by completing the following steps:
   a. Make cell C14 active.
   b. Click the Formulas tab.
   c. Click the Logical button in the Function Library group.
   d. Click *IF* at the drop-down list.
   e. At the Function Arguments dialog box, type b14>599 in the *Logical_test* text box and then press the Tab key.
   f. Type b14*0.95 in the *Value_if_true* text box and then press the Tab key.
   g. Type b14 in the *Value_if_false* text box.
   h. Click OK to close the Function Arguments dialog box.
2. Copy the formula in cell C14 down into the range C15:C26.
3. Apply the Accounting format with a dollar symbol and two digits after the decimal point to cell C14.
4. Save **7-CMPReports.xlsx**.

Check Your Work

Writing IF Statements Containing Text

When writing a formula with an IF statement, if text is to be inserted in a cell rather than a value, insert quotation marks around the text. For example, in Step 2 of Project 6c, you will write a formula with an IF function that looks like this when written out:

> *If* the student averages more than 79 on the quizzes, ***then*** the student passes.

> *If* the student does not average more than 79 on the quizzes, ***then*** the student fails.

In Project 6c, you will write the formula so the word *PASS* is inserted in a cell if the average of the new employee quizzes is greater than 79 and the word *FAIL* is inserted if the condition is not met. The formula would be *=IF(E31>79, "PASS", "FAIL")*. The quotation marks before and after *PASS* and *FAIL* identify the data as text rather than values.

The Function Arguments dialog box can be used to write a formula with an IF function that contains text. For example, in Step 3 of Project 6c, you will write a formula with an IF function using the Function Arguments dialog box that looks like this when written out:

> *If* the product price is greater than $599, ***then*** insert *YES*.

> *If* the product price is not greater than $599, ***then*** insert *NO*.

To create the formula in Step 3 using the Function Arguments dialog box, display the dialog box and then type *b14>599* in the *Logical_test* text box, *YES* in the *Value_if_true* text box, and *NO* in the *Value_if_false* text box. When you press the Enter key after typing *YES* in the *Value_if_true* text box, Excel automatically inserts quotation marks around the text. Excel will do the same thing for *NO* in the *Value_if_false* text box.

Project 6c Writing IF Statements Containing Text

Part 3 of 3

1. With **7-CMPReports.xlsx** open, insert quiz averages by completing the following steps:
   a. Make cell E31 active and then insert a formula that calculates the average of the test scores in the range B31:D31.
   b. Copy the formula in cell E31 down into the range E32:E35.
2. Write a formula with an IF function that inserts the word *PASS* if the quiz average is greater than 79 and inserts the word *FAIL* if the quiz average is not greater than 79. Write the formula by completing the following steps:
   a. Make cell F31 active.
   b. Type =if(e31>79,"PASS","FAIL") and then press the Enter key.

SUM	▾	⋮	✕ ✓	*fx*	=if(e31>79,"PASS","FAIL")	

◢	A	B	C	D	E	F	G
28							
29			New Employee Orientation				
30	Name	Quiz 1	Quiz 2	Quiz 3	Average	Grade	
31	Angelo	78	69	88		=if(e31>79,"PASS","FAIL")	
32	Cunningham	90	95	86	90		

2b

   c. Copy the formula in cell F31 down into the range F32:F35.

3. Write a formula with an IF function using the Function Arguments dialog box that inserts the word *YES* in the cell if the product price is greater than $599 and inserts the word *NO* if the price is not greater than $599. Write the formula by completing the following steps:
   a. Make cell D14 active.
   b. Click the Formulas tab.
   c. Click the Logical button in the Function Library group.
   d. Click *IF* at the drop-down list.
   e. Type b14>599 in the *Logical_test* text box and then press the Tab key.
   f. Type YES in the *Value_if_true* text box and then press the Tab key.
   g. Type NO in the *Value_if_false* text box.
   h. Click OK to close the Function Arguments dialog box.
   i. Copy the formula in cell D14 down into the range D15:D26.

4. Save and then print **7-CMPReports.xlsx**.
5. Press Ctrl + ` to turn on the display of formulas.
6. Print the worksheet again. (The worksheet will print on two pages.)
7. Press Ctrl + ` to turn off the display of formulas.
8. Save and then close **7-CMPReports.xlsx**.

Check Your Work

Chapter Summary

- A chart is a visual presentation of data. Excel provides 15 basic chart types: Area, Bar, Box & Whisker, Column, Combo, Histogram, Line, Pie, Radar, Stock, Sunburst, Surface, Treemap, X Y (Scatter), and Waterfall.

- To create a chart, select the cells, click the Insert tab, and then click the chart button in the Charts group. Click the Recommended Charts button in the Charts group and Excel will recommend a type of chart for the data.

- A chart is inserted in the same worksheet as the selected cells by default.

- Change the size of a chart using the mouse by dragging one of the sizing handles that display around the border of the chart. When changing the chart size, maintain the proportions of the chart by pressing and holding down the Shift key while dragging a sizing handle.

- Move a chart by positioning the mouse pointer on the chart border until the pointer displays with a four-headed arrow attached and then dragging with the mouse.

- The data in the cells used to create the chart are linked to the chart. Changes made to the data are reflected in the chart.

- Three buttons appear outside the right border of a selected chart. Use the Chart Elements button to insert or remove chart elements, use the Chart Styles button to apply chart styles, and use the Chart Filters button to isolate specific data in the chart.

- Print a chart by selecting it, displaying the Print backstage area, and then clicking the Print button.
- When a chart is inserted in a worksheet, the Chart Tools Design tab is active. Use options on this tab to add chart elements, change the chart type, specify a different layout or style, and change the location of the chart.
- Choose a chart style with options in the Chart Styles group on the Chart Tools Design tab or at the Change Chart Type dialog box.
- Click the Switch Row/Column button in the Data group to change what Excel uses to determine the grouping of data along the horizontal axis and legend.
- Use the Quick Layout button in the Chart Layouts group to change the chart layout.
- Use the Change Colors button to apply different colors to a chart.
- By default, a chart is inserted in the active worksheet. The chart can be moved to a new worksheet within the workbook with the *New sheet* option at the Move Chart dialog box.
- Add chart elements with the Add Chart Element button arrow in the Chart Layouts group on the Chart Tools Design tab.
- Move a chart element by selecting it and then dragging it with the mouse. Use the sizing handles that display around a chart element to change its size. Delete a chart element by selecting it and then pressing the Delete key or by right-clicking the selected element and then clicking *Delete* at the shortcut menu.
- Customize the formatting of a chart and chart elements with options on the Chart Tools Format tab. Use these options to identify specific elements in the chart for formatting, insert a shape, apply formatting to a shape, apply WordArt formatting to data in a chart, and arrange, align, and size a chart.
- Insert a shape by clicking it in the Insert Shapes group on the Chart Tools Format tab and then clicking or dragging in the chart.
- Excel provides additional formatting options at a formatting task pane. A formatting task pane displays at the right side of the screen; the name and the contents in the task pane vary depending on whether the entire chart or an element in the chart is selected. Display a task pane by clicking the chart or element in the chart and then clicking the Format Selection button in the Current Selection group on the Chart Tools Format tab.
- Change the size of a chart with the *Shape Height* and *Shape Width* measurement boxes on the Chart Tools Format tab or at the Format Chart Area task pane.
- To delete a chart in a worksheet, click the chart to select it and then press the Delete key. To delete a chart created in a separate sheet, position the mouse pointer on the chart sheet tab, click the right mouse button, and then click *Delete*.
- Write a formula with the PMT function to calculate the payment for a loan based on constant payments and a constant interest rate. Write a formula with the FV function to calculate the future value of an investment based on periodic constant payments and a constant interest rate.
- A logical test is a question that can be answered true or false. Use the IF function to create a logical test that performs one action if the answer is true (condition met) or another action if the answer is false (condition not met).

Commands Review

FEATURE	RIBBON TAB, GROUP	BUTTON	KEYBOARD SHORTCUT
Change Chart Type dialog box	Chart Tools Design, Type		
chart or chart element task pane	Chart Tools Format, Current Selection		
financial functions	Formulas, Function Library		
logical functions	Formulas, Function Library		
Move Chart dialog box	Chart Tools Design, Location		
recommended chart	Insert, Charts		Alt + F1
recommended chart in separate sheet			F11

Microsoft® Excel

Adding Visual Interest to Workbooks

Performance Objectives

Upon successful completion of Chapter 8, you will be able to:

1 Insert symbols and special characters

2 Insert, size, move, and format images

3 Insert screenshots

4 Draw, format, and copy shapes

5 Insert, format, and type text in text boxes

6 Insert and format SmartArt graphics

7 Insert and format WordArt

Precheck

Check your current skills to help focus your study.

Microsoft Excel includes a variety of features that you can use to enhance the appearance of a workbook. Some methods for adding visual appeal that you will learn in this chapter include inserting and modifying images, screenshots, shapes, text boxes, SmartArt, and WordArt.

SNAP

If you are a SNAP user, launch the Precheck and Tutorials from your Assignments page.

Data Files

Before beginning the projects, copy the EL1C8 folder to your storage medium and then make EL1C8 the active folder.

Inserting Symbols and Special Characters

Use the Symbol button on the Insert tab to insert symbols in a worksheet. Click the Symbol button in the Symbols group and the Symbol dialog box displays, as shown in Figure 8.1. At the Symbol dialog box, double-click a symbol and then click the Close button or click the symbol, click the Insert button, and then click the Close button. At the Symbol dialog box with the Symbols tab selected, additional symbols are available with different fonts. Change the font by clicking the *Font* option box arrow and then clicking a font at the drop-down list. Click the Special Characters tab at the Symbol dialog box and a list of special characters displays. Insert a special character by double-clicking a character and then clicking the Close button or by clicking the character, clicking the Insert button, and then clicking the Close button.

Figure 8.1 Symbol Dialog Box with Symbols Tab Selected

Click this tab to display a list of special characters.

Use the *Font* option box to select a font with a set of characters.

This section of the dialog box displays the most recently used symbols.

The *Character code* text box displays the code that can be entered at the keyboard to insert the symbol.

1. Open **SMFFinCon.xlsx** and then save it with the name **8-SMFFinCon**.
2. Insert a symbol by completing the following steps:
   a. Double-click in cell A2.
   b. Delete the *e* that displays at the end of *Qualite*.
   c. With the insertion point positioned immediately right of the *t* in *Qualit*, click the Insert tab.
   d. Click the Symbol button in the Symbols group.
   e. At the Symbol dialog box, scroll down the list box and then click the *é* symbol (located in approximately the ninth through eleventh rows). (You can also type *00E9* in the *Character code* text box to select the symbol.)
   f. Click the Insert button and then click the Close button.

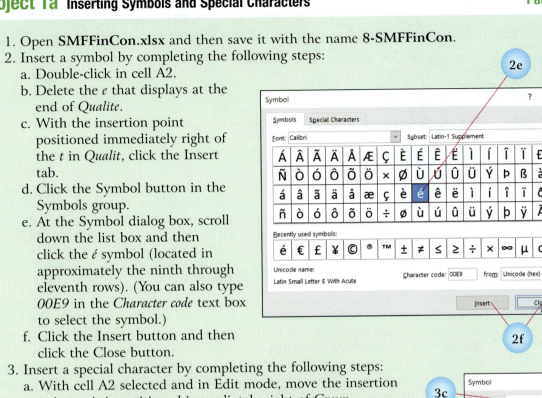

3. Insert a special character by completing the following steps:
   a. With cell A2 selected and in Edit mode, move the insertion point so it is positioned immediately right of *Group*.
   b. Click the Symbol button in the Symbols group.
   c. At the Symbol dialog box, click the Special Characters tab.
   d. Double-click the ® *Registered* symbol (tenth option from the top).
   e. Click the Close button.
4. Insert a symbol by completing the following steps:
   a. With cell A2 selected and in Edit mode, move the insertion point so it is positioned immediately left of the *Q* in *Qualité*.
   b. Click the Symbol button in the Symbols group.
   c. At the Symbol dialog box, click the *Font* option box arrow and then click *Wingdings* at the drop-down list. (You will need to scroll down the list to display this option.)
   d. Click the ❖ symbol (located in approximately the fifth or sixth row). (You can also type *118* in the *Character code* text box to select the symbol.)
   e. Click the Insert button and then click the Close button.
5. Click in cell A3.
6. Save **8-SMFFinCon.xlsx**.

Check Your Work

Figure 8.2 Picture Tools Format Tab

Inserting an Image

Tutorial

Inserting an Image

Pictures

Insert an image, such as a picture or clip art image, in an Excel workbook with buttons in the Illustrations group on the Insert tab. Click the Pictures button to display the Insert Picture dialog box with options for inserting an image from a folder on the computer or a removable drive. Or click the Online Pictures button and search for images online. When an image is inserted in a worksheet, the Picture Tools Format tab displays, as shown in Figure 8.2.

Customizing and Formatting an Image

Tutorial

Modifying Images

Compress Pictures

Quick Steps

Insert an Image
1. Click Insert tab.
2. Click Pictures button.
3. Navigate to folder.
4. Double-click image.

Use buttons in the Adjust group on the Picture Tools Format tab to remove unwanted parts of an image, correct the image brightness and contrast, change the image color, apply artistic effects to the image, change to a different image, and restore the original image formatting. Use the Compress Pictures button in the Adjust group to compress the size of an image file and reduce the amount of space the image requires on the storage medium. Use buttons in the Picture Styles group to apply a predesigned style to the image, change the image border, or apply other effects to the image. With options in the Arrange group, position the image on the page, specify how text will wrap around the image, align the image with other elements in the worksheet, and rotate the image. Use the Crop button in the Size group to remove any unwanted parts of the image and use the *Shape Height* and *Shape Width* measurement boxes to specify the image size.

In addition to options at the Picture Tools Format tab, options at the shortcut menu can be used to format an image. Display this menu by right-clicking the image. Use options at the shortcut menu to change the image, insert a caption, choose text wrapping around the image, size and position the image, and display the Format Picture task pane.

Sizing and Moving an Image

Change the size of an image with the *Shape Height* and *Shape Width* measurement boxes in the Size group on the Picture Tools Format tab or with the sizing handles that display around the selected image. To change size with a sizing handle, position the mouse pointer on a sizing handle until the pointer turns into a double-headed arrow and then drag in or out to decrease or increase the size of the image. Use the middle sizing handles at the left and right sides of the image to make the image wider or thinner. Use the middle sizing handles at the top and bottom of the image to make the image taller or shorter. Use the sizing handles at the corners of the image to change both the width and height at the same time. Press and hold down the Shift key while dragging a sizing handle to maintain the proportions of the image.

Move an image by positioning the mouse pointer on the image border until the pointer displays with a four-headed arrow attached and then dragging the image to the new location. Rotate the image by positioning the mouse pointer on the white round rotation handle until the pointer displays as a circular arrow. Click and hold down the left mouse button, drag in the desired direction, and then release the mouse button.

1. With **8-SMFFinCon.xlsx** open, insert an image by completing the following steps:
   a. Click the Insert tab and then click the Pictures button in the Illustrations group.
   b. At the Insert Picture dialog box, navigate to the EL1C8 folder on your storage medium and then double-click *WallStreet.jpg*.
2. Change the size of the image by clicking in the *Shape Height* measurement box in the Size group on the Picture Tools Format tab, typing 2, and then pressing the Enter key.
3. Remove the yellow background from the image by completing the following steps:
   a. Click the Remove Background button in the Adjust group.
   b. Position the mouse pointer on the middle sizing handle at the top of the image until the pointer displays as an up-and-down-pointing arrow.
   c. Click and hold down the left mouse button, drag the border up to the top of the image, and then release the mouse button.
   d. Position the mouse pointer on the middle sizing handle at the bottom of the image until the pointer displays as an up-and-down-pointing arrow.
   e. Click and hold down the left mouse button, drag the border up 0.25 inch, and then release the mouse button.
   f. Click the Keep Changes button in the Close group on the Background Removal tab.

4. Change the color by clicking the Color button in the Adjust group and then clicking the *Blue, Accent color 1 Light* option (second column, third row in the *Recolor* section).
5. Apply a correction by clicking the Corrections button and then clicking the *Brightness: +20% Contrast: +20%* option (fourth column, fourth row in the *Brightness/Contrast* section).
6. Apply an artistic effect by clicking the Artistic Effects button and then clicking the *Glow Edges* option (last option in the drop-down gallery).

7. Move the image by completing the following steps:
   a. Position the mouse pointer on the image (displays with a four-headed arrow attached).
   b. Click and hold down the left mouse button, drag the image to the upper left corner of the worksheet, and then release the mouse button.
8. Save and then print **8-SMFFinCon.xlsx**.

Check Your Work

Formatting an Image at the Format Picture Task Pane

In addition to the Picture Tools Format tab, the Format Picture task pane provides options for formatting an image. Click the Picture Styles group task pane launcher or the Size group task pane launcher and the Format Picture task pane displays at the right side of the screen. Click the Picture Styles group task pane launcher and the task pane displays with the Effects icon selected; click the Size group task pane launcher and the Size & Properties icon is selected. Two other icons are also available in this task pane: the Fill & Line icon and the Picture icon. The formatting options may need to be expanded. For example, click *Size* with the Size & Properties icon selected and options for changing the size of the image display. Close the task pane by clicking the Close button in the upper right corner.

Tutorial

Inserting an Online Image

 Online Pictures

Quick Steps

Insert an Online Image
1. Click Insert tab.
2. Click Online Pictures button.
3. Type search word or topic.
4. Press Enter.
5. Double-click image.

Inserting an Online Image

Use the Bing Image Search feature to search for images online. To use this feature, click the Insert tab and then click the Online Pictures button in the Illustrations group. This displays the Insert Pictures window, shown in Figure 8.3. Click in the search text box, type the search term or topic, and then press the Enter key. Images that match the search term or topic display in the window. To insert an image, click the image and then click the Insert button or double-click the image. This downloads the image to the document. Customize the image with options and buttons on the Picture Tools Format tab.

Figure 8.3 Insert Pictures Window

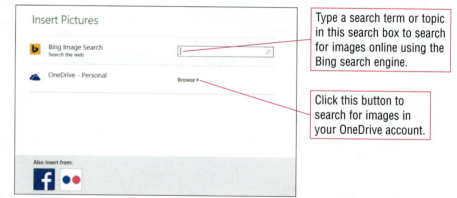

Type a search term or topic in this search box to search for images online using the Bing search engine.

Click this button to search for images in your OneDrive account.

Project 1c Inserting and Formatting an Image

Part 3 of 5

1. With **8-SMFFinCon.xlsx** open, delete the Wall Street sign image by clicking the image and then pressing the Delete key.
2. Insert a different image by completing the following steps:
   a. Make cell A1 active.
   b. Click the Insert tab and then click the Online Pictures button in the Illustrations group.

c. At the Insert Pictures window, type stock market clip art in the search box and then press the Enter key.

d. Double-click the graph image shown below and to the right. (If this image is not available online, click the Pictures button on the Insert tab. At the Insert Picture dialog box, navigate to your EL1C8 folder and then double-click *StockMarket.png*.)

3. Display the Format Picture task pane with the Size & Properties icon selected by clicking the Size group task pane launcher on the Picture Tools Format tab.

4. If necessary, click *Size* in the task pane to display the sizing options.

5. Change the height of the image by selecting the current measurement in the *Height* measurement box, typing 1.65, and then pressing the Enter key. (The width automatically changes to maintain the proportions of the image.)

6. Change the properties of the image by clicking *Properties* to expand the options and then clicking the *Move and size with cells* option. (With this option selected, changing the size of the row also changes the size of the image.)

7. Make a correction to the image by completing the following steps:
   a. Click the Picture icon at the top of the task pane.
   b. Click *Picture Corrections* to expand the options.
   c. Select the current percentage in the *Brightness* text box and then type -25.
   d. Select the current percentage in the *Contrast* text box, type 45, and then press the Enter key.

8. Close the Format Picture task pane by clicking the Close button in the upper right corner.

9. Click outside the image to deselect it.

10. Increase the height of row 1 to 126.00 points and notice that the image size increases with the row height.

11. Save **8-SMFFinCon.xlsx**.

Check Your Work

Tutorial

Creating and
Inserting a
Screenshot

Screenshot

Quick Steps

Insert a Screenshot
1. Open workbook.
2. Open another file.
3. Display information.
4. Make workbook active.
5. Click Insert tab.
6. Click Screenshot button.
7. Click window at drop-down list.
OR
1. Click Screenshot button and then *Screen Clipping*.
2. Drag to specify capture area.

Creating and Inserting a Screenshot

The Illustrations group on the Insert tab contains a Screenshot button that can be used to capture all or part of the contents of a screen as an image. This is useful for capturing information from a web page or a file in another program. To capture the entire screen, display a web page or open a file from a program, make Excel active, and then open a workbook or blank workbook. Click the Insert tab, click the Screenshot button, and then click the screen thumbnail at the drop-down list. The currently active worksheet does not display as a thumbnail at the drop-down list—only any other open file or program displays. If no other file or program is open, the Windows desktop displays. Click the thumbnail at the drop-down list and the screenshot is inserted as an image in the open workbook, the image is selected, and the Picture Tools Format tab is active. Use buttons on this tab to customize the screenshot image.

A screenshot can also be made of a specific portion of the screen by clicking the *Screen Clipping* option at the Screenshot button drop-down list. Click this option and the open web page, file, or Windows desktop displays in a dimmed manner and the mouse pointer displays as crosshairs (a plus symbol [+]). Using the mouse, draw a border around the specific area of the screen to be captured. The area identified is inserted in the workbook as an image, the image is selected, and the Picture Tools Format tab is active.

Project 1d Inserting and Formatting a Screenshot

Part 4 of 5

1. With **8-SMFFinCon.xlsx** open, make sure that no other programs are open.
2. Open Word and then open **SMFProfile.docx** from your EL1C8 folder.
3. Click the Excel button on the taskbar.
4. Insert a screenshot of the table in the Word document by completing the following steps:
   a. Click the Insert tab.
   b. Click the Screenshot button in the Illustrations group and then click *Screen Clipping* at the drop-down list.
   c. When **SMFProfile.docx** displays in a dimmed manner, position the mouse crosshairs in the upper left corner of the table, click and hold down the left mouse button, drag down to the lower right corner of the table, and then release the mouse button. (This creates a screenshot of the entire table.)
5. With the screenshot image inserted in **8-SMFFinCon.xlsx**, make the following changes:
   a. Click in the *Shape Width* measurement box in the Size group on the Picture Tools Format tab, type 3.7, and then press the Enter key.

b. Click the Corrections button and then click the *Sharpen: 25%* option (fourth option in the *Sharpen/Soften* section).

c. Click the Corrections button and then click the *Brightness: 0% (Normal) Contrast: -40%* (third column, first row in the *Brightness/Contrast* section).

d. Using the mouse, drag the screenshot image one row below the data in row 10.

6. Make cell A4 active.

7. Save **8-SMFFinCon.xlsx**.

8. Click the Word button on the taskbar, close **SMFProfile.docx**, and then close Word.

Check Your Work

Tutorial

Inserting a Shape

Tutorial

Formatting a Shape

 Shapes

Quick Steps

Insert a Shape
1. Click Insert tab.
2. Click Shapes button.
3. Click desired shape at drop-down list.
4. Click or drag in worksheet.

Copy a Shape
1. Select shape.
2. Click Copy button.
3. Position insertion point in new location.
4. Click Paste button.
OR
1. Select shape.
2. Press and hold down Ctrl key.
3. Drag shape to new location.

Inserting and Formatting a Shape

Chapter 7 covered how to insert shapes in a chart with options on the Chart Tools Format tab. Shapes can also be inserted in a worksheet with the Shapes button in the Illustrations group on the Insert tab. Use the Shapes button to draw shapes in a worksheet, including lines, basic shapes, block arrows, flow chart symbols, callouts, stars, and banners. Click a shape and the mouse pointer displays as crosshairs. Click in the worksheet or position the crosshairs where the shape is to begin, click and hold down the left mouse button, drag to create the shape, and then release the mouse button. Click or drag in the worksheet and the shape is inserted and the Drawing Tools Format tab, shown in Figure 8.4, becomes active. Use options and buttons on this tab to choose a shape, apply a style to a shape, arrange a shape, and change the size of a shape.

Choose a shape in the *Lines* section of the Shapes button drop-down list and the shape that is drawn is considered a line drawing. Choose an option in another section of the drop-down list and the shape drawn is considered an enclosed object. When drawing an enclosed object, maintain the proportions of the shape by pressing and holding down the Shift key while dragging with the mouse. Text can be typed in an enclosed object and then formatted using buttons in the WordArt Styles group (or options on the Home tab).

Copy a shape in a worksheet by selecting the shape and then clicking the Copy button in the Clipboard group on the Home tab. Make active the cell where the shape is to be copied and then click the Paste button. A shape can also be copied by pressing and holding down the Ctrl key while dragging the shape to the new location.

Figure 8.4 Drawing Tools Format Tab

Chapter 8 | Adding Visual Interest to Workbooks **219**

1. With **8-SMFFinCon.xlsx** open, create the larger arrow shown in Figure 8.5 by completing the following steps:
   a. Click the Insert tab.
   b. Click the Shapes button in the Illustrations group and then click the *Up Arrow* shape (third column, first row in the *Block Arrows* section).
   c. Position the mouse pointer (displays as crosshairs) near the upper left corner of cell D1 and then click the left mouse button. (This inserts the arrow in the worksheet.)

   d. Click in the *Shape Height* measurement box and then type 3.7.
   e. Click in the *Shape Width* measurement box, type 2.1, and then press the Enter key.
   f. If necessary, drag the arrow so it is positioned as shown in Figure 8.5. (To drag the arrow, position the mouse pointer on the border of the selected arrow until the pointer displays with a four-headed arrow attached, click and hold down the left mouse button, drag the arrow to the new position, and then release the mouse button.)
   g. Click the More Shape Styles button in the Shape Styles group on the Drawing Tools Format tab and then click the *Intense Effect - Blue, Accent 1* option (second column, last row in the *Theme Styles* section).
   h. Click the Shape Effects button in the Shape Styles group, point to *Glow*, and then click the *Orange, 11 pt glow, Accent color 2* option (second column, third row in the *Glow Variations* section).

2. Insert text in the arrow by completing the following steps:
   a. With the arrow selected, type McGuire Mutual Shares 5.33%.
   b. Select the text you just typed (*McGuire Mutual Shares 5.33%*).
   c. Click the More WordArt Styles button in the WordArt Styles group and then click the *Fill - White, Outline - Accent 2, Hard Shadow - Accent 2* option (fourth column, third row).
   d. Press Ctrl + E to center the text.

3. With the arrow selected, copy it by completing the following steps:
   a. Press and hold down the Ctrl key.
   b. Position the mouse pointer on the arrow border until the pointer displays with a square box and plus symbol attached.
   c. Click and hold down the left mouse button and drag to the right so the outline of the arrow is positioned at the right side of the existing arrow.
   d. Release the mouse button and then release the Ctrl key.

4. Format the second arrow by completing the following steps:
   a. With the second arrow selected, click in the *Shape Height* measurement box on the Drawing Tools Format tab and then type 2.
   b. Click in the *Shape Width* measurement box, type 1.6, and then press the Enter key.
   c. Select the text *McGuire Mutual Shares 5.33%* and then type SR Linus Fund 0.22%.
   d. Drag the arrow so it is positioned as shown in Figure 8.5.

5. Change to landscape orientation. (Make sure the cells containing the data, screenshot image, and arrows will print on the same page.)

6. Save, print, and then close **8-SMFFinCon.xlsx**.

Check Your Work

Figure 8.5 Project 1e

<table>
<tr><td>**Project 2**</td><td>**Insert an Image and Text Box in a Division Sales Workbook**</td><td>**1 Part**</td></tr>
</table>

Project 2 **Insert an Image and Text Box in a Division Sales Workbook** **1 Part**

You will open a division sales workbook and then insert, move, and size an image. You will also insert a text box and then format the text.

Preview Finished Project

Tutorial

Inserting and Modifying Text Boxes

Text Box

Quick Steps

Draw a Text Box
1. Click Insert tab.
2. Click Text Box button.
3. Click or drag in worksheet to create text box.

Inserting and Modifying Text Boxes

Use the Text Box button on the Insert tab to draw a text box in a worksheet. To draw a text box, click the Insert tab and then click the Text Box button in the Text group. This causes the mouse pointer to display as a long, thin, crosslike pointer. Position the pointer in the worksheet and then drag to create the text box. When a text box is selected, the Drawing Tools Format tab displays with options for customizing it.

Click a text box to select it and a dashed border and sizing handles display around it. To delete the text box, click the border again to change the dashed lines to solid lines and then press the Delete key.

Project 2 **Inserting and Customizing an Image and a Text Box** **Part 1 of 1**

1. Open **SPDivSales.xlsx** and then save it with the name **8-SPDivSales**.
2. Make the following changes to the bird image:
   a. Click the image to select it.
   b. Click the Picture Tools Format tab.
   c. Click the Rotate button in the Arrange group and then click *Flip Horizontal* at the drop-down list.
3. Insert and format an image by completing the following steps:
   a. Click in cell A1 outside the bird image.
   b. Click the Insert tab.
   c. Click the Pictures button in the Illustrations group.
   d. At the Insert Picture dialog box, navigate to the EL1C8 folder on your storage medium and then double-click *Ocean.jpg*.
   e. With the image selected, click the Send Backward button in the Arrange group on the Picture Tools Format tab.
   f. Use the sizing handles that display around the image to move and size it so it fills cell A1, as shown in Figure 8.6.
   g. If necessary, click the bird image and then drag it so it is positioned as shown in Figure 8.6.
4. Save **8-SPDivSales.xlsx**.

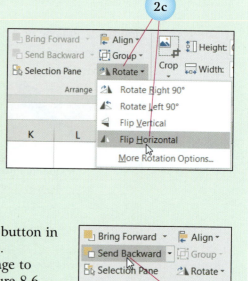

222   Excel Level 1 | Unit 2   Chapter 8 | Adding Visual Interest to Workbooks

5. Draw a text box by completing the following steps:
   a. Click the Insert tab.
   b. Click the Text Box button in the Text group.
   c. Drag into cell A1 to draw a text box the approximate size and shape shown at the right.
6. Format the text box by completing the following steps:
   a. Click the Drawing Tools Format tab.
   b. Click the Shape Fill button arrow in the Shape Styles group and then click *No Fill* at the drop-down gallery.
   c. Click the Shape Outline button arrow in the Shape Styles group and then click *No Outline* at the drop-down gallery.
7. Insert text in the text box by completing the following steps:
   a. With the text box selected, click the Home tab.
   b. Click the *Font* option box arrow and then click *Lucida Calligraphy* at the drop-down gallery. (Scroll down the gallery to display this font.)
   c. Click the *Font Size* option box arrow and then click *32* at the drop-down gallery.
   d. Click the Font Color button arrow and then click *White, Background 1* (first column, first row in the *Theme Colors* section).
   e. Type Seabird Productions.
8. Move the text box so the text is positioned in cell A1 as shown in Figure 8.6.
9. Save, print, and then close **8-SPDivSales.xlsx**.

Check Your Work

Figure 8.6 Project 2

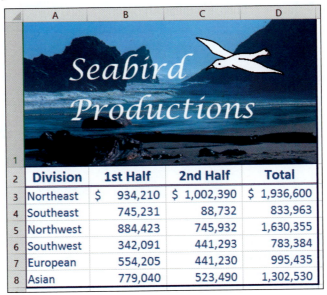

Project 3   Insert and Format SmartArt Graphics in a Company Sales Workbook   4 Parts

You will open a workbook that contains two company sales worksheets. You will insert and format a SmartArt cycle graphic in one worksheet and a SmartArt relationship graphic in the other. You will also create and format WordArt text.

Preview Finished Project

Tutorial

Inserting a
SmartArt Graphic

 SmartArt

ⓠuick Steps

Insert a SmartArt Graphic
1. Click Insert tab.
2. Click SmartArt button.
3. Double-click graphic.

Text Pane

💡 **Hint** Generally, you would use a SmartArt graphic to represent text and a chart to represent numbers.

Inserting a SmartArt Graphic

Use the SmartArt feature included in Excel to insert graphics, such as diagrams and organizational charts, in a worksheet. SmartArt offers a variety of predesigned graphics that are available at the Choose a SmartArt Graphic dialog box, shown in Figure 8.7. Display this dialog box by clicking the Insert tab and then clicking the SmartArt button in the Illustrations group. At the dialog box, *All* is selected in the left panel and all the available predesigned graphics display in the middle panel. Use the scroll bar at the right side of the middle panel to scroll down the list of graphic choices. Click a graphic in the middle panel and the name of the graphic displays in the right panel along with a description of the graphic type. SmartArt includes graphics for presenting lists of data; showing data processes, cycles, and relationships; and presenting data in a matrix or pyramid. Double-click a graphic in the middle panel of the dialog box and the graphic is inserted in the worksheet.

Entering Data in a SmartArt Graphic

Some SmartArt graphics are designed to include text. Type text in a graphic by selecting a shape in the graphic and then typing text in the shape or display a text pane and then type text in the pane. Display the text pane by clicking the Text Pane button in the Create Graphic group on the SmartArt Tools Design tab. Turn off the display of the pane by clicking the Text Pane button or clicking the Close button in the upper right corner of the pane.

Figure 8.7 Choose a SmartArt Graphic Dialog Box

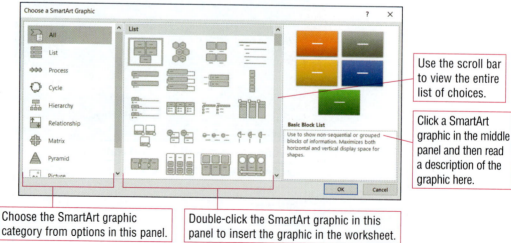

Sizing, Moving, and Deleting a SmartArt Graphic

Increase or decrease the size of a SmartArt graphic by dragging one of the sizing handles that display around the selected graphic. Use the corner sizing handles to increase or decrease the height and width at the same time. Use the middle sizing handles to increase or decrease the height or width of the SmartArt graphic.

To move a SmartArt graphic, select it and then position the mouse pointer on the graphic border until the pointer displays with a four-headed arrow attached. Click and hold down the left mouse button, drag the graphic to the new position, and then release the mouse button. Delete a graphic by selecting it and then pressing the Delete key.

Project 3a Inserting, Moving, and Sizing a SmartArt Graphic in a Worksheet   **Part 1 of 4**

1. Open **EPCoSales.xlsx** and then save it with the name **8-EPCoSales**.
2. Create the SmartArt graphic shown in Figure 8.8. To begin, click the Insert tab.
3. Click the SmartArt button in the Illustrations group.
4. At the Choose a SmartArt Graphic dialog box, click *Cycle* in the left panel.
5. Double-click *Radial Cycle* in the middle panel.
6. If the text pane is not open, click the Text Pane button in the Create Graphic group. (The text pane will display at the left side of the SmartArt graphic.)
7. With the insertion point positioned after the top bullet in the text pane, type Evergreen Products.
8. Click in the *[Text]* placeholder below *Evergreen Products* and then type Seattle.
9. Click in the next *[Text]* placeholder and then type Olympia.
10. Click in the next *[Text]* placeholder and then type Portland.
11. Click in the next *[Text]* placeholder and then type Spokane.
12. Click the Text Pane button to turn off the display of the text pane.
13. Drag the SmartArt graphic so it is positioned as shown in Figure 8.8. To drag the graphic, position the mouse pointer on the graphic border until the pointer displays with a four-headed arrow attached. Click and hold down the left mouse button, drag the graphic to the new position, and then release the mouse button.
14. Use the sizing handles that display around the SmartArt graphic to increase or decrease the size so it displays as shown in Figure 8.8. Note: The color of the graphic will be changed in Project 3b.
15. Save **8-EPCoSales.xlsx**.

Check Your Work

Figure 8.8 Projects 3a and 3b

	A	B	C	D	E	F	G	H	I
1	**Evergreen Products**								
2	**2018 Company Sales**								
3	**Division**	**First Half**	**Second Half**	**Total Sales**					
4	Seattle	$ 1,250,360	$ 1,345,200	$ 2,595,560					
5	Spokane	905,250	987,550	1,892,800					
6	Portland	1,125,000	1,200,500	2,325,500					
7	Olympia	705,610	789,450	1,495,060					
8	Total	3,986,220	4,322,700	8,308,920					
9									

Changing the SmartArt Graphic Design

Hint To restore the SmartArt default layout and color, click the Reset Graphic button in the Reset group on the SmartArt Tools Design tab.

Double-click a SmartArt graphic at the Choose a SmartArt Graphic dialog box and the graphic is inserted in the worksheet and the SmartArt Tools Design tab is active. Use options and buttons on this tab to add objects, change the graphic layout, apply a style to the graphic, and reset the original formatting of the graphic.

Project 3b Changing the SmartArt Graphic Design

Part 2 of 4

1. With **8-EPCoSales.xlsx** open, make sure the SmartArt Tools Design tab is active and then click the *Spokane* circle shape in the graphic to select it.
2. Click the Right to Left button in the Create Graphic group. (This switches *Olympia* and *Spokane*.)
3. Click the More SmartArt Styles button in the SmartArt Styles group and then click the *Polished* option at the drop-down list (first column, first row in the *3-D* section).

4. Click the Change Colors button in the SmartArt Styles group, scroll down the drop-down gallery, and then click the *Gradient Range - Accent 6* option (third option in the *Accent 6* section).
5. Click outside the SmartArt graphic to deselect it.
6. Change to landscape orientation. (Make sure the graphic fits on the first page.)
7. Save **8-EPCoSales.xlsx** and then print the Total Sales worksheet.

Check Your Work

Changing the SmartArt Graphic Formatting

Click the SmartArt Tools Format tab and options display for formatting a SmartArt graphic. Use buttons on this tab to insert and customize shapes; apply a shape style; apply WordArt styles; and specify the position, alignment, rotation, wrapping style, height, and width of a graphic.

Project 3c Changing the SmartArt Graphic Formatting   **Part 3 of 4**

1. With **8-EPCoSales.xlsx** open, click the Seattle Sales worksheet tab.
2. Create the SmartArt graphic shown in Figure 8.9. To begin, click the Insert tab and then click the SmartArt button in the Illustrations group.
3. At the Choose a SmartArt Graphic dialog box, click *Relationship* in the left panel and then double-click *Gear* in the middle panel.

4. Click in the *[Text]* placeholder in the bottom gear and then type Quality Products.
5. Click in the *[Text]* placeholder in the left gear and then type Customized Plans.
6. Click in the *[Text]* placeholder in the top gear and then type Exemplary Service.
7. Click inside the SmartArt graphic border but outside any specific shape.
8. Click the More SmartArt Styles button in the SmartArt Styles group and then click the *Inset* option (second column, first row in the *3-D* section).
9. Click the Change Colors button in the SmartArt Styles group and then click the *Gradient Loop - Accent 6* option (fourth option in the *Accent 6* section).
10. Click the SmartArt Tools Format tab.
11. Click in the *Shape Height* measurement box in the Size group and then type 4.
12. Click in the *Shape Width* measurement box, type 4.5, and then press the Enter key.

13. Click the bottom gear to select it.

14. Click the Shape Fill button arrow in the Shape Styles group and then click the *Green, Accent 6, Darker 50%* option (last column, last row in the *Theme Colors* section).
15. Click the top gear to select it.
16. Click the Shape Fill button arrow and then click the *Green, Accent 6, Darker 25%* option (last column, fifth row in the *Theme Colors* section).
17. Change to landscape orientation.
18. Move the SmartArt graphic so it fits on the first page and displays as shown in Figure 8.9.
19. Click outside the SmartArt graphic to deselect it.
20. Save **8-EPCoSales.xlsx** and then print the Seattle Sales worksheet.

Check Your Work

Figure 8.9 Project 3c

Creating, Sizing, and Moving WordArt

Use the WordArt feature to distort or modify text so it conforms to a variety of shapes. This is useful for creating company logos and headings. Change the font, style, and alignment of text with WordArt and use fill patterns and colors, customize border lines, and add shadow and three-dimensional effects.

To insert WordArt in an Excel worksheet, click the Insert tab, click the Insert WordArt button in the Text group, and then click an option at the drop-down list. This inserts the text *Your text here* in the worksheet, formatted in the WordArt option selected at the drop-down list. Type text and then use the options and buttons on the Drawing Tools Format tab to format the WordArt.

Creating WordArt

Insert WordArt

Quick Steps

Create WordArt
1. Click Insert tab.
2. Click Insert WordArt button.
3. Click WordArt style at drop-down list.
4. Type text.

WordArt text inserted in a worksheet is surrounded by white sizing handles. Use these sizing handles to change the height and width of the WordArt text. To move WordArt text, position the mouse pointer on the border of the WordArt text box until the pointer displays with a four-headed arrow attached and then drag the outline of the text box to the new location.

Make WordArt text conform to a variety of shapes using the *Transform* option from the Text Effects button drop-down list. Apply a transform shape and a small yellow circle displays below the WordArt text. Use this circle to change the slant of the WordArt text.

💡**Hint** To remove a WordArt style from text and retain the text, click the More Styles button in the WordArt Styles group on the Drawing Tools Format tab and then click *Clear WordArt.*

Project 3d   Inserting and Formatting WordArt

Part 4 of 4

1. With **8-EPCoSales.xlsx** open, click the Total Sales worksheet tab.
2. Make cell A1 active and then press the Delete key. (This removes the text from the cell.)
3. Increase the height of row 1 to 138 points.
4. Click the Insert tab.
5. Click the Insert WordArt button in the Text group and then click the *Fill - Black, Text 1, Outline - Background 1, Hard Shadow - Background 1* option (first column, third row).
6. Type Evergreen, press the Enter key, and then type Products.
7. Click the WordArt border to change it to a solid line (not a dashed line).
8. Click the Text Fill button arrow in the WordArt Styles group and then click the *Green, Accent 6, Darker 50%* option (last column, last row in the *Theme Colors* section).
9. Click the Text Effects button in the WordArt Styles group, point to *Transform*, and then click the *Can Up* option (third column, fourth row in the *Warp* section).
10. Position the mouse pointer (turns into a white arrow) on the small yellow circle immediately below the *d* in *Products*, click and hold down the left mouse button, drag up approximately 0.25 inch, and then release the mouse button. (This changes the slant of the text.)
11. Drag the WordArt text so it is positioned in cell A1.
12. If necessary, size the SmartArt graphic and position it so it prints on one page with the data.
13. Click the Seattle Sales worksheet tab and then complete steps similar to those in Steps 2 through 11 to insert *Evergreen Products* as WordArt in cell A1.
14. Make sure the SmartArt graphic fits on one page with the data. If necessary, decrease the size of the graphic.
15. Save **8-EPCoSales.xlsx** and then print both worksheets.
16. Close **8-EPCoSales.xlsx**.

Check Your Work

Chapter Summary

- Insert symbols with options at the Symbol dialog box with the Symbols tab or Special Characters tab selected.

- Use buttons in the Illustrations group on the Insert tab to insert an image such as a picture, clip art image, screenshot, shape, or SmartArt graphic.

- Insert an image by clicking the Insert tab, clicking the Pictures button in the Illustrations group, and then double-clicking an image at the Insert Picture dialog box.

- Insert an image in a worksheet and the Picture Tools Format tab is active. It provides options for adjusting the image, applying preformatted styles to the image, and arranging and sizing the image.

- Change the size of an image with the *Shape Height* and *Shape Width* measurement boxes in the Size group on the Picture Tools Format tab or with the sizing handles that display around a selected image.

- Move an image by positioning the mouse pointer on the image border until the pointer displays with a four-headed arrow attached and then dragging the image to the new location.

- Insert an online image with options at the Insert Pictures window. Display this window by clicking the Insert tab and then clicking the Online Pictures button in the Illustrations group.

- Use the Screenshot button in the Illustrations group on the Insert tab to capture all or part of the contents of a screen.

- To draw a shape in a workbook, click the Insert tab, click the Shapes button in the Illustrations group, and then click a shape at the drop-down list. Click or drag in the worksheet to insert the shape. To maintain the proportions of the shape, press and hold down the Shift key while dragging in the worksheet.

- Copy a shape by using the Copy and Paste buttons in the Clipboard group on the Home tab or by pressing and holding down the Ctrl key while dragging the shape.

- Draw a text box in a worksheet by clicking the Insert tab, clicking the Text Box button in the Text group, and then clicking or dragging in the worksheet. Use options on the Drawing Tools Format tab to format and customize the text box.

- Insert a SmartArt graphic in a worksheet by clicking the Insert tab, clicking the SmartArt button in the Illustrations group, and then double-clicking a graphic at the Choose a SmartArt Graphic dialog box. Customize a SmartArt graphic with options on the SmartArt Tools Design tab and SmartArt Tools Format tab.

- Use WordArt to create, distort, and modify text and to make it conform to a variety of shapes. Insert WordArt in a worksheet with the WordArt button in the Text group on the Insert tab. Customize WordArt text with options on the Drawing Tools Format tab.

Commands Review

FEATURE	RIBBON TAB, GROUP	BUTTON
Choose a SmartArt Graphic dialog box	Insert, Illustrations	
Insert Picture dialog box	Insert, Illustrations	
Insert Pictures window	Insert, Illustrations	
Insert WordArt button drop-down list	Insert, Text	
screenshot	Insert, Illustrations	
Shapes button drop-down list	Insert, Illustrations	
Symbol dialog box	Insert, Symbols	
text box	Insert, Text	

Index

with Chart Tools Format
tab, 191–192
Format Chart Area task
pane, 195
line chart, 191–192
pie chart, 196–198
Quick Analysis feature,
196–197
treemap chart, 199
inserting and customizing
shapes, 192–194
moving, 179–180
printing, 184–185
sizing, 179–180
types of, 178–179
Chart Styles button, 182
Chart Tools Design tab, 185,
186
Chart Tools Format tab, 191
Clear button, 58
clip art, inserting and
formatting, 216–217
Clipboard task pane, 120–121
Close button, 135
closing
Excel, 12
workbook, 11
Collapse the Ribbon button, 4,
5
color
change colors in charts, 187
change worksheet color, 124
font formatting and, 59
column boundary line, changing
width with, 52–53
column chart, 178
column header, 5
columns
deleting, 57–58
formatting
row height, 54–55
width, 20–21, 52–53
hiding and unhiding, 75–76
inserting, 56–57
printing column headings, 89
printing titles on multiple
pages, 86–87
sorting in more than one, 106
switching in charts, 186–187
Column Width dialog box,
changing column width at,
53
combo chart, 178

comma formatting, 22
Comma Style button, 22
Compress Pictures button, 214
constant, defined, 38
Copy button, 117
copying
cell styles, 164, 165
data, 136
between programs, 138–139
formulas
with fill handle, 18
with relative cell references,
32–33
formulas with relative cell
references, 32–33
shapes, 219–221
workbook, 148–149
worksheet, 123–124
to another workbook,
154–155
copying and pasting, cells
with Clipboard task pane,
120–121
pasting values only, 122–123
selected cells, 119–120
using Paste Options button,
118–119
COUNTA function, 43
COUNT function, 40
writing formulas with, 43
Crop button, 214
Currency, as category in Format
Cells dialog box, 66
Currency format, 63
Custom, as category in Format
Cells dialog box, 66
customizing
images, 214–215
print jobs, 96–97
shapes in charts, 192–194
Cut button, 117
cutting
cells, 117–118
workbooks, 149–150

D

data
aligning, 67–69
clearing, in cells, 58
copying, 136
editing
in cell, 9–10

in chart, 180
entering into cells
with fill handle, 14, 15–16
typing in, 6–7
filtering, 106–108
finding and replacing, 99–101
indenting, 67–68
linking, 137–138
moving, 136
rotating, 68–69
scaling, 87–88
selecting within cell
with keyboard, 20
with mouse, 20
sorting, 104–106
data series, adding to chart, 180
Date, as category in Format
Cells dialog box, 66
Date & Time button, 44
Decrease Decimal button, 22, 64
Decrease Font Size button, 59
Define Name button, 130
Delete button, 57
Delete dialog box, 57
Delete key, 58
deleting
cells, 57
cell styles, 165
chart, 196–199
chart element, 188
columns, 57
data in cell, 9
folder, 147, 151
hyperlink, 170–171
to Recycle Bin, 147
rows, 57–58
SmartArt graphic, 225
workbook, 147–148
worksheet, 116–118, 123–124
dependent worksheet, 137
dialog box launcher, 4, 5
division
order of operations, 35
writing formula with, 32
DIV/O error code, 36
down time, writing formula to
calculate percentage of, 37
drawing
arrow shapes, 220–221
text boxes, 222–223
Drawing Tools Format tab, 219,
222

symbols and special characters, 212–213
WordArt, 228–229
Insert WordArt button, 228
integration, 138–139
interest, simple, formula with mixed cell references, 48
Italic button, 59

K

keyboard shortcuts
   to activate cells, 6
   closing Excel, 12
   closing workbook, 11
   displaying Open backstage area, 15
   display Print backstage area, 10
   insert SUM function, 17
   Open dialog box, 15
   repeat last action, 73
   selecting cell with, 19, 20
   selecting data within cell, 19–20

L

landscape orientation, 82
line chart, 178
   creating and formatting, 191–192
linking
   cells between worksheets, 137–138
   data, 137–138
live preview feature, 62
loan, finding periodic payments for, 201–203
logical test, 204

M

margins
   changing in worksheet, 80–82
   default settings, 80
Margins button, 80
marquee, 117
mathematical operations, writing formulas with, 32–38
MAX function, 40

writing formulas with, 41–43
Maximize button, 135
Merge & Center button, 21, 59–60
Merge Styles dialog box, 165
merging, cells, 21
MIN function, 40
   writing formulas with, 41–43
Minimize button, 135
Mini toolbar, formatting with, 59
mixed cell reference, 45
mouse
   to activate cells, 7
   moving split lines, 128
   selecting cell with, 19
   selecting data within cell, 20
Move Chart button, 188
Move Chart dialog box, 188
Move or Copy dialog box, 154
moving
   chart, 179–180
   chart element, 188
   chart location, 188–190
   data, 136
   images, 214
   SmartArt graphic, 225
   split lines, 128
   WordArt, 229
   workbook, 135
   worksheet, 123–124
      to another workbook, 155–157
multiple cell reference, using in formula, 46
multiplication, 32
   order of operations, 35

N

N/A error code, 36
Name box, 4, 5, 6
NAME? error code, 36
navigating, using hyperlinks, 167–168
nested parentheses, 35
New folder button, 145
New sheet button, 4, 5, 116
New Window button, 132
Normal button, 84
NOW function, writing formulas with, 44
Nper, in financial functions, 200

Number, as category in Format Cells dialog box, 66
Number Format option box, 64
numbers
   AutoSum
      to add, 17–18
      to average numbers, 18
   formatting, 22–23
      with Format Cells dialog box, 65–67
      with Number group buttons, 63–65
   number symbol (###) for exceeding space in cell, 7
NUM! error code, 36

O

100% button, 127
Online Pictures button, 214
Open dialog box, 15
   copying workbook to another folder, 149
   creating folder, 145
   cutting and pasting workbook, 149–150
   deleting workbooks and folders, 147–148
   elements of, 144
   renaming folder, 146
   renaming workbook, 150–151
   selecting workbook, 146–148
opening, workbook
   multiple, 132, 134
   from Open dialog box, 15
   from *Recent* option list, 15
order of operations, 35
Organize button, 146
Orientation button, 60, 82

P

page break, inserting and removing, 83–86
Page Break Preview button, 84–85
page orientation
   changing, 82–83
   default, 80
Page Setup dialog box
   centering horizontally/ vertically, 81–82